GOING PLATINUM

Going Platinum

KISS, Donna Summer, and How Neil Bogart Built
Casablanca Records

Brett Ermilio & Josh Levine

B SCOTT, N. ERM
Ermilio, Brett
Going platinum

CENTRAL

$25.95
319940 14883869

LYONS PRESS
Guilford, Connecticut
Helena, Montana
An imprint of Rowman & Littlefield

Lyons Press is an imprint of Rowman & Littlefield

Distributed by NATIONAL BOOK NETWORK

British Library Cataloguing-in-Publication Information available

Ermilio, Brett.
  Going platinum: KISS, Donna Summer, and How Neil Bogart Built Casablanca Records / Brett Ermilio and Josh Levine; foreword by Jylle Bogart Barker.
    pages cm
  ISBN 978-0-7627-9133-0
  1. Bogart, Neil, 1943-1982. 2. Sound recording executives and producers—United States—Biography. 3. Casablanca Records. I. Levine, Josh, 1975- II. Title.
  ML429.B62E76 2014
  781.64092--dc23
  [B]
                                   2014015149

♾️™ The paper used in this publication meets the minimum requirements of American National Standard for Information Sciences—Permanence of Paper for Printed Library Materials, ANSI/NISO Z39.48-1992.

In Memory of Al Bogart

Contents

Foreword

There have been so many things attributed to my father, to things he said and did. Even some of his own most riveting stories came from him, to create excitement around himself and the project he was working on. There are, I am sure, some stories more and some less flattering. Some will be true, some exaggerated, and some just made up by people who wanted to *claim* a part of his success.

I would like readers to know that the truth of the story, that no one can deny, is that he was a poor kid from Brooklyn who was able to change his life's course through hard work, determination, and dreams. And isn't that amazing?

He was devoted to all his children. When I was very young he would put me up on a little table and if I danced to the song, he said it would be a hit. He called this "record review."

Yes, he met presidents of the United States and other incredibly influential people, but he came home early from work to see us after school and made me sandwiches for camp with a note in them.

His latter life was influenced by the disco era and all that went along with that. Some readers won't understand the wild excitement that fed on itself. Some readers do because they were part of it.

Please remember as you read or see any materials about my father that it has been 32 years since his death and people's memories change.

The favor I ask of you who follow his life is to remember that he was by no means lucky. He drove himself. You can do this too. You can make anything you want of yourself and I guess that is what my dad's message would be to all of us.

Jylle Bogart Barker
April 2014

Introduction

The man who became music mogul Neil Bogart started as a kid named Neil Bogatz from the humble streets of Brooklyn, New York—far from the glamour and glitz of a Los Angeles that, to some degree, he would help create. As fascinating a figure as he would become, the story of how he got there is even more so. The development of Neil's talent and hunger for success started when he was a youth; he grew up in a home where his parents fostered and, in some ways, incessantly drove that desire. They fashioned him into the man and dynamic producer he would become—the King of Bubblegum, Casablanca Records founder, the man responsible for bringing KISS to the masses, and, perhaps most famously, the Disco King.

I am his only nephew, son of his lone sibling, Bonnie Ellen Ermilio (formerly Bogatz). With the help of my close friend, Josh Levine, we retraced the steps of Neil Bogart's life from prior to his birth to the impact he made beyond his death. This book contains interviews from his closest relatives, personal accounts from childhood friends, and never-before-shared stories from the first love of his life, his first wife, Beth. We have compiled extraordinary tales from colleagues who worked with Neil from his time in promotions on the East Coast all the way to his incredible run at Casablanca Records. We sifted through thousands of pages of documents, books, articles, and interviews to help reconstruct Neil Bogart's life.

Neil's life was the extraordinary ride of a dreamer, a man with incredible expectations and historic import who was both a creature of his success and a victim of its trappings. He succumbed to the temptations of fame and lived a life many could only dream of. In that process, Neil faced his own mortality at the height of his success. He rose and fell with tremendous thunder and left a positive imprint on our culture that will be felt for decades to come. Many of the stories in this book have never seen the light of day. This is the only complete account of Neil Bogart's life and how he became the Disco King.

Brett Ermilio and Josh Levine
April 2014

Prologue

On May 8, 1982, at Cedars Sinai Hospital in Los Angeles, California, the Disco King lay dying.

The now-weakened man had once been a larger-than-life figure, the grand orchestrator of parties, promotions, and shows, releasing gold record after gold record—and discovering music that would far outlast him. Neil Scott Bogatz, a man whose name would be all but forgotten twenty years later, helped to create some of the most memorable and relevant music of his and of our time. Acts such as the Village People, KISS, Parliament, and Donna Summer highlighted his list of talent. Their contributions drove the 1970's music industry like a freight train. Neil was its brilliant conductor.

On that day in 1982, there was no disco ball or music blasting through the hospital. There was only a man with cancer dying in a hospital bed. With all hope lost and his oxygen mask removed, Neil was drawing his final breath in the late morning hours. With his sister, Bonnie, by his side and his brother-in-law, Joseph, standing by, and the rest of the family waiting outside the room, the Disco King's fight was over. At 10:20 a.m. he was gone. He died on Mother's Day and was buried on his father's birthday.

From the streets of Brooklyn, New York, to the penthouse of the music industry, Neil Bogart's story is unique. He lived his life like a Roman candle—burning brightly until his untimely demise, considering how much he accomplished, at the very young age of thirty-nine.

Throughout his life, Neil managed to rise above circumstances and adversity. His beginnings in the Glenwood housing projects were humble.

His mother, Ruth, a rigid and difficult woman, physically and verbally abused him. His father, Al, a World War II veteran and postal worker, was a creative influence on his son who turned a blind eye to his wife's behavior. On his way up, Neil received rejection after rejection from the music industry; success seemed always just out of reach until he clawed his way to the top. One can even argue that the abuse that Neil endured from his mother was a driving spark that ultimately stoked the fires of his own success.

Neil began his career in the music industry in his late teens, launching a singing career based on the music his father had written, even scoring a hit with the song "Bobby." The industry, as it tends to do, moved on without him when he could not muster a follow-up. A hustler at heart, Neil never turned down an opportunity to appear in the public eye; he shifted his energies to getting featured in teen magazines to raise his profile. Though singing and dancing were in his blood, his acumen for business and self-promotion were evident early on. He quickly learned that, strangely enough, being the talent was not where the money was. Neil didn't want to be the one onstage—he wanted to *own* the people onstage.

Within three years of entering the industry, Neil landed a job as president of Buddah Records, making him a twenty-four-year-old music executive, the youngest ever. From the late 1960s to the early 1970s, Neil was called the "Bubblegum King" for his ability to turn out a litany of chart-topping successes. As that era came to an end, Neil transitioned successfully into the R&B arena. His rise at Buddah was not quite enough for him; Neil wanted his own company. Like a lot of people in the twentieth century, he moved west to achieve this dream—and Casablanca Records was born.

Casablanca Records, the home of KISS, the Village People, and Donna Summer, has become a story within a story, a legendary tale of drug abuse, innovative music, success, wasted talent, women, money, blown opportunity, and some of the biggest names in the music industry. At the time, the wild ride seemed like it would last forever. In truth, it lasted only five years.

Neil was a visionary, a creative and sharp businessman who drove others hard, himself harder. In an era where big was hip and bigger was hipper, Neil became an absolute juggernaut. He left the impoverished streets of New York to live out west among some of the most powerful, influential, and respected people in the entertainment industry. He was a self-made multi-millionaire, a dreamer who literally thought he could not be stopped.

In 1979, just three years prior to his death, Neil offered this perspective on his unlikely success:

> *Hey, I'm just an ordinary guy from Brooklyn having a good time. Two and a half years ago I was flat on my ass in debt, down to my last warning from American Express, and now I've got this company that's grossing fifty million dollars a year, that's making the hottest records and movies around. Who would believe a guy from PS 203 could live like this? Who would believe anyone could make so much money from his fantasies?*[1]

CHAPTER 1

The Creative Seed

Why head for the mountaintop when you're reaching for the sky?[1]
—NEIL SCOTT BOGART

In 1943, the year Neil Scott Bogatz was born in Brooklyn Jewish Hospital, the average working wage in America was two thousand dollars a year, the average cost of a gallon of gas was fifteen cents, a bottle of Coca-Cola was five cents, and Bing Crosby's "White Christmas" had just finished a triumphant eleven-month run on the charts. The Great Depression was officially over as the US economy moved into overdrive, while war production reached a feverish pace. The Academy Award for best picture of the year went to *Casablanca*, starring Humphrey Bogart. That movie that would have a great impact on Neil over the course of his life, providing both inspiration and a namesake.

Neil's parents, Abraham "Al" Bogatz and Ruth Bogatz, met as children in the 1930s and quickly became inseparable. They didn't grow up poor, per se, but they certainly were limited. Their lives seemed to run in parallel; they both scurried through the streets of New York in the pre–World War II days, when economic and military crises had not yet burdened the lives of the nation's citizens. Al and Ruth were happy, and the atmosphere was ripe for romance. Fumbling flirtations soon turned into love, and their marriage would ultimately last more than five decades.

Al was shy and handsome, a creative young man who loved to write music. Ruth was a beautiful and outspoken woman with a flair for making costumes. They were a socially dynamic couple who shared a passion for music and looked for any opportunity to dance. They did so as often as they could during a time in America when this was quite common; dancing through the tough years of the Great Depression provided a release and an outlet for their mutual creativity.

During high school, Al spent much of his idle time penning songs and stories with aspirations of going to college to study writing. However, the Great Depression sidetracked countless dreams, and Al's were one of its many victims. Instead of heading off to college and improving his chances at succeeding as a writer, Al was forced to make other arrangements. In the 1930s, wanting to become a writer meant one thing; living as one was something else entirely. The fact was, he needed to make a living as one. He started off as a shipfitter in the Brooklyn Naval Yard for Bethlehem Steel Corporation to make ends meet, while Ruth kept the home.

In the summer of 1943, a few short months after Neil's birth, Al was drafted to fight for his country. Because of his skills and experience reconditioning ships, he was enlisted into the US Navy as a Shipfitter First Class during World War II. He was first sent to mainland locations and then stationed at Pearl Harbor, remaining there until 1945. During his time there, he couldn't resist writing. When handed the opportunity to write for *Patrol*, the wartime paper issued by the Navy about the seamen at Pearl Harbor, he took it.

Al's "The Voice" became a featured column. Jim Gaffney, a writer for a naval publication called *Topside Watch*, called Al "earthy" and wrote of how Al "broke the monotony of War Bond promotions, editorials on the importance of censorship, tomes of baseball stories and the jokes . . . his columns echoed the hope, praise, fear, resentment, and humor of people at war."[2]

Al was also not afraid to speak his mind, and his articles reveal an honesty and forthrightness that one can imagine spoke to the men who put their lives on hold to fight for their country:

I believe in Freedom of Press where a man can "voice" his opinion on right or wrong. My first thought, as everyone else, is to get this war over with as soon as possible and get back to my family. I believe in fighting for the next guy and helping people along.[3]

Back at home, Ruth regularly sent love letters to her husband stationed more than five thousand miles away. She kept Al up to speed on the family and their activities, especially what was going on with baby "Neilly." The time apart was difficult on Ruth. Like many other wives left to fend for themselves during the war, she longed for her husband to come home. It was particularly tough for the young mother, since she and Al had been best friends as children; they hadn't spent any time apart.

Al finally returned home, unscathed from the war, in 1945, but it was a short-lived homecoming. Rent was due, Neil was growing, and the bills were piling up. Al was immediately confronted with the responsibility of providing for his family. The Great Depression had diverted him from a college degree and a writing career, and the war had further pushed back any hope of pursuing either. He once again put his pen down and joined the US Post Office so that he could support his family. Putting his dreams aside had become commonplace for Al, but he wouldn't let that stop him from writing songs on his own. Al would make up melodies, write lyrics, and eventually teach the songs to his children (for them to record with his help). He never played an instrument, but as family members recall, if you stood close to him, he could usually be heard humming a tune.

Two years after returning home from war, the Bogatz clan expanded again with a girl, Bonnie Ellen Bogatz. Despite being four years apart in age, she and Neil would become extremely close. Bonnie always cherished the way Neil looked after his little sister—she referred to him as her "protector."

The Bogatz household flourished with creativity, especially music. At night the Bogatzes gathered in the living room and danced to all kinds of music—from Big Band and swing greats like Duke Ellington, Benny Goodman, and Count Basie, to the standards of Bing Crosby, to the newer, pre–rock-and-roll sounds of Buddy Holly and Little Richard. They laughed, danced, and sang along with songs that filled their home—music was an important ritual the family shared together. Sometimes they'd even pretend to ballroom dance. The walls of their cozy Brooklyn apartment in the projects broke away, and the space outside their home filled with rows and rows of chairs upon which sat their cheering fans. There they were, the Bogatz clan, dressed to the nines, exchanging partners and pretending to be stars in front of an audience. They weren't just performing for them-selves—they were performing for the *world*. For the Bogatz children, the art of entertainment was an education unto itself. Neil learned to play to the audience before the audience even existed.

The Ed Sullivan Show and comedians like Bob Hope and Sid Caesar were also popular with the Bogatz kids as breaks from the monotony of homework. Neil mimicked his idols from his favorite variety shows on the small screen. When they sang, he sang. When they danced, he danced. When they told a joke, he would commit it to memory, make it his own, and send his sister into fits of uncontrollable laughter.

Movie stars also played a huge role in young Neil's life. He would sit on his parents' quietly fading furniture and marvel at the screen leg-ends who seemed so much larger than life—Shirley Temple, Fred Astaire, and Humphrey Bogart—and dream that one day *he* would be coming back through the screen into people's homes. Though Neil was known for his musical prowess, his hidden passion was always the movies. In fact, though music became his vocation, he embraced all types of art. He wasn't limited to simply dance or song or film; it was the idea of perfor-mance in general that attracted him. Perhaps it was a lack of focus, but the landscape inside Neil's mind allowed for all these possibilities. The merging of music and movies, the ability of entertainment to take you to a fantasy world, the creation of personas for performance, all would heavily influence Neil throughout his career. These innocent childhood dreams, which began in his parents' living room in front of a black-and-white RCA television, formed the basis for a career that would lead to a number of musical movements in the 1960s and 1970s.

Ruth and Al fostered a creative environment for their children, exposing them to "the Arts," which were pivotal in their growth. It was something both children would pass on to their own children. From an early age, Al taught songs to his children—one of his favorites being Bil-lie Holiday's version of "Pennies from Heaven." They sang Frank Sinatra, Perry Como, and Johnny Mathis—the great crooners of Al's generation. Neil would come home from school and run right to the radio, where the two would listen together to the big band music his dad loved. This music greatly affected Neil's own musical trajectory and drove him to learn to play the bongo drums, saxophone, and the clarinet—the same instruments that were standard in these songs. He wanted to re-create in his own music the sounds he first heard in that room.

Al also wrote his own songs for Neil and Bonnie to sing. He took his kids to a twenty-five-cent record press box, a machine common in the city at the time, and had them record his tunes. The booth was similar to the photo booths where people take candid, and often silly, pictures. The Bogatzes headed out to one on Coney Island, where anyone could go inside the soundproof booth, put in a quarter, and sing when the light came on. Upon completion, a record was pressed and came out of a slot for you to take. This is where Al took Neil and Bonnie to record early songs from the time Neil was eleven until he was thirteen years old. In fact, Neil's first released singles in 1959, "Go Bohemian" and its B-side, "Oh Genie," were written and produced by Al Bogatz and Neil Scott, Neil's first stage name.

Al and Ruth made it a practice to show their kids as much of the world as they could. Giving them opportunities to get out of their neighborhood was important, especially when the kids were young. Al and Ruth vacationed in the Catskills, headed to old US Army forts, and visited local Native American villages up and down the East Coast. The parents wanted to give their kids some perspective on the world and get them out of the often-isolated confines of Brooklyn. Not many families could afford the travel, and though it was a stretch for the Bogatzes, giving the children venues to expand their education and experience was worth any expense.

The Bogatzes practiced a broad philosophy of education. They believed that schoolwork was only half of the equation to becoming a productive member of society. It was just as important to make their kids comfortable with America's past, with their own history, with all types of people and a litany of different cultures.

Ruth also exhibited her own creativity in the house, hand-knitting clothes for school and creating lavish costumes for the kids' performances and special occasions like Halloween. She took any opportunity to create something extraordinary from scratch for her kids. This worked both as a creative outlet for the talented mother and as a way to save the household money. Instead of purchasing clothes, she made everything they needed. She was also a fantastic cook, not merely a housewife with a gift for making a good brisket or lasagna. She inspired other women in the neighborhood, who would come to get a taste of her culinary treats. There were no cooking shows to learn from back then; it all came from her imagination. People began asking her to cater local events, but Ruth had little time for this. Her kitchen in the projects was barely bigger than their linen closet. Instead she focused much of her time on helping her son develop his already obvious and burgeoning talents.

Neil displayed a lot of confidence early on. As his father would say years later: Neil "started singing at the age of ten, and he never stopped." He had an almost desperate drive to rise from his humble beginnings and become famous. When his sister, Bonnie, was just four, a teenager named Yvonne escorted her back to the house after she had wandered off. A grateful Ruth quickly proclaimed that Yvonne was to be their babysitter. Yvonne accepted because that's what most people did when Ruth had already decided something. Yvonne then made her way into the living room, where Neil was lying upside down on the couch, watching television. She mimicked the precocious boy, lying upside down beside him and introducing herself. She playfully asked the eight-year-old, "So . . . what do you want to be when you grow up?" Neil, without hesitation, eyes locked on the TV, said, "I want to be a star." To him, it was the most obvious answer in the world. What else was there to be?

As Neil grew older, Ruth got the sense that something special was developing in her son, and she decided to dedicate her life to ensuring he made it out of Brooklyn. His dream would become her dream. She glommed onto her eldest child and went to any lengths to remove all obstacles that might have blocked him. No one would deny that Ruth Bogatz had tremendously high expectations and ruled with a decidedly iron fist. Neither Neil nor Bonnie could afford to disappoint their mother—they learned quickly that the ramifications were costly when they did.

CHAPTER 2

The Glenwood Projects

We all knew, even at that time, music was a very serious subject to him.
—LYNN CAMPOLO, CHILDHOOD FRIEND

Growing up in the diverse Glenwood Projects in Brooklyn created a variety of challenges for a skinny Jewish kid like Neil. If you didn't have street smarts, you didn't thrive. Neil had to develop those skill sets as quickly as possible. Street savvy, quick thinking and—most important—toughness were hallmarks of Neil Bogart from an early age.

The Glenwood Houses (or "Glenwood Projects," as residents called it) was a moderate- to low-income housing development in the Flatbush section of Brooklyn. The housing project began in 1949 during the post–World War II era, when the New York City Housing Authority reached its peak in constructing public housing. The apartments were built around parks, which served as the cultural epicenters of the community. The buildings were not high-rises but moderate-size towers lifting above and around the parks in a "tower by the park" style.

Completed in 1950, Glenwood had twenty six-story buildings, with 1,186 apartments and more than 2,700 residents. Children's playgrounds, numerous city parks, recreation centers, and senior centers were sprinkled throughout the developments. Often the parks served as the social mecca of activity for the development's youth.

Today Glenwood is far different. There is more crime and drug use today than there was sixty years ago. But the challenges of growing up in tough communities with people of different backgrounds living on top of one another has been a common theme throughout Glenwood's history. It was certainly true back when Neil Bogart was stomping around there.

Back in the early 1950s, Jewish families dominated the streets of the Glenwood Projects. More than 60 percent of the families that lived there were Jewish, although families from a variety of other backgrounds—Italian, Irish, black, Puerto Rican—made up the diverse group of residents. The Jewish community wasn't religious—they only really celebrated the High Holy Days of Rosh Hashanah (New Year) and Yom Kippur (Day of Atonement). During any other time of year, an outsider would never have known that the majority of the people living in the community were part of any religion.

The qualifications at the time to live in the neighborhood were strictly financial. You had to make some money, but not too much. The land behind Glenwood stood vacant, a place for kids to get themselves in all kinds of trouble. The world was expanding quickly, but not in the "projects." Although opportunity could be found in America in the 1950s—a lot of it right across the East River in Manhattan—to the residents of Glenwood it seemed as though that world was thousands of miles away.

The park was the nucleus of the neighborhood around the Bogatz apartment. It was the hub where the majority of local kids spent their time playing, socializing, and unknowingly establishing themselves in grade-school hierarchies that would stick with them through their entire lives. A long bench crisscrossed the park. The girls sat arm in arm and watched the boys play tackle football and stickball on the hard asphalt. Neil and Bonnie liked the part of the bench near the water spouts, which shot up into the air and landed in a moss-filled wading pool. The pool allowed kids some relief in the hot summers and served as a monument to better days in winter.

Neil didn't frequent the park much, but when he did, he often regretted going there. Joseph Ermilio, Bonnie's future husband and one of the future directors under Neil at Casablanca Records, recalls a time when Neil's mother interrupted one of his softball games (a rarity for Neil, who tended to stay indoors practicing his music) and made him go get bread for the house. "Neil was mortified," he noted, "but he wouldn't dare question his mother's wishes."

While many kids socialized at the park, Neil spent countless hours practicing his craft, taking singing and dancing lessons. Neil also took music lessons: bongo drums, the saxophone, and the clarinet. Even in his early teens, Bogart was driven to succeed in show business; he had greater goals in mind and cared little for juvenile activities.

Neil's uncle, Seymour Bogatz, remembers the girls chasing him, but the teenager wasn't interested. "He was always too busy promoting himself," he says. "He always had a lot of girls running after him. But his focus was on being successful. I'd drive him to many of his gigs. We would see numerous girls. They would run to him. But he never had any time for chance encounters. Having a girlfriend wasn't in his vocabulary."

To help pay for all of Neil's music lessons (and Bonnie's dance lessons), Ruth left the comfortable confines of home to get a job as an assistant at a doctor's office. Ruth considered it a sacrifice to do this for her children, and in some ways she never let them forget it. But since performing was always at their core, she also viewed working outside the home as her duty. It fit in with her and Al's philosophy to facilitate all opportunities for their children. Her son's creative development moved along nicely, and with all the encouragement he received from his teachers and peers, an added toughness, almost cockiness, came along with it.

Bonnie was continually amazed at how protective her brother was. One time a boy was mean to Bonnie just outside their complex. Upset, Bonnie ran up to their apartment and told her brother what had happened. He rushed down the stairs with his eyes bulging right out of his head and got in the boy's face, nose to chin. Neil was never physically imposing, but he was fierce when he needed to be. Bonnie heard her brother yell, "If you ever talk to my sister that way again, you and I are going to have a problem!" The other boy wanted no part of Neil and backed down.

When Neil got angry, when his eyes flared with rage, he looked downright rabid. There was an edge to Neil people sometimes didn't see coming, as he usually came off as an affable guy. But you never wanted to see his dark side. It was something passed to him by his mother, whose darkness was decidedly less hidden.

Sometimes Neil played the role of big brother to a fault. Once Neil started performing publicly, Bonnie and her close friend, Eileen Freidman, became a fixture at Neil's shows. Ruth tried to maintain a home court advantage for Neil wherever he performed, which often included putting Bonnie and her friends in the audience to be sure the cheers were appropriately raucous.

Eileen can remember countless times Neil got them into trouble for overstepping his bounds. Recalls Eileen:

> *When I was about thirteen, that would put Neil at about seventeen, I remember he was trying to make it as a singer. He was singing at a hotel in Spring Lake, in the Catskills. My parents were staying at a bungalow colony not far away, so they drove me to the hotel so I could stay with Bonnie for a few days and see Neil perform. Ruth kind of left us alone, and our only requirement was to check in once in a while and scream when Neil came on to sing.*

Bonnie was seeing someone at the time and asked Eileen to vanish for the night, which she agreed to do. Since Ruth and Al were so occupied with managing Neil during his shows, Bonnie felt like the odd family member out. On one occasion she took the opportunity to sneak out on a date with a boy and left Eileen alone in their room. Neil came into the room to find Eileen alone watching *Lassie*—and took off as soon as he saw that Bonnie wasn't there. Meanwhile, Ruth had no idea that Bonnie had disappeared with a boy. Eileen remembers that Neil must have been pissed that Bonnie was missing. Al and Ruth were upset at Bonnie's behavior and were not at all pleased with Eileen either. "Al and Ruth called my parents because I was found alone with a boy too," Eileen says. "They were upset. But Neil felt terrible I got in trouble, because really I did nothing wrong. He kept apologizing to me. Neil always was a big brother to all of us. He looked after us. But Neil, either directly or indirectly, would get us into trouble pretty often."

Neil was always actively engaged in Bonnie's life, even with her friends. Staying close to his sister and her friends wasn't just selfless brothering—it also gave him an audience and helped him shape his ear for music. He could see what got them excited and learned to play off the crowd; the young performer was diligent, and he would tweak and adapt based on their response. This skill would prove invaluable when he began to perform.

Lynn Campolo was one of Bonnie's friends. Neil would sit in his and Bonnie's bedroom with Lynn and play "Name That Tune" with his records. Lynn told us:

> *You have to remember that back then, we weren't poor but just about okay. Neil, being so into music, had a record player on a table near the bedroom door. He would "test" my knowledge of songs by playing just the first few notes of the record, then take the needle off the record and see if I knew the song.*

Neil took the game seriously. He'd refined his tastes over the years and wanted to prove to anyone and everyone that he was an expert. And Lynn always played along, happy to watch his infectious behavior:

> *I would sit up on the desk in front of the window and keep my back to him so I couldn't see the record label. Back then, records had distinctive labels and you could tell by the label itself what song, or artist, a record might be from. . . . We all knew, even at that time, music was a very serious subject to him.*

Neil's mother helped Neil foster his talents, which meant that she also took some responsibility for his daily activities. She was not only his guardian and keeper but also his manager and advisor; it was an odd relationship for a mother and child to have, especially back then. Perhaps she took too personal an interest in her son and his career. When a parental relationship goes from guidance to something more akin to management, it can take a nasty turn, especially if the parent has little life of her own and feels she must live vicariously through her child.

Ruth loved to be with people and be the center of attention. This was a trait picked up by Neil; socializing, holding court, taking over a room—all came natural to him, just as it did to her. But sooner or later, relationships between two people with similar personalities, especially when they are tied to the same boat, tend to come up against rocks.

Ruth also passed on to her son a strikingly violent temper. As much love as there was between them, and for all the attention Ruth gave Neil, the two clashed often. While Ruth certainly supported and almost idolized her son because of his abilities, the mother made sure to let the son know who was in charge. There was little doubt that she held the power over her son, and as much as she loved Neil—as much as he was her baby boy—she maintained complete psychological control over him and, for that matter, her entire family. Neil's burgeoning talent and voracious energy seemed larger than life, but in the tiny Bogatz apartment, Ruth's rule was even bigger. As intense as Ruth's love for Neil was, it was matched by the intensity of her anger.

CHAPTER 3

The Dark Ages

We never ever talked back to her. We wouldn't dare. We were petrified of her.

—Bonnie Ermilio

At times the atmosphere inside the Bogatz home could be chaotic. With Al working and the children at play or practice or school, Ruth had to keep the home together. She could be a tyrant when she wasn't accorded the respect she thought she deserved. At other times she was a dedicated mother who went to great lengths to make certain of her children's—particularly Neil's—success. But more often than not, family and friends remembered her as a controlling woman who ordered her husband around and instilled the fear of God into Neil and Bonnie.

The woman nicknamed "Chippy" by her husband could be downright brutish. She was a fearless and fierce woman who could be ruthless in achieving her goals. Though she put on one sociable face to the world, those who knew her most intimately knew the truth. Ruth could be extremely dark. Demeaning to her children and cruel when she wanted to be, Ruth spawned a kind of fragility in her children, her temper triggering future stresses that were impossible to repair. She would unleash both physical and mental abuse, some subtle and some overt.

Ruth treated strangers on the street, people she barely knew, far better than the people close to her. This behavior continued through her entire life. She had Russian blood running through her veins and ruled her house the way she saw fit, knowing full well that Al was subservient to her. Joseph Ermilio, Al and Ruth's son-in-law, told us:

[Al] was a man that didn't stand up for himself or his kids. He was a mouse. In front of the kids he would never show Ruth up. I remember once Ruth was sitting next to the phone when it rang and she shouted over and over again at Al who was across the house to come and get it. She shouted multiple times until he walked over and answered the phone right next to her. That was Ruth. That's who she was.

Ruth's mean streak wasn't necessarily genetic—it was likely taught to her by her Russian mother, Edith. Edith, like Ruth, cared very much about how the world perceived her. Bonnie remembers her grandmother vividly: "My grandmother always dressed up and tried to wear fancy clothes. She always wanted to appear like she had more money than she did. She wore frilly hats and coats, anything that was popular at the time. Appearances were very important to her."

In addition to Edith's attempts to impress everyone around her, she harbored a hardened attitude and wicked temper. "She was so mean. Just a very mean woman," Bonnie shivered as she recalled.

Edith was not around often, but Neil and Bonnie still felt her impact. Edith definitely left her footprint on Ruth, and a cycle of behavior was passed from mother to daughter. Ruth too aspired to rise from the depths of the lower class and dreamed of being rich. She carried her mother's desire to be more than she was, and by extension, her family needed to be more as well. Her hardness partly came from her need to realize this desire.

Ruth took an alternative tack with Neil. Instead of consistently tearing him down, she drove him to be better and stronger. The appearance of these "two Ruths" probably stemmed from something she saw in her son. She thought he was simply more talented than other children. While other young boys played mindlessly in the park, Neil spent his time practicing instruments and mapping out his track to fame and fortune. Ruth sensed that Neil would get out of Brooklyn and achieve something bigger than all of them. Al may have had dreams of being a great writer and entertainer, but to Ruth, those were exactly that: dreams. Dreams were nothing more than a fantasy. She once said, "I hate fantasies. Fantasies aren't real." Ruth made sure her son held no illusions about what "shooting for the stars" actually meant—it involved grit and hard work—and clearly she thought it involved someone driving him toward them.

Ruth attempted to expose her children to the faces of success, as she understood it. She wanted her kids to see the stars up close and in person. "My mother always wanted to show us what we could be," Bonnie says. "Especially with Neil, she wanted him to know he could be a star if he worked hard enough. That's why she took us to so many places."

Al and Ruth took the children to places like the Catskills to show them where and how "rich" people lived. They wanted to be part of that world, despite not being able to afford it themselves. Ruth ingrained these images of money and success into her children, believing that "successful people were respected people." Ruth always tried to hold that image out before her children's eyes, persuading them to reach for it and do what she and Al could not.

When Ruth took her son around to friends and relatives, she stood back and watched, beaming, as he performed and demonstrated his many talents. Despite her pushing, Neil was not a classic "show-biz child," merely acting out his parents' fantasies. Neil performed because he loved to, not because Ruth asked him to. Both of them had far greater goals for Neil than simple living room performances.

On his thirteenth birthday, Neil stepped on center stage on the dance floor at his own bar mitzvah and belted out a rousing rendition of the family favorite, "Pennies from Heaven," a song Al had taught his children (and later recorded with them on Coney Island). Already the ultimate showman, Neil sang the chorus and tossed pennies all around the dance floor, causing the children to scurry about and snatch up as many as they could. With that gimmick, he gained a captive audience.

As he would show later in life as a promotions man and founder of his own label, Neil had a knack for "selling" acts and performances. He could figure out what the audience wanted and bring it to them with a hook, or a plan, or sometimes a simple gimmick. Whether it was at home in front of his sister and her friends or out in public, the teenage Neil quickly learned the effect he could have on people with his performances.

Ruth felt empowered by her son's charisma and was determined for him to be famous. She focused on Neil's blossoming career and drove him hard to be successful. Numerous family members remember that making Neil a star was her greatest priority. Ruth wanted more for her family and more for Neil; she knew he could get it.

As Al worked long hours, Ruth not only worked but also ran the household. All married couples fall into their roles, and the Bogatzes were no exception. He was more passive; she was direct and aggressive. Perhaps that was just the way Al was. Perhaps his timidity arose from the fact that when Ruth got angry, she got *real* angry. If Neil or Bonnie got in trouble, a slew of insults and crazed shouting from their mother would be a blessing, because if you disappointed or upset Ruth, a slap could easily come your way. However, Neil rarely faced the physical punishment that Bonnie had to endure.

A favorite tool of punishment in Ruth's arsenal was "the straps," a harsh reprimand she used when her children were not playing by her rules. The straps had a twofold use for Bonnie. The first was to tie her to the dining room chair in order to force her to finish her vegetables. The second use was far worse: Ruth beat Bonnie with them when she got particularly enraged.

Another special tool Ruth had at her disposal was wooden hangers. Both the straps and hangers would leave Bonnie with visible welts. Neil was always protective of his sister and was constantly finding creative ways of protecting her against regular beatings from their mother. "I remember when my mother would get angry and reach for the straps," Bonnie recalls:

She would come after me, but my brother wouldn't allow her to get to me. He would pretend he was a monkey. He flailed his arms about and chased my mother around the apartment before she had a chance to get to me. He would chase her, making crazy monkey sounds and flapping his arms all around. She would laugh and give in. She put the straps down and just laughed. He saved me.

Ruth inflicted the kind of pain and suffering on a child that today would be considered out-and-out child abuse, but in those days she got away with it. Although Neil got some share of the abuse, he was always the rising star and so was spared the worst of her wrath. When Ruth got upset, her anger often barreled down on her daughter. "My mother would make me sit at the table until I ate [my vegetables]," Bonnie says. "Neil would sneak over and eat the vegetables for me so I wouldn't get into trouble."

The damage Ruth could cause wasn't limited to straps and wooden hangers. She abused her children psychologically as well. Bonnie was treated as her mother's live-in help. Bonnie recalls:

> *I had to do the laundry and clean the house. If I didn't do everything exactly right, she could fly off the handle and beat me. Sometimes she would snap for nothing. She once made me go to the store and get bread three different times, each time changing her mind on the bread she wanted. She did this to my brother all the time too. I think she just did it on purpose to torture us.*

Another form of punishment Ruth inflicted on both of her children was locking them out of their apartment naked, stranding them in the halls of the complex to face their neighbors and friends. She ignored their pleas to be allowed back inside, committed to embarrassing them as much as possible. Neil and Bonnie's only salvation was six stories up, where their Aunt Dottie and Uncle Seymour lived. Riding that elevator naked, they prayed no one else would get on. Dottie and Seymour regularly opened their door to whichever sibling needed help, temporarily taking them in. Seymour remembers:

> *I came home and found Neil in the hallway, curled in a ball, naked, crying. Ruth had sent him out of the apartment and wouldn't let him back in. Neil didn't tell me what had happened or why, but I knew. She was always very hard on him. She pushed him hard to be success-ful. But she could be very cruel. Neil was a good boy. It was terrible what she did to him. I'll never forget that day. I'll never forget finding him naked on the floor. That kind of thing, it sticks with you.*

Neil's cousin, Sheryl Feinberg, Dottie's daughter, also remembers some of the abuse the Bogatz children received at the hand of their mother. "I was trying to get off the elevator and Neil wouldn't let me. He was covering himself, embarrassed. I don't know why his mother punished him by locking him out of the apartment naked, but that's when my mom would come in to help."

Ruth loved her children. She just had a unique way of showing it. She wanted so badly for Neil to reach the heights that both she and Al would never reach. At the same time, there was a selfish purpose that drove this desire. Ruth wanted Neil's success for herself as much as for her son; essentially, she wanted to be the mother of a star and all that came with it. She sought to bask in the glory of her son's fame and rise up the social ranks with him. To do that, she needed to drive Neil hard.

Ruth instilled in her children a refusal to fail that remained within them. Both Neil and Bonnie would become dedicated perfectionists who remained constantly haunted by their mother. Although Ruth idolized her son, not even he escaped her brutality growing up. Neil's relationship with his mother was no doubt complex. Whether this treatment helped drive Neil single-mindedly toward success can be argued; nevertheless, the abuse was something he would never forget.

CHAPTER 4

The Dreamer Casts Off

I remember Neil would come home and make me sit on my bed and watch him. He'd make me wait as he fixed himself into a strange pose. He'd stand there and ask me, "Tell me if I look like a weeping willow tree blowing in the wind?" It was so funny . . . he had all kinds of strange things like that he came home with.

—Bonnie Ermilio

Neil realized early on that for a small Jewish boy to stand out in the New York streets, he had to learn how to hustle. To the other immigrants who resided in this tiny corner of Brooklyn, he was an easy target. His quick wit and moxie yielded their own set of challenges in a neighborhood where boys were judged by how well they could swing a bat or run a 440. Neil figured he had to be a quick thinker, and the quicker he was, the more notoriety he garnered. With mostly brains and hints of brawn, Neil not only survived—he thrived.

One of Neil's first jobs was as a newspaper delivery boy, and he brought his characteristic entrepreneurship to the task. Rather than just taking a paper route like a regular kid, he negotiated deals with *several* newspapers whereby he would acquire six paper routes throughout the surrounding neighborhoods. After negotiating a payment price on each route, he went through the neighborhood in search of other kids to deliver the papers for him. He had the other kids take less money, and they were grateful to do it. Neil essentially subcontracted the job of paperboy out to more naïve kids in the neighborhood. In fact, he never delivered a single paper. Instead he slept comfortably while others got up early to make the deliveries—all he had to do was collect the money. It's obvious that early on, Neil planned on running things.

Neil started high school at Samuel J. Tilden High School in Brooklyn, New York, but he had other aspirations; he wanted more out of high school than just a standard education. He left the confines of Brooklyn in 1958 for Manhattan and the famed High School of Performing Arts, later popularized by the film and television show *Fame*. At first Neil failed to gain acceptance into the drama department. Not to be denied a place at the esteemed school, he showed up a second time with a saxophone and was accepted into the music program. He then began to master the clarinet and bongo drums, instruments popular in the big band era that he had always loved from listening to music with his father.

Neil relished the opportunity to play in front of students and administrators alike. His dedication was impressive for someone his age, as was his ability to block out the distractions of teenage life. After school, when the other kids were gathered in the park, Neil was home practicing the mental and physical exercises the school had given him as homework. The teenager put absolutely no limitations on when, where, and how much he would practice. School and home became little more than places to perfect his craft.

In 1958, when Neil was fifteen, Ruth took her son for a series of professional headshots in the hopes of landing him a gig as a model. Neil was game, assuming the photos would help him to better promote himself. He concocted the stage name Neil Scott to hide the Jewishness associated with Bogatz, a common practice in show business throughout the twentieth century. Some of those headshots were featured in multiple teen magazines. He also appeared in advertisements for Lipton Tea and Acne Skin Control; the ads brought exposure and would soon provide a nice springboard for his singing career.

Changing his last name for his desired profession wasn't just a gimmick; he did it strategically a couple of times in his career. He didn't just change his own name but also encouraged others to do so. Bonnie's friend, Eileen Freidman, remembers:

When I worked for Neil, he had me use the name Eileen Scott. I asked him why the name Scott? He said it was strong, short, and easy to remember. He thought Friedman was too Jewish at the time and felt like the world was too narrow-minded and biased. I knew he had used that name when he recorded a few years earlier. . . . Any time he wanted to use an "alias" or made-up name, that's the name he would come up with.

Once Neil's modeling career brought some much-needed cash into the Bogatz family, the family began to focus on developing material for Neil to sing. Al wrote the songs "Oh Genie" and "Go Bohemian," and working on them together was a bonding experience for father and son. The experience also legitimized the desire Neil had to pursue a career in show business.

Neil wanted to pursue show business from an early age. He threw himself into the entertainment universe to see what might make him a star, attacking multiple avenues at the same time. His personality opened doors, and by the time he was fifteen, while still a student at the High School of Performing Arts, Neil was a professional singer and model. Numerous other students at the school were hell-bent on being famous, and Neil forged a successful relationship with one of them, Erminie McNaulty. Erminie was an attractive girl and a highly skilled dancer. They immediately recognized in each other a kindred spirit, a desire for success. In 1959 the two became a formidable dance team, traveling together during summers away from school. Their relationship would take them to a variety of locations, professionally and personally. Erminie would also be Neil's first real girlfriend.

They visited the Catskills and performed at numerous hotels, such as the Spring Lake Hotel, Laurels Country Club, Laurel in the Pines Hotel, and many others. These locations in the Catskills were often referred to as the "Borscht Belt," or the "Jewish Alps," and were popular vacation destinations for Jewish-Americans living in and around New York. The hotels were a mountain oasis for a variety of entertainment. The area drew a distinguished list of performers and was a small hub for high-quality entertainment. However, the bread and butter of the Catskills' hotel circuit were the comedians. People like George Burns, Gracie Allen, Sid Caesar, Buddy Hackett, Don Rickles, Woody Allen, and Jerry Stiller performed regularly.

As he graced the dance floors of the Borscht Belt, Neil had the opportunity to hobnob with some extraordinary talent. He continued to use the name Neil Scott as he performed with Erminie, and despite their young age, the two danced with the flair of seasoned professionals. The duo not only performed in the Catskills but also moved their talents abroad, hitting the high seas and performing on the cruise ship *Queen of Bermuda*.

When school was back in session, Neil and Erminie landed a job dancing at a local restaurant in the heart of Manhattan. While other kids went to movies on Friday and Saturday nights, Neil and Erminie worked. The gig was an opportunity for more exposure and highlighted both Neil's singing and dancing. The Luau 400 was a Hawaiian restaurant in midtown Manhattan featuring Polynesian cuisine. It was not a normal dinner joint; its owner, Harry Bloomfield, built a stage reminiscent of a lavishly conceived Hawaiian movie set, "with tropical trees, waterfalls and exotic birds."[1] He renovated a simple restaurant into an evening of dining and escapist entertainment for its customers that still exists today. The Luau 400 was the perfect setting for Neil and Erminie to display their talents. Neil put himself in the right place at the right time—and fate would soon walk through the door.

Neil was seventeen years old when Bill Darnell was in attendance one night at the Luau 400 in 1960. Darnell was heading up a new record company called Portrait Records. Neil and Erminie were dancing on the stage when Darnell took notice—not of them at first, but of the captivated patrons watching their performance. He then turned toward the source. As Darnell feasted on the Luau's famous pupu platter, he watched the personable young man gripping the audience. After Neil finished singing, Darnell approached him and asked if he was interested in recording on the label.

At seventeen, Bogart had already been waiting years to hear that question.

Neil's first album, which he put together with his father, had been small potatoes. This, however, was the big time. His singing career officially began when he recorded two songs for Portrait Records. Neil landed a hit with his song, "Bobby," which got immediate airplay and seemed to strike a chord with the public. The Bogatzes tried to ensure the song's success on two fronts. Neil kept a close eye on what Darnell was doing to help promote the songs and help guarantee the success of Neil's single, and Ruth began a grassroots campaign by his family and friends to call local DJs and get the song played on the air. She also handed out bags of dimes to all the kids in the neighborhood and pressured them to call the local radio stations to ensure her son's record continued to get air time and had the opportunity to move up the charts. The scheme worked; the calls got the DJs to keep "Bobby" in rotation and helped thrust it onto the charts. Getting a single on the charts garnered immediate success for young up-and-comer Neil Scott.

The song's lyrics centered on a dying youth, which was too dramatic for radio play in the conservative radio market at the time, but the music itself was reminiscent of the early pre-country sounds of Kenny Rogers or the more poppy tunes from Pat Boone. Boston radio stations even banned the song because of its dark tone. Regardless of the banning, and perhaps because of it in some places, "Bobby" gave Neil Scott notoriety and some attention from big players. Almost immediately, Dick Clark, America's oldest teenager and a prime star maker, took notice of Neil Scott's talents. In 1961 Neil became a regular on Dick Clark's highly successful *American Bandstand.* Clark also brought Neil out to his Palisades Park Rock Show in upstate New York as a regular performer. His relationship with Clark (who'd remain America's oldest teenager for another fifty years) lasted long after his initial success. The two remained industry friends until the day Neil died.

In 1961 Neil Scott's stock was rising. Landing on the charts with a hit song was a big deal for a boy from the streets of Brooklyn. He even had his own fan club. There was a lot to keep up with, so his sister, Bonnie, and her friend Eileen Freidman and others helped distribute information for *The Neil Scott Fan Club*, a newsletter that in the early 1960s regularly updated fans on their young hero. Common for pop stars of the era, the fan club focused on keeping all his young fans abreast of what Neil was up to and where he would be making an appearance. Knowing the importance of staying loyal to his local fans, and showing a soft spot for his roots, Neil also performed at the local Jewish Center with Bonnie.

Despite the burst of success, Neil quickly hit a professional plateau. Other than "Bobby," Neil Scott never had another hit—"a has-been who never was," his Grandma Edith claimed.[2] Grandma Edith, much like Neil's own mother, Ruth, could be quite nasty. "The meanest grandmother in the world," Bonnie says. The negativity only seemed to drive Neil harder; he remained undeterred by the flameout.

As requests for his appearances dwindled, Neil went to plan B and tried his hand at acting. Neil's first foray into movies was a soft-core porn feature film called *Sin in the Suburbs*, in which he appeared under his acting pseudonym, Wayne Roberts. A running joke for his family and friends was that Wayne was the "only clothed person in the entire movie." Unfazed, Neil was so excited he brought his entire family to a movie theater in Philadelphia to see it. They thought they were going to see a mainstream movie and had no idea there was so much sex and nudity involved.

Caught up in the excitement, Neil failed to mention that the film was a pornographic one. Needless to say, some family members were mortified. But to Neil, all that mattered was that he was on the big screen, a performer. He felt it was a step in the right direction. His sole focus was to be successful, and sometimes that created blindness. He saw even a low-budget porn film as climbing another rung on the show business ladder.

Neil may have had a hidden passion for movies, but his strength was music, and that industry would one day butter his bread. He just didn't know how yet. He continued to travel and hustle for any kind of job he could get.

One steady gig he could always rely on was at the Laurel in the Pines Hotel in the Catskills, where he performed with Erminie. He also served as dance instructor to the wives and girls while their husbands were off golfing or otherwise engaged. One evening in December 1959, he found himself face-to-face on the dance floor with a beautiful young socialite named Beth Weiss. Nothing would ever be the same. Neil's personal relationship with Erminie would come to an end. Their professional relationship would last a few more years and then fizzle out as well. Beth entered his life and things changed for both of them—in ways they couldn't have imagined.

～～

Neil was magnetic, unlike any boy I had known. I came from a very wealthy family, went to private school, and only dated guys like me. I was only seventeen, and he appealed to the rebel teenager that I was.

—BETH WEISS GUBER

In the late 1950s, Beth Weiss's family went to the Laurel in the Pines Hotel in the Catskills at regular intervals throughout the year. Occasions such as birthdays, religious holidays, Wednesdays—they were all times to celebrate. The Weisses were a family of means, and as regulars and close friends of the owners, they were treated like royalty by the staff. On a lazy afternoon in December 1959, during one such holiday getaway, the family split up for the day to enjoy the hotel's considerable amenities.

Beth had an appointment for a "tea dance," a mid-afternoon event in one of the ballrooms adjacent to the garden. Neil was the dance instructor and was on duty at the time, paid to dance with the guests. Expecting the usual fair, husband-less wives looking to mix it up with the help. Neil was taken aback when he saw Beth all alone on the dance floor. Beth remembers Neil moving over and asking her to dance. Although Neil's job *required* him to dance with the various women he taught at the hotel, dancing with Beth was different. They were smitten from the get-go. The magnetic teenager and the privileged guest fell in love.

There were, however, some obstacles as their relationship progressed. The greatest challenge was the culture clash between a lower-class kid from the Brooklyn projects and the wealthy "princess" who grew up in the penthouses of New York. In a way, it had the tenor of a classic love story: The rich girl fell hard for the poor boy with big dreams. The greatest issue was Beth's family, in particular, Beth's father—"a real son of a bitch" according to Joe Ermilio, Neil's future brother-in-law. "My parents hated Neil," Beth admitted to us. "He always tried to prove to them he was worthy." Despite her parents' disapproval (or maybe because of it), she kept seeing Neil.

As Neil traveled around promoting "Bobby," money was scarce. The subsequent follow-up records, "It Happened All Over Again," "Tomboy," "One Piece Bathing Suit," and even his *Greatest Hits* album (just a repackaging of all those songs and their B-sides) never seemed to connect with an audience. Neither did his final song "(I Don't Stand) A Ghost of a Chance with You," recorded at the tail end of his singing career on Cameo-Parkway's label. He even withdrew his name from the credits of "One Piece Bathing Suit," instead listing his porn moniker, Wayne Roberts, as the lead singer. Neil's singing career was floundering. He had hit a giant creative wall and wasn't able to produce another hit. The record company even took to billing him as Neil "Bobby" Scott to capitalize on his one hit—an example of how he was being forced to live up to early expectations.

The reality was that he had peaked and, like countless singers before him, had fallen victim to the business's need for a performer to churn out hit after hit to stay relevant. Neil was learning the way the business could chew you up, get every last bit of flavor, and then spit you out. It's likely that this experience gave Neil insight into the performer's psyche that would become invaluable later on—when *he* was the one doing the chewing.

In the midst of his struggle to repeat his success as a singer, Neil was called upon to serve his time in the US Army Reserves. Stationed in Fort Dix, New Jersey, Neil wouldn't have to travel too far from home, and his sister and friends could visit him at the base. After a short six-month stint in the reserves, Neil returned to a steeper uphill battle if he was to win over his potential in-laws and find a good job. However, he refused to let his lack of money prevent his relationship with Beth from moving forward. He was going to see that they were married. Neil wasn't about to let anything stop him.

Neil and Beth were engaged in December 1963. Neil had to juggle three different jobs to pay for the engagement ring. He worked at a shoe store and at the post office with his father, and he appeared in the aforementioned soft-core porn film, *Sin in the Suburbs*. In desperate need for legitimate work, he went door to door with a camera to take professional baby pictures, a job that brought out his natural salesmanship. Perhaps unsurprisingly, these odd jobs were not promising enough to win over Beth's parents.

Beth made Neil take night classes at New York University (NYU) in hopes of developing Neil's "overall" skills, though she couldn't change the fact that he had never been much of a student. Beth remembers doing nearly all of Neil's NYU papers for him while he attended night classes. Whether Neil earned the grades or had significant help, the method itself seemed to take a backseat to the results. Beth wanted Neil to gain stature through his schooling. With Neil's singing career on the rocks, Beth saw a college degree as another avenue to success for him. Her support for him was unwavering, though his commitment to school was decidedly less so.

It was Beth's drive that brought Neil to NYU—she was attending Syracuse University herself—but Neil had virtually no interest in college. He wasn't a big fan of traditional school, especially considering the cost and his lack of a real income, even if Beth was the one paying. He stayed at NYU for a short while and then bowed out. His heart just wasn't in it; he only stuck with it to appease his love.

While he was still enrolled at NYU, one of Beth's good friends from Syracuse, Lynda, was dating a young man named Peter Guber. Peter and Neil first met, quite serendipitously, on a double date with the women and hit it off immediately. They would forge a professional and personal relationship that would last throughout Neil's life. Guber and Bogart traveled in and out of the same circles for years and ultimately became dynamic business partners. At the time of their first meeting, Neil was still struggling to find his path; he had no way of knowing what lay in store for the two of them.

Realizing his path at NYU was likely to lead nowhere, Neil searched the *New York Times* want ads for anything, any tip that would lead to a better career. Some of the motivation was no doubt to get a better footing with his in-laws. Ruth Bogatz, meanwhile, still held out hope that Neil could break big into the entertainment field. All that mattered to his mother was Neil's being a success. As Neil's sister, Bonnie, told us, "My mother supported Neil in anything and everything he did. It didn't matter what it was. As long as Neil's career was moving forward, she supported him. He could do no wrong in her eyes." She still believed her son could be (and would be) a big success, but the clock was ticking. Neil was in his early twenties by then, and both his singing and acting careers were floundering. He needed another way in.

Neil took a job at Fortune Personnel, an employment agency in Manhattan. Just as teenage Neil had gotten the neighborhood kids to do the legwork on his paper route, Neil sought the aid of a friend to "hit the pavement" to help him fill jobs for the company. He employed Bonnie's friend Eileen to make cold calls for him to find any available jobs in Manhattan at the time. This enabled Neil to swoop in and help the company in need find a temp to fill the open spot.

Neil paid Eileen a dollar per call, under the table, to help out—essentially she was splitting the work with him. Eileen remembers, "Neil scripted what I was to say on the phone. Hopefully they would have job openings and they would let me know about them. Neil even tried to get *me* a better paying job, even though it meant he would lose me." Some moral compass inside Neil led him to try to land Bonnie a job; he knew he was taking advantage of his sister's friend, and it likely didn't sit well with him. The reality is that Neil understood he would get credit for doing the work of two people. The risk was worth it—the business cared about results, and Neil brought them. The issue of how didn't seem to matter much.

Neil's bosses at Fortune Personnel liked him so much they decided to give him a job working there as a copywriter. Using his creativity and gall, Neil poured some real imagination into the ads he wrote, which garnered him a lot of attention for their originality. In an interview he gave to Anthony Cook, Neil mused about how "people used to come up to the office just to see who wrote the screwball ads."[3] He found himself writing headlines like "Life Is Just a Chair of Bowlies" to grab job seekers' attention in the classifieds. It was a simple play on words off the saying "Life is just a bowl of cherries." Many years later, artist Mary Engelbreit found success with the same phrase, using it on greeting cards as well as for the title of a book she published in 1992.

Working at Fortune Personnel allowed Neil to use his natural skills of promotion. Although he wasn't yet promoting the next big music act, his boss praised his work and the clients were so pleased that the agency offered to make him a partner. He had managed to literally walk in off the street and in just a few months become a valued member of the team.

In 1964 a job came across Neil's desk that would allow him to cross the threshold. It was a campaign for an ad at *Cash Box* magazine, the second largest record magazine in the country behind *Billboard*. The job was to sell ads directly for *Cash Box*. Neil called *Cash Box* under the name Neil Stewart and let them know he had the perfect individual for the job—a young man by the name of Neil Bogart. Unbeknownst to them, Neil set up his own interview and followed up with numerous calls, pushing for them to hire the young upstart Bogart. Neil's relentless promotion—and clever roundabout—paid off; he was hired. With some fancy maneuvering, and certain amount of rule-bending, Neil Bogart was born.

After a detour in the ad world, Neil was now going back to his one true love, music. Not as a singer—he was still only selling ads—but it was a start. He was on his way. More often than not, all Neil needed was a crack of opportunity and he could kick any door in.

With Beth's support, Neil stepped confidently into the job at *Cash Box* magazine. There he developed relations with upper management that would serve him well, but it was his ability to sell ads that set him apart from everyone else. His networking skills took over, and his rise back into the music industry began. "My mother was happy Neil got back into the business," says Bonnie. "Although it was only at a magazine writing ads, it was a way back in. And that's all that mattered to her."

For Neil it was the chance he had been looking for. *Cash Box* gave Bogart an inside view of how the industry worked. It would be the basis for a hands-on education in the music world, far more important than any night classes he took. It was just a few months, but those months would be the catalyst for a new start and new opportunities.

His life with Beth was evolving, and his in-laws began to see that he was trying hard to impress them. But trying wasn't exactly cutting it. They expected him to succeed, and there would be no moving forward with Beth until that was assured. Being a kid from the streets, Neil knew how to wheel and deal. He knew how to network and never forgot a name or a face—hugely important traits in his business—and he got far on these abilities. However, Neil desperately needed something that Beth provided. She gave us some unique insight into what Neil gained during this time:

Neil used the connections and stature of my family to rise up out of his sociology and learn to be comfortable with wealthy, self-confident men. He needed to deal with these men on equal footing. A lot of the entertainment industry is after-hour socializing; contacts were very important. I believe our marriage gave him credibility and enabled him to mingle on equal footing.

He had all the pressures he put on himself, along with some more from his wife's family, as well as the expectations of his own family bearing down upon him. He had doubts, but he would outrace them. And once Neil Bogart got the chance, he would race up the ladder without stopping or looking down.

CHAPTER 5

Trading Up

Neil never had a plan to become a record executive. He just followed the road and it ended where it did.

—BETH WEISS

The 1960s saw its share of dynamic events, many of which molded Neil's own creative decisions. The time period had an undeniable ripple effect on the creative world. The Vietnam War, the civil rights and women's rights movements, JFK and LBJ and RFK and Nixon, student protests, payola scandals, urban riots—it was an era of sweeping and chaotic change, and the music industry was not immune to the winds. Simply writing or talking about the 1960s conjures up certain images; it's a language shared both by the generations who lived through that time and by the ones who've only read about it and listened to its soundtrack.

War dominated the mood of the 1960s. John F. Kennedy was elected in 1960 and in the next two years went head to head with the Soviets for two Cold War showdowns: the Bay of Pigs Invasion and the Cuban Missile Crisis. Both added to the hysteria in the United States that nuclear war was one step away. A game of chess between the democracy in the United States and communism in the Soviet Union played out, constantly hanging over everyone's head. Something, somewhere, had to give.

The Vietnam saga began ramping up in 1961 and would continue to dominate headlines for the next thirteen years, eventually killing fifty-eight thousand young Americans. In 1963 Kennedy, a president embraced by the baby boomers and a champion of racial equality, was assassinated in Dallas. In 1965 Malcolm X was assassinated by members of the Nation of

Islam. In 1968 civil rights icon Martin Luther King Jr. was assassinated; two months later, beloved presidential candidate Robert F. Kennedy was murdered as well. The string of high-profile political executions added to the turmoil and created an anxiety that rippled through all of American society and the world at large.

The music industry followed right along, reflecting this tension and uncertainty. Neil helped spearhead some oldies but goodies in the early 1960s, but the game was about to change as nobody had predicted it would. The United States was about to be invaded.

There was only one large-scale invasion that actually landed on American soil, and it wasn't sent from Moscow. It was the so-called "British Invasion"—the term used to describe the major influx of rock and roll and pseudo-pop performers from Great Britain who, following the Beatles, were thrust into popularity from 1964 to 1966.

Ironically, the roots of the British music invasion actually came from America: blues music from the South and cities like Memphis and Chicago. American blues musicians, many of whom languished in obscurity in their homeland, had a huge impact on the British youth and music community abroad in the late 1950s. The Rolling Stones were enormously influenced by these black American musicians (Keith Richards and Mick Jagger famously chatted about these records upon first meeting). British bands such as the Beatles also combined the American sounds with skiffle, early rock and roll (American artists like Jerry Lee Lewis and Little Richard), and other British music. This fusing of styles would create a music revolution, as an incredible influx of British music poured into American culture. Fifty years later, our musical landscape is still indebted to the artists that broke though during this time of enormous change.

On December 10, 1963, a few weeks after JFK's assassination, the nation was still in shock and mourning, and the people looking for something to embrace. The *CBS Evening News with Walter Cronkite*—at the time the most trusted broadcast in the nation—ran a story about "Beatlemania." The phenomenon was already running rampant across the United Kingdom, and soon people began requesting their music on our shores.

On December 17, disc jockey Carroll James at radio station WWDC in Washington, DC, introduced "I Want to Hold Your Hand," the first ever live airing of a Beatles song in the United States. This spurred a massive uprising of musical interest in the Beatles in the Washington, DC, area. People flocked to stores for the records that weren't even released yet. Capitol Records would release the album three weeks ahead of schedule. By January 1964, "I Want to Hold Your Hand" had reached #1 on the *Cash Box* chart. The following week it hit #1 on the *Billboard* chart. Then, on Sunday, February 9, 1964, the Beatles appeared on *The Ed Sullivan Show.* At the end of the twentieth century, the appearance would become universally accepted as a seminal moment in music history. Other British artists such as Dusty Springfield, Manfred Mann, Freddie and the Dreamers, Herman's Hermits, the Kinks, and the Rolling Stones shot up the American charts and began to take over US radio.

❧

Neil Bogart had developed an eclectic ear for music from growing up listening to big band music in his parents' living room and choosing to learn to play the bongo drums and the saxophone in high school. As head of a major music label, he was not yet ready to jump on the bandwagon. American mainstays were falling by the wayside, unable to maintain their usual place at the top of the *Billboard* charts. There was a new wave of music, and many companies were hopping on board. Chubby Checker, Fats Domino, and the dynamic dance music of yesteryear had been replaced with a different kind of beat: a blues-driven rock beat. Still, Bogart didn't bite. His inner ear heard a different tune.

Drug use exploded in the second half of the 1960s, as a distinct countercultural revolution sought to fight the conservative norms that dominated the previous decade. With the baby boom explosion, there were a lot of teenagers in the 1960s who sought to upend their parents' carefully groomed society. In particular, the youth were in an uproar about US involvement in Vietnam. It was a "young" war, being fought by kids who were being drafted and sent over by the tens of thousands to die.

The movement, marked by widespread, socially acceptable drug use, highlighted by marijuana, led to a wave of psychedelic music by bands such as the Velvet Underground, the Doors, and a new, matured Beatles. Sexual liberation exploded as women broke free of the mold set in place by their mothers and began a "free love" revolution. Music transcended mere entertainment and became tied to movements and cultural statements. Johnny Cash rebelled against conservative controls and roared his messages—daring to record live performances at both Folsom and San Quentin Prisons. Bob Dylan sang his antiestablishment tunes, becoming a spokesman to millions of fans, whether he wanted to be or not. While on stage in London, Jimi Hendrix lit his guitar on fire, perhaps the single greatest act of protest toward . . . well, nobody knew exactly what. Boring guitar solos, most likely. The end of the decade saw an attempt to coalesce this all into three days of music, drugs, and communal living: the Woodstock Festival in upstate New York.

The 1960s seemed to have a bit of everything from political turmoil to social and musical triumphs. Change was in the air and the decade of the 1960s would be no different for Neil Bogart. Though the job at *Cash Box* brought some legitimacy to Bogart's music ambitions, he'd already started laying the groundwork a few years earlier in a more creative capacity. In spring 1962, at the very green age of nineteen, Bogart had produced a record—the first production credit of his career. Mark Stevens, who would become famous a few years later as the front man for the band Vanilla Fudge, cut his first record on Allison Records at the young age of fifteen. Stevens was born Mark Stein—making him another in a long line of performers who dropped their ethnic-sounding name on their way to fame and fortune.

Bogart and Stevens had actually met years earlier, in 1959 on the set of *The Milt Grant Show*. Milt Grant, a local radio personality, hosted a Washington, DC–based TV show featuring teenagers dancing to albums, a sort of precursor to *American Bandstand* and later *Soul Train*. Bogart was an MC on the show, while Stevens, who had genuine musical talent, was placed in front of the camera because his father, acting as manager, wanted to get his eleven-year-old son exposure. Among other guests for that episode was soul icon Sam Cooke. Stevens told an interviewer, "I remember one time [my father] heard about this thing . . . he got me this audition, it was this rock 'n' roll show. I just remember going into this rehearsal hall and being scared, ten years old and all these teenage rock 'n' roll guys and stuff, you know, and I auditioned and I got the gig, and that's where I met Neil Bogart. . . .[1]"

Bogart and Stevens took an almost immediate liking to each other. Bogart, ever the optimist, took Mark under his wing and managed to get him into the Brill Building. Since World War II, the Brill Building in Manhattan had been synonymous with American mainstream popular music. In the 1950s it was *the* place to go to cut a record. Neil introduced Mark to a sound engineer, and a record was soon produced. "I just went in and I cut this thing," Stevens remembers. "I don't even remember, we were gonna get a deal with this small record label, and next thing you know I had this record out and we were singing it in the show. . . . I remember I was real excited. . . . That thing lasted like a few months and it was over. I was still in grammar school, and my mother was like freakin' out because I was missing school, you know what I mean?"[2]

Stevens's record featured the two songs "Come Back to My Heart" on side A and "Magic Rose" on side B. Neil saw a burgeoning talent in the young man that he wanted to develop—Stevens's success five years later with Vanilla Fudge would prove Neil's foresight.

Producing the record was a key point in Neil's development as he realized two important things: He had the skill to spot talent in others, and he knew where the *real* money was. While musicians got paid pennies for records sold at the time, producers got paid *dollars*. Neil had his sights set on making dollars, lots of them. "Neil never had a plan to become a record executive," Beth Weiss says now. "He just followed the road and it ended where it did."

<hr />

Neil may have played the system to get inside *Cash Box* magazine, but once he was there, he learned the value of working hard and trading up. In fact, he put an entire career together this way. Neil dealt with a variety of clients in the music business while at *Cash Box*, including MGM Records, which in the early to mid-1960s was producing and promoting bands as successful (and varied) as the Righteous Brothers, the Velvet Underground, the Mothers of Invention (with new guitarist Frank Zappa), and, under the newly founded Kama Sutra label, the Lovin' Spoonful. The sheer diversity of this list drives home how much was changing in the music industry at the time. It was a rich and exciting time to be in the music business, with an influx of styles and genres regularly breaking through into the mainstream.

After selling and creating ads for *Cash Box*, Neil built up such a good relationship at MGM and their promotional team that, in winter 1962, they offered him a job as promoter. Once again, he traded up and snatched the opportunity. Neil hit the road and promoted a variety of music acts for MGM, from pop act Herman's Hermits to Rat Pack legend Sammy Davis Jr., up and down the East Coast, spending most of his time in New England.

Neil's travel schedule was simply grueling; the job took him out on the road from Monday through Friday, leaving his wife at home and the young couple very little time together. Despite the long time apart, and though it was tough at times, Beth stood by Neil's side. Things weren't easy at home, with Neil traveling all over the East Coast. But both Neil and Beth believed the work and sacrifice would pay off in the end. And it did.

Bogart's reputation as a dynamic ad and promotional man was growing in the business. Before corporations and conglomerates bought up most of the labels, the music industry was a tightly knit world. Back then, a good reputation was as valuable as anything. Neil's success as promoter for MGM didn't go unnoticed by Jerry Shifrin, head of Cameo-Parkway Records, a Philadelphia-based record label that was a combination of two previous separate labels, Cameo Records and Parkway Records.

Cameo produced numerous R&B groups as well and played a big role in popular music through the early 1960s. Bobby Rydell's "Kissin' Time" was also a big hit for them in 1959. (Later, Neil would get KISS to rewrite and record a wildly different version of the track.) Chubby Checker's monster hits "The Twist" (1960) and "Pony Time" (1961) were huge for the record label, both hitting #1 on the charts. Cameo rode Rydell's and Checker's backs to become a real industry player. Chubby Checker's "The Twist" and his follow-up "Let's Twist Again" were landmarks in a long line of dance crazes that swept the United States. (Almost fifty years later, in 2008, Checker's "The Twist" was named the biggest chart hit of all time by *Billboard* magazine.) The avalanche of success yielded stunning results for Cameo, but it also proved to be their swan song.

Cameo peaked in those years before the British Invasion. Like a lot of labels, they were unceremoniously drowned out when they failed to adapt to the new musical landscape and the new generation of listeners. Chubby Checker's "Limbo Rock" in 1962 would be his last top-ten hit. Cameo, along with Checker and a lot of acts from the 1950s, was simply ignored—and then trampled by new acts and their screaming teenage fans. All the success at Cameo-Parkway came to a crashing halt with the arrival of bands like the Beatles and the Rolling Stones to US stores around 1963–64. Music's popularity in American culture often happens in swings, and labels that don't stay ahead of the curve to anticipate what's coming are doomed. Cameo was a textbook example.

Much of 1962 and early 1963 was characterized by a big dry spell at Cameo-Parkway. By 1963 Cameo desperately needed an injection of fresh ideas and someone hungry to keep the company afloat. Neil Bogart was brought in to replace Jerry Shifrin as the head of sales at Cameo and to provide the energy necessary to help revive the struggling label. Neil and Beth liked the prospect of Cameo for a number of reasons, not least of which was the fact that he could stay closer to home, working from the office instead of on the road. Also, Bogart was becoming something of an industry player. The job move was newsworthy enough for *Billboard* magazine to run a piece on the young up-and-comer and his new role.[3]

Under Bogart, Cameo would go on to sign and promote groups like the Kinks and give Bob Seger his first recording contract. Though neither took off while at Cameo, they ended up having enormous careers later on—another testament to Neil's ability to spot talent. A 1966 newspaper article in *Cash Box* magazine highlighted an up-and-coming band out of Flint, Michigan, that was making all kinds of noise on local radio shows. They had the wonderfully bizarre name of Question Mark and the Mysterians. Long before bands like the Ramones or the Sex Pistols were heard on the airwaves, they were one of the first bands to be called "punk rock"; in the mid 1960s, this was a very rare, raw, and unproven sound. But new was in, as was "authentic," so labels from all over were sniffing around them.

There was only one problem: An airline strike had delayed all the major record label executives from getting to see the band. The executives expected the strike to end soon; they assumed their rivals couldn't get to the band either, so nobody seemed to be in a big rush. That is, nobody except Neil Bogart. Bogart sensed the opportunity before him and capitalized immediately. He rented a private plane and flew to Michigan—ahead of everyone else—to meet Question Mark and the Mysterians. The band's eccentric front man was actually named Question Mark. Claiming he was from another planet, he would actually change his name to "?" years before Prince took a symbol for a name. As would be his calling card (and strategy) throughout his career, Neil wasted little time in signing talent once he saw it. He signed the group immediately, and in fall 1966, their smash hit, the organ-infused "96 Tears," went to #1 on the *Billboard* Hot 100. They went gold (selling over a million records) and received the BMI award for over three million airplays. The group also had the distinction of being the first Latino group with a mainstream hit record in the United States.

One of the main reasons for Neil Bogart's success was his almost supernatural ability to quickly spot a good hook—the part of a song that grabs a listener, catches his ear, and stays with him long after the song has stopped playing. In real-world terms, the hook equals dollars. Neil's hold over listeners and record buyers depended on his ability to recognize hooks—and he made the most of it.

The hook is everything in music, especially in pop music, where the tune needs to be digested quicker, and after just one or two listens on the radio. Neil had a distinct gift of recognizing hooks. Throughout his career, he would sign bands merely after listening to them once over the phone. Years later, he would sign KISS after hearing them play over a scratchy telephone line. Neil could home in on a sound and not get bogged down by needing to see the performance. He wasn't limited in that way—if anything, seeing the performance was a *distraction* from the sound. In the 1960s (and 1970s), it was all about radio; if a band couldn't pass his keen sensibilities, there was no place for them on the national dial.

After only eighteen months as a salesman at Cameo-Parkway, Neil received a promotion to vice president. He saw the company's bottom line finally turn a profit after signing bands such as Question Mark and the Mysterians, Terry Knight, and the Hardly Worthit Players, as well as churning out twenty-four charting singles and five charting albums in that time. However, Neil could smell the change in the air, and he knew Cameo was still a sinking ship. Rydell and Checker were off contract, the new British bands had forever changed America's ears, and Bernie Lowe, one of the label's founding members, had become disillusioned with the business and was increasingly absent from decision making.

Since Bogart's MO was to trade his way up the industry ladder, he didn't have unrealistic expectations at Cameo-Parkway. He accepted that the label was just a stepping-stone to the next move, and he diligently kept his eyes peeled for other opportunities. Through his position at Cameo, Neil made friends with Artie Ripp of Kama Sutra Records. Kama Sutra had a distribution deal with MGM that they weren't happy with. They were looking to start a new label and wanted a fresh creative force in the industry to take on the challenge. Artie Ripp's partner, Art Kass, offered Neil something too good to pass up—his own New York City–based label. Bogart knew his future lay elsewhere, away from Cameo-Parkway. In February 1964 *American Bandstand* moved from its East Coast home in Philadelphia to Los Angeles, taking away Cameo's proximity and access to an enormous source of promotion and exposure.

Jim Dawson's fascinating book *The Twist* explores the checkered history of that iconic song and its relationship with *American Bandstand* and Dick Clark. The author also touches on the thread between Cameo-Parkway and Casablanca Records. Dawson told us: "Neil Bogart joined Cameo-Parkway as a VP and sales manager in 1967 before moving on to . . . Buddah, where he fine-tuned the art of hyping studio creations, i.e., artists that didn't exist outside the studio, like the Archies. Cameo-Parkway without doubt suffered the loss of Dick Clark's promotion; Clark was a silent partner in Cameo at one point and owned other companies with Cameo head Bernie Lowe. The label was also a victim of changing musical tastes and new owners, especially Allen Klein, who seemed more interested in owning music and 'tying it up' than selling records."[4]

Thus, in 1967 Buddah Records was born. Bogart, at the astonishingly young age of twenty-four, was the youngest label head in the music industry.

—◦—

From 1963 to 1967 Neil Bogart lived inside a whirlwind. He went from a fledgling singer/dancer/actor, to door-to-door salesman, to green record executive, to head of his own label. Obviously it was not a traditional blueprint that others could follow. As a young kid in Brooklyn with outsize dreams, he couldn't have figured this way into the business if he had tried.

Perhaps more important to him, at this point he finally showed his worth to his in-laws. Jylle, the first of Beth and Neil's three children, was born in 1967. It seemed that he'd finally achieved the kind of success his mother had envisioned for him—and his wife's family had required of him. Neil Bogart was now a somebody. To maintain that level of respect, he needed to devote his life to his career. Simply getting a record label wasn't enough. He needed to have it all; he wanted to be on top, and he was just getting started.

—◦—

Neil Bogart began the 1960s as a teenager with a dream to strike gold in the entertainment business by whatever means necessary, but his destiny manifested along more unconventional routes. This is a common theme for him. At the time he seemed to be blessed by a growing family, a bizarre career trajectory pasted together through sheer tenacity, and the kind of respect that yielded power. He also noticed a gap, a hole that couldn't be filled by the counterculture. Neil Bogart was the chief decision maker at a major record label, and he noticed that one key demographic was without a voice. While twenty-somethings and older teenagers were burning their bras and draft cards and tuning out, their younger siblings (and sometimes their parents) were left searching for something that appealed to them. There needed to be another option.

Neil was not a man who followed trends—he created them. Cameo-Parkway got trampled by the screaming teenagers of Beatlemania and its offspring, and highly successful established artists like Bobby Darin and Bobby Rydell drowned in their wake. Even Elvis Presley struggled on the charts for a while, unable to crack through what was an overwhelming sea change in public taste; he too almost drowned in the tidal wave. Bogart's signing of Question Mark and the Mysterians in 1966, a Latin punk group of all things, shows he wasn't swayed too much by trends. His success with them showed he wasn't crazy either.

Neil also found success with Terry Knight, a former disc jockey who had talent writing and singing, producing a convergence of pop and rock. With the Hardly Worthit Players, a group of comedians and radio personalities who made gag records, he also found broad appeal with younger audiences. Bogart had a soft spot for comedians and records, releasing numerous comedy albums throughout his career with varying success. Neil made some diverse choices at Cameo, but they would be nothing compared to the choices he made later in the decade at Buddah Records.

In the latter half of the 1960s, Neil Bogart responded to the counterculture by driving a new kind of music into the hearts and minds of Americans: "bubblegum pop." Bubblegum is most easily associated with the kinds of pop music songs generated for younger teens. It was a fun-loving, nonpolitical, non-drug-induced form of music that lent itself to three minutes of mindless, finger-snapping fun. The quintessential bubblegum song centered on catchy hooks that people could immediately enjoy. As the whole world was seemingly up in arms and going to war and the mood in America was all about choosing sides, Neil gave the country a sound it could—in theory—all agree on. Betting against the sure thing, the musical gambler hit it big. The public ate it up; Buddah Records made millions off this strategy of going against the grain of the typical 1960's sounds.

Neil's musical choices were seemingly at odds with what was going on in the world around him, and that focus paid off big. Bogart made his bets on pop music, the kind of music that made people happy and energetic, and it completely bucked the contemporary music trend. He led the counterrevolution. Bogart and bubblegum pop answered a basic question: *When everyone is rebelling against the same thing, how do you stand out?* As British rock, blues-based rock, and psychedelic music got more complex and experimental, Bogart kept it simple—fun, hook-y songs to rope in the pre-teens and young teenagers. There was something nostalgic, almost 1950s, about it, which drew in the parents, and something rebellious about its lack of rebelliousness, which brought in the younger crowds.

As Neil found success with a new gig at Buddah Records, his family began to move up in the world as well. In the second half of the 1960s, the Bogatz household moved to a much nicer neighborhood on Foster Avenue in Brooklyn. The three-story house featured a wraparound porch and a nice, finished basement. Their home more than doubled in size. Unthinkable just a few years earlier, Ruth even managed a staff at her home. The Jewish Foster Federation System hired a housekeeper by the name of Mabel to help Ruth take care of the children. Al was still a postal worker, but now they started a foster home. With Neil out of the house and Bonnie almost out of her teens, Ruth focused her attention on the foster home.

True to form, Ruth would treat her foster children, complete strangers when they came through the door, far better than Neil or Bonnie. It would be a sore spot for both of the Bogatz children throughout their entire lives. "That stuck with us always," Bonnie says. "Both Neil and I never understood how our mother could treat the foster kids so much better than her own children." There were likely more practical reasons for this. Legally speaking, Ruth had no choice but to be accommodating to the foster kids, also adhering to numerous interviews and psychological tests by the state in order to be awarded the right to even have the foster home. The rent on their home was subsidized by the state, financially enabling Al and Ruth for the first time in their lives. The state also paid for Mable.

Nevertheless, Al and Ruth were good people who wanted to help children. Despite Ruth's issues with her own children, she was a savior for numerous others. Al and Ruth provided a home and shelter to dozens and dozens of foster children, trying to give them something they never had themselves: caring parents. They would go on to adopt two of the foster children, brothers Lance and Ira. The brothers would change their last name to Bogatz (later changed again to Bogart). The Bogatzes were entering a new class, one that Ruth had hoped to join from her earliest days with Al. With a new home and more money, they were no longer living in the shadows of the projects.

Buddah Records kept Neil busy, but in spite of this (or maybe because of it), his relationship with his family back East remained extremely close. There were so many relatives that they established their own club. The "Cousin's Club" was a series of parties and events that were held by Neil and his relatives to get together and reconnect. Each party was hosted by a different cousin, featuring food, alcohol, and even a little pot. The meetings were innocent and provided the extended family members a great opportunity to get together and spend some time with Bogart. Howie Bogatz, Renee Freeman, Edith and Paul Fisherman, Neil, Bonnie, and many cousins from Al's side, which yielded even more cousins, came together regularly to bond and blow off steam.

Neil generously hosted Cousin's Club events at his beautiful new home in New Jersey. Early in his career, Neil was close and extremely loyal to his family, even providing some of them with jobs when he could. In some ways he was still the boy from Brooklyn who made good, and he didn't forget it. He saw himself as just another member of the clan. Despite his early success, Neil showed humility.

As Neil soared, his focus and dedication to his family wilted and he became consumed with work and its accompanying nightlife. This turn would take him personally along a very slippery slope. To quote an old Arabian proverb, "If the camel once gets his nose in the tent, his body will soon follow."

CHAPTER 6

The Bubblegum King

We sold eighteen million records that year, but it took me a long time to live down the title.[1]

—NEIL BOGART

In 1967, at twenty-four years of age, Neil Scott Bogart was handed the keys to the kingdom. And it was good to be the king. He was charged with the enviable position of running Buddah Records, an MGM Records label during the "Summer of Love" when bands like the Beatles, the Doors, Jefferson Airplane, and the Rolling Stones were changing the industry and the psychedelic rock movement was at its apex.

Art Kass, head of Kama Sutra Records at the time, took a leap of faith on the young Bogart. Despite Neil's age and lack of experience, Art was convinced that Neil was the right man for the job. Kass was impressed with Bogart's proven ability to sell and his impressive track record at Cameo-Parkway. By the time Kass tapped him to run Buddah, Neil had already shown his gift for identifying and promoting talent. Russ Bach, an industry insider and adept promotions man himself, worked with Neil on the road up and down the East Coast. He told us that he remembers Neil as a "terrific promotions manager. He *always* delivered. Neil had the great capability of finding acts and betting on those acts."

Right at the time that Neil took the reins of his first company, he was also balancing being a father for the first time with Jylle. Beth saw Neil's love for children shine during early fatherhood. "Early on, Neil was a good dad," Beth points out. He was focused on his career, and anything short of the kind of success he was looking for would not be enough.

He did his best to balance both worlds—in the beginning, at least, he succeeded.

Though Neil was running Buddah Records, he had loftier goals in mind. It was hard—almost unnatural—for him to squelch his voracious appetite for success. Neil was a workaholic, something engrained in him by his mother; nothing was ever good enough for him. He made a habit of being the first man into the office and the last man out.

Neil knew that he couldn't build Buddah Records all by himself. Experience told him that success in music—and in business—came about through collaboration, each player taking on his or her role. He already knew how to identify a great song, but just as important, he knew to scout for a solid production team and fold them into the Buddah family. Neil made the prescient decision to bring with him from Cameo-Parkway two little-known producers, Jerry Kasenetz and Jeff Katz. The move would help make Buddah a dominant force of the era.

Jerry Kasenetz and Jeff Katz were mere rookies in the music business when Bogart recruited them to join Buddah Records. The duo was just a couple of Brooklynites who met at the University of Arizona, where Katz played football and Kasenetz was a team manager. They made the trek back to New York, where they tried their luck at managing groups in Greenwich Village in the late 1960s. Their adventure in New York fizzled out, so they made the next logical step: They opted to produce instead. Katz told *Goldmine* magazine how they got started:

> *We had this black group, King Ernest and the Palace Guards, and they were sensational. We got them signed to Mercury, and I don't remember who did the record, a single, and we heard the record—it was terrible. We said, "We could do better than that." And that's actually how we got into producing.*[2]

Kasenetz and Katz were picked up by Cameo-Parkway as it was floundering and ultimately folding; that's where and how Neil met them. Recognizing talent when he saw it, Neil knew the duo was languishing and threw them a lifeline by bringing them along to Buddah Records. There they headed Super K Productions, a label operating under its parent, Buddah. Super K helped further Neil's vision of what popular music could be with acts like Ohio Express, 1910 Fruit Company, Crazy Elephant, and Music Explosion. "Beg Borrow and Steal" by Ohio Express busted into the Top 40 and proved the duo's ability to produce a hit right out of the gate. The trio of Bogart, Kasenetz, and Katz would produce a sound soon known to the world by a moniker as catchy as the music itself: "bubblegum pop."

If Neil was the conductor of the bubblegum train, then Kasenetz and Katz were its engine. In an era of war, civil unrest, drug use, and sweeping change, Bogart, Kasenetz, and Katz sought to produce an alternate source of music for the younger kids—something more innocent and accessible. That audience's voice had gotten lost in the political turmoil and the chaos swirling around them at the time. "It was music for the younger brothers and sisters of the acid generation, kids who weren't into psychedelics,"[3] Bogart explained. In the late 1960s this was an untapped market, and Bogart went right after them. At a time when the traditional outsiders got all the attention, there was room for a more traditional pop music audience too. Bubblegum pop ran counter to the counterculture, reinventing pop music for the mainstream.

Clearly, Bogart had been on to something. The years 1967 to 1972 would bring the bubblegum pop explosion, "pop music" for its generation. The groups tended to be hip but clean-cut, good-looking boys pulled from talent pools across the country. Every generation has its "bubblegum" acts, music that has specific commercial and formulaic appeal. The music was accessible and, in a way, naive, but it was honest. Writer Bill Pitzonka described it well: "The whole thing that really makes a record bubblegum is just an inherently contrived innocence that somehow transcends ... the contrivance ... it has to sound like they mean it."[4]

As an alternative to the big groups and artists of the 1960s, there were no high-profile front men in bubblegum pop, no "rock gods" who went on to storied fame. In fact, many bubblegum bands flamed out shortly after their short run on the charts. Nowadays they'd be called "one-hit wonders." But when the acts broke through, when they were big, they were enormous; bubblegum pop made Buddha a big deal. The music raked in the dough for Buddha Records, making it a good year for the fledgling company. The big sales also proved Neil's formula could work—on a large scale.

Though Bogart sold the innocence of bubblegum pop, some people noticed something more subversive going on. The only rock critic who ever became a legend in his own right—Lester Bangs—saw something much deeper going on in bubblegum. "The irony, which everybody missed at the time," Bangs said, "was that while rock was trying to be so hip and 'adult,' many bubblegum songs had some of the most lubriciously explicit lyrics in the world."[5]

Buddah's first release, from the bubblegum-sounding Mulberry Fruit Band, featured two singles, "Yes, We Have No Bananas" and "The Audition." But strangely enough, Buddah's first album was the seminal cult classic *Safe as Milk* by Captain Beefheart & His Magic Band, who scored a surprise hit with a cover of Bo Diddley's "Diddy Wah Diddy." Beefheart was decidedly *not* bubblegum, which Bogart found out soon enough. Neil loved to take chances on eclectic artists, as indicated by his signing Beefheart and later KISS and Parliament, but in the 1960s Bogart was focused on the bubblegum formula. (Beefheart proved to be too experimental for a lot of labels, and the band was dropped by a series of them before finding a home with the more progressive Frank Zappa's Straight Records.) Bogart, along with Kasenetz and Katz, set forth with one specific goal: Make hits that would sell records. Since his producers were hitting their stride, it was time for Neil to focus on what he did best—promotion.

There are a lot of unwritten rules, tiny details, and subtle nuances to the promotion game, and Neil Bogart seemed to hold the blueprint. He was an industry man, having cut his teeth as a singer-for-hire when he was a kid. Back when Bill Darnell, head of Portrait Records, gave Neil his first shot at recording, which produced his one and only true hit, "Bobby," Neil paid close attention to every step of the process. It wasn't just about writing a song; it was about *telling the truth*. It wasn't just about producing a song either; it was about how to get the song heard by the right people *at the right time*. It was the *strategy* involved that impressed Neil. So much of a song's success or failure was luck, as Neil knew, but he saw how Darnell helped promote the song, and saw the results that came from his mother's support and effort to get "Bobby" played.

Neil was smart enough to understand there wasn't one single thing that got a song off the ground; a combination of many things was needed for it to break out. It had been years since "Bobby" hit the radio, but Neil had seen many things since then. He had become the guru, the master of talk. Not only did he know his own game but he knew what everyone else was doing too. And because of his early experiences, he knew how to get records played, how to get exposure for his songs, and how to land them on the charts.

During his brush with fame on the radio with "Bobby," Neil witnessed first-hand how local radio stations were used to get a song played, heard, and popularized. It continued at MGM when he needed to create buzz for artists he promoted on the road throughout the Northeast. He knew that in order to have and maintain success, his songs would need to make it on the charts and on the air—by any means necessary. Neil had the personality, charisma, and know-how to stand out above the noise and force the industry to take notice. He put in hours and hours of face time every week with local DJs and station managers; he mastered the schmooze-fest that was promotion back in those days. Any traveling salesman with a vinyl album could make the effort. It took someone with fortitude and charm to make it happen. So, when necessary, Neil greased the occasional wheel. He spent boatloads of money on people at *Billboard* and *Cash Box* by taking them to dinner, buying them drinks, whatever it took—a very common practice at the time.

Meanwhile, Kasenetz and Katz (K&K) got to work. The first Buddah release to highlight the direction the company was going in was the 1910 Fruitgum Company's song "Simon Says." It was a soft rock nursery rhyme remake at best, but they combined it with a garage-band sound that became pure K&K. The song reached #4 on the charts. The band was originally named Jekyll and the Hydes, but the K&K team remained firm that there'd be no record without a name change. Much like Neil, K&K made sure things were done their way; it's one of the things Neil respected about them. The 1910 Fruitgum Company's "Simon Says" was followed by "May I Take a Giant Step (Into Your Heart)," which hit #63 on the charts. Not earthshaking numbers just yet, but K&K were still tinkering.

Buddah had its first legitimate hit in 1967, but it was more of an accident than part of the strategy. This would be okay if K&K were interested in competing with Pink Floyd and the Beatles, but not consistent with Buddah's game plan to create a new sound. The Lemon Pipers' "Green Tambourine" was clearly not bubblegum—the fact that they had success with the song was chalked up to their being a product of the times, swept into popularity by the force of the genre. The Lemon Pipers were a little garage band from Oxford, Ohio, lucky enough to have been given the opportunity to put out an album heavy with psychedelic lyrics and musical arrangements in 1967. As hopeful as the Lemon Pipers appeared to be, they were short-lived. They would disband after a few other minor hits.

Neil reminded K&K that they were there to produce bubblegum for *the people*. The only problem was that the people might reject bubblegum, since it was seemingly out of step with the times. Always hedging his bets, Neil coyly signed a talented black group named the Stairsteps (later known as the Five Stairsteps & Cubie). The group was originally under contract with Cameo-Parkway, but Neil liked the sound of their single "Something's Missing" so much, he pinched them for Buddah; the group rocketed to #17 on the charts after Neil got his hands on them.

By this point, Buddah's bubblegum pop releases had yet to gain traction with the public. In fact, in early 1968, despite some minor hits, Buddah suffered numerous nonstarters. Until bubblegum was embraced by the mainstream, Bogart had to hedge his bets with other sounds, but studio concoctions by groups called the Frosted Flakes, Chicago Prohibition 1931, and the Carnaby Street Runners had little impact on the music scene. Additional albums by Salt Water Taffy, Lt. Garcia's Magic Music Box, Cowboys 'N' Indians, and J.C.W. Ratfinks came and went with little fanfare.

Then, in 1968, it happened. Ohio Express released the single "Yummy Yummy Yummy." Neil had provided the masses with three minutes of fun that could inject something into their day beyond the dark news of the times.

Ohio Express would be one of Buddah's biggest success stories and would help anchor the bubblegum pop movement. The song was simple and fun (e.g., "I got love in my tummy"). It was what the country's youth craved—to step away from all the dark clouds hanging over their heads.

Bubblegum connotes three essential things: flavor, repetition, and cheap entertainment. Legend has it that Kasenetz or Katz was chewing gum while listening to their music in the studio one day, and one of them made a snide comment that the music was akin to bubblegum. "Easy to chew on," one of them supposedly said. When Neil overheard the moniker he immediately loved the analogy. Bogart began using the slogan to promote the music from coast to coast and everywhere in between. Bubblegum pop was born, coined by the men who produced and developed the music themselves, and Neil was its king. "We sold eighteen million records that year," Neil said, "but it took me a long time to live down the title."[6]

In his fawning essay about bubblegum pop in *The Rolling Stone Illustrated History of Rock and Roll*, rock critic Lester Bangs didn't care about the genre's seeming disposability; in fact, he believed the exact opposite: "Bubblegum, after all, is the bottom line of rock and roll. It matters because the real truth is that there will always be at least one tender spot deep in the heart of rock and roll which should never grow up and never will." Bangs knew what Bogart was going for and understood it as an "inevitable" offshoot of rock music: "The basic bubblegum sound could be described as the basic sound of rock & roll—minus the rage, violence, and anomie."[7]

Bangs and others have pointed out that though bubblegum music put forth a "calculated innocence," there was a lot of adult and sexual innuendo buried within the seemingly simple lyrics. Joey Levine, of the Ohio Express, admitted, "We were told to write these innocent songs, but we were all in our late teens, so we wanted to slide some double entendres past them if we could."[8]

"Yummy" and other bubblegum tunes just like it flowed out from radio stations across the country in summer 1968. The driving guitar openings combined with a low-fi K&K garage band–like sound and simple, catchy lyrics combined to form the quintessential bubblegum sound. "Yummy" started a series of hits from the 1910 Fruit Company and the

Ohio Express that drove Buddah to the top of the charts. In fact, as "Yummy, Yummy, Yummy" hit #4 on the billboard charts, the 1910 Fruit Company landed their biggest hit, "1, 2, 3 Red Light." The song rocketed up to #5 on the charts right behind "Yummy."

Bogart's focus on the next generation, the one he felt was getting ignored, was prescient—and it was working. Buddah's music became the focus of younger kids across the country. While the counterculture turned on, tuned in, and dropped out, their younger brothers and sisters were feeding off every song Buddah Records was putting out. The string of hits led to quick success at Buddah, and the money started rolling in.

In 1968, about a year before Woodstock would set the tone for music festivals for a generation, the K&K team had a novel idea. They invented a fictitious music festival, took some of the best bubblegum talent, marketed them together as a "supergroup," and had them perform "live" at Carnegie Hall. The idea was to sell the record, not promote a music festival. The festival itself was just the carrot—Neil wanted to give the impression that the artists had been recorded at a music festival to sell the record. It was a brilliant marketing ploy on Bogart's part. K&K assembled members from the Ohio Express, 1910 Fruitgum Company, Music Explosion, St. Louis Invisible Marching Band, Teri Nelson Group, and J.C.W. Ratfinks among others and billed them as the Kasenetz-Katz Singing Orchestral Circus.

The Circus recorded songs, some of which hit the billboard charts, including "Quick Joey Small (Run, Joey Run)," which hit the Top 25. Around the same time, the Ohio Express broke the Top 20 with "Chewy Chewy," and the 1910 Fruitgum Company landed another hit with "Goody Goody Gumdrops." These hits not only sold well but also acted as a kind of advertising for bubblegum music. The songs were cleverly titled to help remind everyone of the genre itself. It was an example of "branding" before the public even knew to call it that. The Buddah formula was working; MGM started to take notice.

After the Kasenetz-Katz Singing Orchestral Circus had a few hits, the Buddah team went at it again with another supergroup called Captain Groovy and His Bubblegum Army. Most companies at the time might score a hit with every twenty singles released, but Buddah Records landed about one in five on the charts. This success in such a short period allowed the Buddah team to explore more and more options. This staggering number would lead to *Time* magazine in 1968 hailing Bogart as the "king of bubblegum." In the article and interview, Bogart explained the music's appeal:

> *Bubblegum music is pure entertainment. It's about sunshine and going places and falling in love and dancing for the fun of it. It's not about war and poverty and disease and rioting, and frustration and making money and lying and all the things that "really" matter. It's not about these things, and that is why it is so popular. It's about the good things in life . . . that sometimes [you] lose sight of . . . but can find again.*[9]

When your promotions man is labeled a "king" and your producers are seemingly taking credit for your work, it can feel to a humble artist like he's an afterthought. "[Kasenetz and Katz] were difficult to work with. It was strictly a money game with them," former Ohio Express guitarist Doug Grassel said about all the success at Buddah. "They'd tell us, 'Keep it simple. Hurry up. You're costing us money.' They'd tell us what songs to play. And if we didn't like a particular song, they'd say something like, 'Who do you think you are, Jimi Hendrix?'"[10]

—◆—

Grassel's feelings aside, his point was grounded in a very real strategy at Buddah. To Buddah, it didn't matter who sang the songs. It didn't matter who played the music. The bands, their names, their faces—all of it was interchangeable. That's what gave Bogart the power. The whole arrangement of these groups was manufactured in a studio as K&K developed their sound and force-fed artists to play and sing them their way. They were the men behind the curtain running the show. If bands refused, K&K simply found someone to replace them. They owned the bands. They owned the music. They were conductors through and through. With K&K's stranglehold on their groups, all Neil had to do was promote the heck out of them. Together, they all made millions, and the artists themselves were lucky to have the work. The Buddah Records strategy was decidedly the opposite of letting such musical "geniuses" as Jimi Hendrix, Eric Clapton, and Jimmy Page explore to their hearts' content. To bubble-gum, the artist was, for lack of a better word, replaceable.

Artie Wayne, a producing and writing "lifer" in the music business, was at Buddah for many of these recordings. He was managing lead singer Joey Levine of Ohio Express in 1968 and admired Buddah's strategy for getting the most out of an artist. They played loose with artists' names and who was on what record in order to maximize the bands they had under contract. Wayne explains:

> *It was the idea of Jeff Kasenetz and Jerry Katz, who executive pro-duced the dates, to have Joey [Levine] start singing lead on most of their records. They loved Joey's commercial, young sounding voice with a rock and roll edge and those great tracks he produced, so they released single after single using different names of actual groups they had under contract. When a record was a hit, the real group went on the road to promote it. . . . [Neil] encouraged the concept and put out a string of singles for Buddah.*[11]

How was Buddah Records able to score hits with no-name artists at a much higher clip than their much larger competitors? In addition to his golden ear—everyone from the Talking Heads to Blondie to the Cars would credit bubblegum pop as an influence—this was a big part of Bogart's success. He knew how to create buzz, the feeling in the air that something big was coming, or already had come. Neil famously once said: "*Hype.* What a marvelous, misused word. If you hype something and it succeeds, you're a genius, it wasn't hype; if you hype it and it fails, then it's just a hype."[12]

Bogart made appearances at industry parties and events, visited exec-utives on both coasts, befriended such industry giants as Dick Clark and Merv Griffin, and had his promotional team traveling from radio station to radio station working with DJs to promote Buddah's artists. He knew the game well. Being successful in the music industry meant getting your songs onto the *Billboard* charts, and Buddah did that better than anyone else at the time. "It's a gut feeling," Neil would say a few years later, at the height of his fame. "You make music for yourself as you think you'd like it if you were a fifteen-year-old or a twenty-five-year-old."[13]

━⌣━

As 1969 arrived, Neil Scott Bogart was at his peak, professionally and personally. His days were spent as a highly successful music mogul and his nights, when he could make it home, as a loving father and husband.

Neil was a provider, a worker, a husband, a father, an immensely successful music mogul, and the "king" of an entire musical movement. The signs were all there. The high-water mark had been reached. But when you're the center of the storm, when you *are* the storm, it's impossible to detect the waters receding. Neil achieved a great deal both monetarily and professionally. Maybe his new moniker had gone to his head. Perhaps his personal life just wasn't working out, as is often the case under such stresses. Marriages end. The more power and influence he achieved, the more Neil's character was tested.

CHAPTER 7

Buddah Records

What a team we had. We were lethal.

—JERRY SHARELL

As 1967 turned into 1968, Neil had a seat at the table and a slice of the pie. But like a lot of men sharing the industry pie at this time, he was hungry for more. Neil liked to keep his options open; he was keeping a keen eye on changes and trends in the industry in the late 1960s as well as maintaining his connections all over the music business. He wanted to make sure, for the time being, that Buddah kept up its pace. But as with his run at Cameo-Parkway, somewhere in the back of his head he knew that Buddah was not going to be his last stop.

Still only in his mid-twenties, Neil Bogart had become a legitimate power player in the music business. By the end of 1968, he was stringing together hit after hit, his label regularly charting the tops of *Billboard* and *Cash Box* with seeming ease. Earlier that year, Viewlex, a New York–based visual aids company, purchased a controlling interest in Buddah Records. Now Neil not only had to answer to Art Kass, which for him was enough, but these new overlords at Viewlex as well. Bogart was young, but he was savvy enough not to cause a stink; he realized how the business worked. Neil went along with the new arrangement, certain that success would keep both Kass and his corporate bosses happy. But since he had become boss pretty early in life, he had not spent a lot of time answering to higher-ups before; he couldn't foresee the issues that would come about.

In 1968 Buddah Records prided itself on a light and stress-free environment. The pressure of getting the company off the ground in those first few months had subsided. The early days of Buddah Records never rivaled the extravagance and sensational drug use that went on at Neil's future company, the legendary Casablanca Records. In fact, "when Neil started at Buddah he had been far more conservative . . ." wrote Larry Harris, a cousin of Neil's who worked at Buddah Records at this time. "Drugs and that whole scene were completely verboten as well. Anyone caught doing drugs in the office was fired."[1]

Early on, Neil was strict with his staff. He was dedicated to his work and demanded that his employees match his intensity and focus. With all the hours he put in traveling the country, keeping up with his connections and making new ones, he couldn't afford a staff not up to the task. He worked long nights at the office. His father, Al, had taught him that success was something earned, not given.

Despite initially imposing a "No Smoking Pot" policy at work, Neil was no saint. He had smoked marijuana years before during casual encounters at his cousin's club, as well as at parties and gatherings. After all, it was the 1960s, and smoking pot was par for the course. If it *was* done at Buddah, it had to be kept on the down low. At this point, Neil had not yet combined those elements of fun and excess with his work. But he was bringing the two closer together.

Nineteen seventy marked a change for Bogart. Somewhere between the late nights, the lack of sleep, and all that pressure to keep the train moving, his moral compass wavered. His "whatever it takes" attitude in business finally spilled over into his personal life. Neil was known to have numerous extramarital affairs that began around this time, including one with his secretary (which included numerous sexual encounters on Neil's desk).[2]

Once forbidden in the office, marijuana began to waft its way into after-hours parties and gatherings. The drug use was consistent with the times, but it would start a pattern of behavior that, like everything else in Neil's life, would be driven to extremes. Neil was the type of person who felt that if something was worth doing, it was worth doing right. Buddah's focus was not on partying but on success. By 1970, however, Bogart was beginning to have fun achieving it.

The camaraderie built at Buddah Records was airtight. From top to bottom, Neil on down, the atmosphere was full of vim and vigor. Neil's cousin David Bogatz, an employee in the mailroom at Buddah Records, remembers:

We always got our work done. People loved working there. Working at Buddah in the music industry was like working at the "temple." Everybody wanted to work in the music business. I loved working there. Neil created that environment. And after hours, once we got all our work done, we locked all the doors, smoked pot, and chilled out.

Ira Bogart, Neil's adopted foster brother, also worked in the mailroom at Buddah Records. He told us of a similar balance, recalling:

Things were professional there. People got things done. I remember Keith Moon used to love Bowser from Sha Na Na, and he would hang out at Buddah to see them. It was a great atmosphere, and when we got our work done, we would smoke some pot.

In *And Party Every Day*, Bogart's cousin Larry Harris's personal account of the heyday of Casablanca Records, he describes Buddah as a family, noting, "No business environment I've been in before or since has created a more intimate bond among coworkers than those hangout sessions at Neil's office did. It was us against the world. It was family, and that's exactly the way Neil wanted it."[3]

Jerry Sharell was brought into the fold at Buddah Records around this time. The talented promotions man immediately became part of Neil's Buddah family. In the three years Sharell was there, he forged a friendship with Neil that was as rare and unique as anyone had with Bogart. Neil didn't make too many real friends, though he tended to make countless connections and acquaintances. Genuine friendships were far rarer.

Jerry felt like part of the family right away. "We were all a family," Jerry says now. "It was like a well-connected family of cousins. If one bled, we all bled." When Jerry came to Buddah, his wife was eight and a half months pregnant. She lived in Farrell, Pennsylvania, while Jerry lived Sunday through Friday in the Squire Hotel in New York City. Neil made arrangements to have Jerry flown home on the weekends. It showed the great lengths Bogart would go to for a loyal member of the family, but it was also a sign of Neil's future over-willingness to spend. Neil had little regard for corporate money, believing you had to spend it to make it. In this case, however, he was spending someone else's money, which would become a problem.

After five months of this arrangement with the Sharells, Art Kass, Buddah's owner, grew tired of paying for the hotel and pushed for Jerry to find a permanent place closer to New York. Although Neil wanted to accommodate Sharell and didn't care about the cost, Kass was from a different mold. Kass was a money man, in that it was *his* money. A small rift began to build between Neil's desire to spend and Kass's unwillingness to waste. Usually, Bogart and Kass worked well together. Kass gave Neil room to be creative and guide his team. But Kass had made his point, and Neil had Sharell and his wife move into a home in northern New Jersey.

Bogart always found a way to spend. Sharell was in his office one day when Bogart came in and played two records for Sharell, challenging him to figure out which one was going to be a hit. Sharell chose an R&B track he was certain he could sell; Neil then offered him a fun challenge. Since Sharell had just moved, Neil offered him much needed appliances to fill his new home.

"What do you need?" Neil posed, "a fridge, a washer, a dryer?" Sharell of course needed them all. Bogart, the lifelong gambler, offered Sharell a deal. Jerry vividly remembers his conversation with Neil:

> *"Here's the deal. You make that record Top 10 and I'll buy you new," Neil offered. Neil was going to buy me all new appliances if I was able to get the record into the Top 10. So of course I killed myself working everything and everyone. I took people out to dinner, wining and dining them. The record was a smash, but it died at #11. I walked into Neil's office on a Thursday afternoon. I was afraid to tell him the record didn't make it. I had promised my wife the new set of appliances.*

I went into Neil's office and said, "I let you down. I feel like crap. The record peaked at 11 and it's not going any higher. I'm going to head home."

I turned to walk back out of his office when Neil said, "Where you going?" I stopped at the door and turned back. "Our deal was the Top 10, and it didn't go Top 10. I gotta take my wife out for dinner and explain."

Neil said, "You still want them?" I was confused. "Jer, if you still need them, just step up here and ask me for them."

"Neil, if you can see it in your heart to get us the appliances, I'd love them."

Neil smirked. "All right, then. Tomorrow we'll look through a catalog and order them."

I turned to walk out the office door again but stopped just short of the door and began to cry. I couldn't believe the guy. He came around the desk and gave me a great big hug. He said to me, "Look, everyone should try as hard as you did on that record. Just keep working hard and do what you're doing." That was Neil Bogart to me.

Sharell knew he had to produce. Unlike his previous jobs, such as working promotions for Mercury out of Cleveland, Ohio, or hustling on the distribution end for Main Line Distributors, the atmosphere fostered by Neil was one of dedication, drive, and success. The closeness of the Buddah team only helped create the feeling that the company's success belonged to everyone.

Ron Weisner, another Buddah man—a sort of jack-of-all trades—started off as Neil's assistant but ended up working on the promotions team, involved in marketing and R&D (research & development). Weisner told us that Buddah was "like *Animal House*. Everyone took care of what they needed to take care of, but we had a great time. It was like a circus atmosphere."

If Ron's ascent from assistant to working promotions was a great example of success and advancement at Buddah, then Buck Reingold's could be described as extraordinary. In 1969 Reingold was a New York businessman dating Nancy Weiss, Neil's sister-in-law and close friend.

Buck was in the restaurant business and catered parties but when he met Bogart, through Nancy, he was looking to get out. It didn't really matter what it was, the man had a penchant for selling. Reingold was a natural and Neil had an eye for spotting talent. Neil asked Buck to help him out for a few months and work the New York radio stations as a promotion man. It was a trial run in the business that was supposed to last only three months—but tended up lasting nine amazing years.

Buck had no idea what the record business was when he accepted Neil's offer and the music man knew that. That's what he liked about Reingold. Neil didn't need someone with opinions on the music business. He needed someone who could *sell* the music business. "I never knew what a hit was," Reingold told us. "I got them played. I had a way of getting records played. If Neil bought bananas, I sold bananas. If he bought peaches, I sold peaches. I got it played on thirty stations. I didn't know music. I sold it."

Buddah Records was all about their promotional team. Led by Jerry Sharell, they worked the streets and they worked them hard. "What most people gave in a week we did in a day and a half. We moved fast—we had a great formula," Reingold said.

Buddah promotions had a proven formula, they were strong and they were diligent. They were virtually untouchable too. Neil always had their back and supported their every move come what may.

Returning back from a business trip in which he felt it necessary to spend a great a deal of money, Reingold was confronted by an unhappy controller in Eric Steinmetz. Steinmetz was responsible for controlling all the spending at Buddah and was displeased about a two-thousand dollar bill delivered after Buck's return. Buck explained to Eric that his trips around the East Coast include plane rides, car rentals, breakfast, lunch, and dinner expenditures for both himself and the prospective radio producers and DJ's, not to mention about three hundred dollars in drug expenses depending on the mood of the party. Buck explained that in just a few days, the bills could really pile up.

But Steinmetz was an accountant. He balked and took the argument to Bogart. Buck remembers with delight Neil's emphatic response in support of his promo man. "'Yeah. He spends two grand,'" Buck remembers

Neil saying. "'And when he goes on the road he gets records played and we get 90,000 in sales. Do not fuck with him. Just pay him his expenses. Just leave him alone. Don't ask him what he does with the money.'"

Neil sent around a man who had no music experience and gave him a blank check to promote his artists. He saw in Buck the ability to promote, to drive record sales, to make them money. Spending two thousand dollars to make ninety-thousand was a no-brainer. Neil was a long believer in promotions and the combination of marketing and persistence that sells records.

Neil sold his promo team on a formula of communication and persistence ("When I worked for Neil, I worked sixteen hours a day," Reingold remembers.) It wasn't just about pitching a product. Relationships were the key. The team at Buddah were free to explore any avenue that furthered a relationship. As a result, Buck Reingold grew in importance at Buddah Records.

As the initial three-month trial run had come and gone, Buck found himself in the enviable position of being Jerry Sharell's right hand man. This allowed Buck access to bigger clients and more money to spend accordingly. The proof was in the pudding. While the so-called big companies had five charted records for every 100, Buddah had 20 hits on the top 100. "When I came to town I got my game on," Buck remembers. "We had good times—never talked records. It's not about the record—it's about relationships." For Buck Reingold, it wasn't just fleeting friendships either. He made his friendships last. The key to Buddha's success, the key to Neil's success, was always to foster those relationships. If Buck had to promise DJ's and producers better jobs at different stations then so be it. If they had problems, he made sure to deliver. His word had value and therefore, they trusted him. So when Buck came to town to push a record, it got played. It was the Buddah way.

Neil knew he had to stay ahead of the curve if he wanted to stay in business. The Beatles officially called it quits in the spring of 1970, and a new wave of music was filling their place. The tide was turning. The 1960s were over, tastes were evolving, and Neil recognized a change was needed.

Buddah was still rolling after the bubblegum era ended, but Neil hoped to break free of the moniker "Bubblegum King of the World" and become something else. The decision was made at Buddah to work with R&B artists, partly as a response to changing tastes and partly for Neil to break out of the bubblegum mold, which many at Buddah Records resented, despite its profitability. A lot of Buddha guys hated the attention that bubblegum got; they wanted to promote and work with more challenging artists, especially in R&B, which is what they liked to listen to. They pushed the Isley Brothers, Curtis "Superfly" Mayfield, Gladys Knight and the Pips, the Five Stairsteps, Melanie, and Bill Withers.

"The bubblegum paid the bills. It came and went," Ron Weisner says. "We all felt the success of bubblegum gave us the opportunity. We now needed to get credibility. We reached out to Gladys Knight. Then we were pretty aggressive in going after and signing a gospel record. Neil had heard of this great gospel record being released by a very small company in San Francisco. Neil heard the song, got on a plane, and went there immediately to meet up with the people that produced it. It was the Edward Hawkins Singers and a little song called 'Oh, Happy Day.' Neil signed a distribution deal on the spot, and we aggressively went into the R&B business. We changed hats midstream and went in a different direction."

In the blink of an eye, Buddah Records sought to become an R&B label. It was something their entire staff seemed to relish. Although bubblegum had paid the bills and had made Buddah's name, it was a niche brand and, to some, the butt of a joke. The promo men running Buddah wanted credibility from the industry. They weren't just a dog and pony show. "We excelled at R&B. We knew how to grab an R&B hit and carry it to the other side," says Jerry Sharell.

Once again, promotion drove everything else. Their ability to get people to play Buddah's records was what established them as a wildly successful distributor of bubblegum music. Neil knew how to generate the buzz, get songs on the charts, and get records sold. In fact, shortly after Larry Harris was brought over to Buddah Records, Bogart had a heart-to-heart with his cousin about his spending practices. In his book *And Party Every Day*, Harris writes:

> *[Neil] told me I wasn't living up to his expectations. I couldn't believe Neil was disappointed in my work. When I asked him what he meant, he pointed to my expense account. I cringed. And then I began to get mad, because I knew that I was always very frugal with my expenditures. Then Neil said, "You're not spending enough. Larry, you can't do your job well unless you're spending money, and you're not spending enough of it."*[4]

A boss annoyed that you're *not spending enough*? That was Neil Bogart: Spend, spend, and spend. And when you are almost down to your last cent, spend that too. Bogart was committed to the strategy that in order to make money you needed to spend it. Neil took that motto to an extreme and would increasingly spend as his career went on. "Neil was the consummate promoter—like P. T. Barnum," Ron Weisner remembers:

> *. . . We had an act called Elephants Memory. Neil was very excited about them. They traveled around with enormous inflatable animals that would blow up at shows. Neil was obsessed with making them work. A lot of money was poured into them, but they never caught on. We knew we would spend more money than we'd get back. But it was more important to Neil for a record to be successful. Neil believed we had to do whatever necessary to get things done. He was aggressive, creative, and a hustler. I've never seen anyone like him in the record business since. . . . The word no was unacceptable. You had to make it happen. There was nothing that was impossible.*

Neil was the quintessential hustler in the music business; he got his team to perform and do what was required of them. Neil's "whatever it takes" attitude was not limited to driving sales through promotion. While those qualities were at the crux of his business model, there were cheat codes in the industry, and it appears that Buddah took part. The unspoken truths of the music business were not so different from those of organized crime. (In fact, the music business was known to have mob ties for decades.) Payoffs, bagmen—these were also part of the music business. They had a dirty unspoken word for it: payola.

In the 1930s the federal government tried to control the illegal payments and potential bribes that were rampant in the music industry. They failed. Federal laws were passed in 1960 that forbade the direct payment of compensation to disc jockeys or other radio staff. In 1960 an amendment to the 1934 Communications Act required radio stations to announce on air any song they had been paid to play. It also made the Federal Communications Commission (FCC) the federal regulator of payola.

Payola, in simplest terms, was "pay for play." Small companies relied on this illegal trade-off to compete with larger music companies that had tremendous promotional scope. The most well-known account of the payola scandal involved Alan Freed, a nationally famous rock and roll DJ in the 1950s. Freed's radio and television career ended in 1959 when he was fired after payola accusations surfaced. He pleaded guilty to charges of commercial bribery in 1962, after payola was made illegal. Earlier in his career, Dick Clark, a close friend of Bogart's, was also investigated for payola and was forced to sell his stake in a record company. Many saw Freed and Clark as scapegoats for a common industry practice. "Alan Freed and Dick Clark took the hit for a lot of people," says Ron Weisner.

A *Billboard* magazine article as far back as the late 1940s noted: "Payola, in one form or another, is as old as the music business."[5] In the 1950s and as the 1960s rolled in, payola was still common practice. Small labels relied heavily on payola as a means of survival. The law targeted small independent record labels and made it hard for up-and-coming companies like Buddah to break through.

It was David Bogatz, Neil's cousin, who stepped out of the mailroom to physically drive these packages to various stops along the Interstate 95 corridor in his small compact car. "I would just take the bags and go where Neil told me to," David remembers. "I never looked inside. I wasn't allowed to. I don't know what was inside the bags. But Neil only trusted me or those close to him to deliver the packages."

The "drops," as they were called, were a necessary evil; these gifts also were behind some of Neil's promotional success. It was the lynchpin to guarantee records got played. It was a way to compete with the big boys, and it was commonplace. Inside the brown bag, Scotch-taped shut, was money; the packages were not to be opened before delivery under any circumstances. Usually it was a few thousand dollars a pop. "It bought you prominence on a radio station and a promise for airplay," explains Jerry Sharell.

"It was the industry. . . . It was part of the game that had to be played," adds Ron Weisner.

Buddah paid off radio stations and DJ's all over the eastern seaboard to get its new R&B sounds into new markets. Many of the guys working at Buddah Records were promo men who had an extensive network of contacts. They had wined and dined the radio jocks for years. A man like Buck Reingold had forged the kind of connections that got Buddah Records played and sold. The entire Buddah Records promotion department had these kinds of connections and they knew had to use them to their advantage. The payoffs were easy; they knew exactly whom to approach and how to get what they needed. This was crucial to Buddah's success. Bogart picked up the artists the big companies would never touch, giving him a budding reputation as friend to all musicians. If he believed in them, no matter how big or small, Neil had no problem throwing his full weight behind them.

Neil was the preeminent gambler in the music business, sometimes looking more at originality than reputation. According to Weisner, "Neil took a lot of chances on unknown acts, while the big companies signed only big acts." Bogart was always willing to take risks where other music heavyweights would play it safe. That is what endeared Neil to his staff and his artists—and also what stressed out Art Kass to no end.

Neil's aggressive behavior was a stark contrast to Art Kass's keen business sense. The two men were friends, and their families were close. They even spent weekends together and had a great relationship. But they also were business partners with different philosophies that could clash at times. Neil was a creative force that was willing to do anything and everything to make an act successful, even if it meant *not* turning a profit. Kass, meanwhile, was the man who signed the checks at Buddah. He saw dollars and cents. And often they constructively differed in opinion. "Art and

Neil were conflicted at times," Weisner diplomatically notes. "Neil never looked at numbers, more in a creative mode. They balanced each other."

David Bogatz doesn't mince words. "Neil was *the* music business. Art was a businessman," he says.

Bogart's hunger finally got the better of him. The writing was on the wall at Buddah anyway. Neil wanted more freedom. Having Art Kass with him limited Neil's ability to do things his "own" way. It felt like the right time to make a move.

Neil Bogart took his act west in 1973, shocking the people at Buddah who had no idea he was leaving, including his cousin Larry Harris. "You know I'm not unhappy here," he told Harris. "We've had a lot of success for Buddah, but we can do more, and I think having to answer to Viewlex for everything we do is hindering us."[6]

Having Kass and Viewlex over Neil's shoulder was like having parents overseeing everything he did. Art Kass essentially provided a necessary balance to Neil's creative and free-flowing style, which often crossed the boundary of normal industry practice. In a very practical sense, Art Kass was Neil's conscience. Losing Kass's business sensibilities would greatly hurt Neil in his next venture. "If it cost [Neil] three dollars to make two dollars, he would do it," Art Kass was quoted in Fredric Dannen's *Hit Men: Power Brokers and Fast Money Inside the Music Business*. "He always wanted to live the fast life. I think if he had a choice, Buddah had to go out of business when he left. That's what he really wanted."[7]

Buck Reingold was running the promotions department, a position he got when Jerry Sharell left for the West Coast for a promotion of his own. Buck remembers Art Kass as a very nice man—an accountant and a businessman. "Neil asked Art to come to Casablanca with him," Buck said. "When Neil left he took key men with him. Art couldn't handle the creative side and stayed with Buddah."

Inevitably, Neil would move on from Buddah Records and take key promotion men with him. Larry Harris, Buck Reingold, and Cecil Holmes were tapped by Neil to head west.

What Neil created at Buddah Records was a tremendous accomplishment, especially for such a young music executive. Ohio Express and the 1910 Fruit Company were a big deal in bubblegum rock—and so many other successful artists to come through Buddah's doors. Melanie, Captain Beefheart, The Lemon Pipers, Bill Withers, Curtis Mayfield and Gladys Knight & the Pips, and Sha Na Na were just a few of the many artists and groups whose careers found tremendous success under Neil Bogart's guidance.

"At Buddah Records, Neil was the most hard working executive," Reingold told us. "He scratched his way up by working hard and had the most incredible smile. He did paperwork all weekend. He was an exciting guy that knew how to motivate people. He had a pair of balls on him."

Buddah Records was a juggernaut under Neil, and stepping away from a company nearly at its peak seemed almost insane. But Neil wanted autonomy. He wanted not only to be the creative force making decisions and pulling strings but also wanted to do it without anyone over his shoulder telling him no. *No* was not a word Neil liked hearing, and in his mind, Kass and Viewlex used it too much. In late 1973 Neil took his greatest business leap of faith yet and started his own company. "I had Casablanca in my head," he told a reporter. "I left a note for the people at Buddah, saying, 'This is something I have to do, and here's looking at you, kids.'"[8]

CHAPTER 8

The Beginning of Casablanca

It was an absolutely ferocious performance, and at one point I jumped off the stage and ran up to Neil and forced his two hands to clap together. He must have been scared out of his mind . . .

—GENE SIMMONS
KISS AND MAKE-UP

Hit makers who turn up on the charts over and over again understand not just what makes an album successful but also a lot about the listening public and the culture. It's not really about finding a formula; it's about insight. It's an understanding of the crowds and the waves—those going in and those going out. It's something that can't be taught. Once someone taps into that secret knowledge, he can use that blueprint to keep churning out hits. (It's no coincidence that the famous New York recording studio was called the Hit *Factory*).

Neil Bogart, though never a professional musician, was always gifted musically. If his own musical talents ultimately failed him, he more than made up for it with his ability to recognize the talents of others. Neil's auditory senses were special, maybe even unique within the industry at the time. The only rival to his love for music was his interest in the visual arts.

Neil was tempted by film and television but was too busy to pursue it while he was building his résumé in the music industry. To draw Neil's attention, it had to be the right foray into a new medium. In the early 1970s there was no MTV, and the groundbreaking technology that would merge music and video, permanently changing both, was in its infancy. His ongoing love affair with movies and television led him to a small production team putting together commercials and short videos for a television rock and roll show called *Flipside*. The show was the brainchild of future KISS manager Bill Aucoin. "[Television networks] really didn't want contemporary music on most of their shows. They just didn't think it was the right place." Aucoin remembers:

> *These young rock 'n' rollers didn't belong on the network. Well, I came up with a show called* Flipside, *where actually we went into the studios with the producers these artists were used to. So they felt very comfortable talking and playing, 'cause they knew the sound was gonna be there. That was basically the idea—make artists comfortable, especially with the way their music sounded.*[1]

Whether it was luck or foresight, the decision to enter television at that moment would soon pay huge dividends for Neil Bogart and everyone else involved.

In 1973 Neil met Bill Aucoin and Joyce Biawitz, who would both become hugely influential in his life. Joyce was born to a leather goods maker and a saleswoman in Queens, New York. She attended the University of Buffalo with the intention of becoming a teacher. After school, Joyce gained life experience working as a hospital social worker in Brooklyn, New York. "That sobered me," she said.[2]

Joyce ended up working as a broadcast producer at an advertising agency developing commercials for Buick and Magnavox. On the strength of that work, she became an associate producer for *Flipside* alongside Aucoin. The duo found success producing commercials and short music video cuts. Joyce found that she was hungry for success. No less an authority than Gene Simmons described her as "a powerhouse."[3] Her hustle and determination were admirable, and they would make her a key part of Neil's life.

Neil immediately brought Bill and Joyce to Buddah Records and asked them to produce short commercials for his artists for *Flipside*. Neil was always working on new angles for promotion, and the more visual exposure Buddah could get for its artists, the better his bottom line would be. *Flipside* was a short-lived television show that might have been a precursor to MTV (which would launch eight years later). However, it was something else that would bring Neil, Bill, and Joyce together for the long haul: an unknown, theatrical band that Joyce and Bill co-represented named KISS. The groundbreaking band would provide the springboard and the nucleus for Casablanca Records and help turn it into one of the era's biggest labels.

—~—

In the early 1970s, Neil Bogart seemingly had the Midas touch. It was at this time that he began flirting with various studios in Los Angeles to chase his lifelong dream of combining music and film under one label. And there was no better place to do so than in Tinseltown.

At about the same time, a struggling band in Queens named Wicked Lester was getting dropped by their label, Epic Records, after their first album was a bust—in fact, it was never even officially released. The record was shelved, and the band's founders, vocalist and bass guitarist Gene Simmons and vocalist and rhythm guitarist Paul Stanley, began tinkering with their sound and image in hopes of attracting a new label. In 1972 they picked up a drummer named Peter Criss after reading an ad he had placed in the classifieds of *Rolling Stone*: "EXPD. ROCK & roll drummer looking for orig. grp. doing soft & hard music. Peter, Brooklyn."

The three bandmates then put out an ad in the *Village Voice*: "Lead Guitarist Wanted with Flash and Ability. Album out Shortly. No time wasters please."[4] Ace Frehley famously showed up in mismatched sneakers, but his playing won the job.

With their newfound momentum and harder rock sound in place, Wicked Lester changed its name to KISS, based on a suggestion from Stanley after Criss mentioned he had been in a band called Lips. KISS first performed in January 1973 (their soon-to-be iconic makeup still in its embryonic phrase) at what was then known as the Popcorn Club in Queens. They played for about ten people and were paid fifty dollars for two sets[5]—a none-too-auspicious beginning for what would become a crazy ride for the power rockers.

Bill Aucoin saw KISS play in myriad venues during the summer of that year. He approached them in October 1973 and made a deal to sign the band. KISS agreed to let Aucoin represent them on one condition: He had just two weeks to get the band signed to a label or he would forfeit his rights to be their manager. With the already tight clock ticking, Aucoin approached the biggest gambler in the business: Neil Bogart.

Based on their relationship working on *Flipside*, Bill knew all about the kind of risks Neil was willing to take. Hearing rumors that Neil had secured funding from Warner Brothers Records and was preparing to move west, Bill made a phone call. Listening to the music scratchily played over the phone, Bogart immediately agreed to sign the band to a record contract. Only Neil Bogart knows what he heard in that recording that brought him to this decision. Aucoin was thrilled, but he also insisted that Bogart come see the band play live. The scratchy recording was one thing; seeing the band in person was something else entirely. *Entirely.*

Manhattan would be the scene for one of the craziest auditions of Neil Bogart's career. Aucoin assured Neil that KISS would be like nothing he had ever seen before. Certainly they set out not to disappoint. As Larry Harris describes in *And Party Every Day*, the band gave Bogart and the others a sense of how they saw themselves as well:

> *The room was fairly small, maybe twenty feet wide by thirty feet deep. . . . The stage was elevated about a foot above the worn hardwood floor. Behind a small set of drums were at least six stacks of amplifiers and speaker cabinets, and a huge PA filled the flanked stage. Had it been a twenty-five-hundred-seat theater, this would have been a modest equipment arsenal. In that small room, it was ridiculous.*[6]

The room was tiny, the speakers huge, and if that didn't signal something special was about to arrive, the band entering the room put all doubts to rest. When Aucoin warned that this was something Bogart needed to see, he wasn't kidding. Four decked-out lunatics in black-and-white makeup entered the small studio. Each member stood nearly seven feet tall in giant platform shoes. Harris describes the look that, though now part of music's iconography, at the time must have been just downright bizarre: "Four seven-foot monsters in eight-inch platform boots took the stage," Harris writes. The makeup they wore that night was close to what would become the trademark KISS visage: whiteface, with a different design around the eyes for each band member.[7]

Neil had to be some kind of gambler to place a bet on the scary-looking band from Queens. With Neil intent on selling visual as well as musical artistry, the makeup, hairstyle, and dress seemed like something fresh and new. The look was something; the sound was something else. When KISS played, they rocked the small room to its foundation. The audience couldn't help but feel something for the freaky, unknown band on stage. "KISS's decibel level was so high that standing in the jet intake of the Concorde would have been more restful," Larry Harris remembers. "I couldn't hear for two days afterward."[8]

Peter Criss adds, "When we finished, Neil seemed to be in total shock."[9]

KISS was a sight to see. The musical force alone was incredible, but combined with the look on stage, it was a new way to *see* music. Gene Simmons remembers the audition in his autobiography, *Kiss and Make Up*:

> *It was a small room with about twenty people, and we came out wearing makeup and played at maximum level. We blew out everybody's ears. It was an absolutely ferocious performance, and at one point I jumped off the stage and ran up to Neil and forced his two hands to clap together. He must have been scared out of his mind, because with the heels on, I was close to seven feet tall, and he was about five-seven.*[10]

Buck Reingold was also brought in as part of the newly formed Casablanca team. As head of the promotions department at Casablanca, Buck would have a say in what they had just heard. They were "so ugly, the music so terrible," Buck remembers. Neil asked Buck what he thought of the performance. "Something that makes it in the music business is either really good or really bad. I think they're really bad. So . . . we signed them."

Their sound, their look, their *gall*—everything pointed to KISS being something special. Neil didn't really know what he had, but he knew he had something. He knew the band's value would be in its originality. As a promotions man, he knew there was always value in bringing something new to the table. He clearly had quite a bit to work with and would make the most of it. For Bill Aucoin, Neil Bogart would be a formidable force to help promote KISS.

"We had two wild men, Bill and Neil, behind us," Peter Criss wrote in his memoir, "guys who would do anything to break an act. Guys who didn't think out of the box: They fucking smashed the box to smithereens." [11] KISS would become the backbone for Neil Bogart's fledgling company. As Ace Frehley wrote in his autobiography, *No Regrets*, about why they went with Bogart: Neil was the kind of guy who could "make miracles happen." [12]

❦

Buddah Records had been a subsidiary of Kama Sutra Records, an MGM Records distributed label. What this meant to Neil was that there were many levels of permissions—Neil would've called it "bullshit"—he needed to work through in order to get anything done. Neil wanted autonomy, but it would come at a cost. In 1973 Neil decided it was time to make another move. He badly wanted to own his new company outright, but he had to have a financial champion to get off the ground. Despite his lack of love or respect for the corporate world, Neil needed a big backer with strong promotional outreach. He struck a deal with Warner Brothers to bankroll his start-up company for a 50/50 split. It was a deal with the devil as far as Bogart was concerned, but as with most deals with the devil, it was also a means to an end.

Neil landed on Sunset Boulevard and fell in love with a small office decorated in the style of the movie *Casablanca*: rugs from the Middle East, palm trees, rattan sofas, and a huge stuffed camel that he quickly named Bogie. Neil picked 8255 Sunset Boulevard, the old home of juggernaut A&M Records, in the hopes that their success would rub off.

Though it's now inextricably linked with the music it produced, the name Casablanca Records almost never came to be. Neil originally had wanted to call his company Emerald City for the "magical" connotations that went along with the film *The Wizard of Oz*. However, Warner Brothers, Neil's new parent company, didn't own the rights to the film, and gaining those rights would prove to be a hassle. However, Warner did own the film *Casablanca*. Neil naturally returned to one of his original idols and his stage namesake, Humphrey Bogart, for inspiration.

—◦—

The final contract details with Bill Aucoin were hammered out on November 1, 1973, and KISS was officially signed to Neil's new label, Casablanca Records. KISS was the springboard Neil would use to establish his new West Coast company; his plan was to promote KISS around the world using Warner Brothers' worldwide connections.

A few weeks after signing KISS, Neil filed the papers to incorporate Casablanca Records in California, officially dropping anchor on the West Coast. Shortly after, he and his family, like so many seekers before them, made the move westward. The dynamic Buddah Records promotional squad of Larry Harris, Buck Reingold, and Cecil Holmes established the key components of the Casablanca team. Larry Harris would take on the vice president role and handle artist relations. Cecil Holmes ran the R&B department and Buck Reingold headed the promotions team. All the men were Neil's close allies and were willing to take a leap of faith on the man who knew how to spin solid gold again and again.

It wasn't enough to simply file the paperwork and proceed. Neil Bogart lived his life by the adage "bigger is better." When he started a record company for the first time, he was going to make sure everyone knew about it. His coming-out party was going to be legendary. The promotion party to launch Casablanca Records was likely the biggest thrown for a company to release an album at the time. The massive forty-five-thousand-dollar (two hundred thousand in today's dollars) event was held in the grand ballroom of the Century Plaza Hotel, which was turned into a replica of Rick's Café from the film *Casablanca*, complete with a Humphrey Bogart look-alike to greet guests. An area was set up for gambling (reminiscent of Rick's back room), with the big chip winner taking home the original *Maltese Falcon*, donated by Warner Brothers. The entire evening was a showcase of what was to come at Casablanca Records. Neil Bogart and Casablanca were announcing themselves to the world, and they laid it on thick.

There was another practice that Neil got involved in shortly after arriving in California. "Within the first week of us getting there [Los

Angeles], we got into cocaine," Reingold remembers. "Cocaine became an instrument to use in the early 1970s. If you got the uncut right stuff it was like finding gold." Before Casablanca, Buck was a straight-laced businessman who had never smoked grass or snorted coke. That changed for most of the team once the move west was complete.

Neil knew that in order to be successful in a competitive business, Casablanca needed to create a working relationship with Warner Brothers Music. While Neil came out west to establish Casablanca and plant roots in California, Bill Aucoin and Joyce Biawitz worked with KISS to fine-tune the band's performance and style. "We created the look, the logo, the props," Joyce said. "[We] even went to magic shops to learn the gimmicks."[13]

"Neil was a very hands-on guy, and he immediately came up with the ideas to help us refine our stage show," Peter Criss wrote in *Makeup to Breakup*:

> *He was a big fan of magic, so he brought a magician up to the office one day to see what magic effects we could incorporate into the show. We were nixing everything until he got to fire breathing. Immediately, Ace, Paul, and I refused. "I'll try," Gene said. Gene tried it and he almost burned down the office. Then it became a staple in our live act.* [14]

Casablanca was official, and KISS had a home. Soon after they were signed to the label, the band hit the studio. They made their public debut on New Year's Eve 1974 at the Academy of Music in New York. Simmons, heavily made up and drenched in hairspray, accidentally lit himself on fire while attempting a fire-breathing stunt on stage. Word of mouth began to spread about the incident and about the freakish band. Bogart was right—the band was simply too original to ignore.

With high aspirations for his new company and a potentially electrifying act in his grasp, Neil was excited about his prospects heading into the new year. However, he would once again run into some of the same issues that hampered him at Buddah Records. Warner was a big company, and big companies don't necessarily jump when their smaller subsidiary wants them to.

KISS released their self-entitled album, *KISS*, on February 8, 1974. The experienced crew of promotional men at Casablanca worked their tails off to get the band out into the public eye. Neil was betting heavily on KISS to make an impression; his company hung in the balance. Sales, however, didn't match the group's energetic performances, and the debut was a disappointment.

Other problems began to brew between Casablanca and Warner Brothers, and the pressure for Neil to smooth out the relationship became too much to bear. The promotions men got frustrated with their large corporate partners. Warner Brothers failed to promote KISS like Casablanca had hoped. In his book about Casablanca Records, *And Party Every Day*, Larry Harris explains, "KISS was an uphill battle for us as far as Warner Brothers was concerned, and at the crux of that was the black-and-white contrast between the Casablanca and the Warner ways of doing business."[15]

The clash between the corporate attitude at Warner Brothers and the guerilla style of the Casablanca Records crew was an ongoing issue. Casablanca was made up of a group of young, energetic men who had little patience for schedules and timelines. Neil would sign bands after hearing them over the phone, a practice that was surely ridiculous to Warner Brothers executives. Warner Brothers had a carefully managed blueprint, a strict set of release dates for which their structured environment worked. Casablanca wanted to push KISS, as it was their priority. But for Warner Brothers, KISS was just another band.

The problem was that KISS *was* Casablanca Records in early 1974. It would be the horse the label would ride for most of the year. With KISS working on the East Coast, Neil regularly flew across the country to visit his only commodity. His visits to the East Coast were not limited to business. Joyce Biawitz, now one of KISS's managers, had gotten cozy with Neil. Peter Criss had seen the signs at their audition. "I noticed that Joyce had her arm around Neil, who was a married man, and they looked pretty chummy,"[16] he wrote. People began to talk. Joyce was a fiery, driven woman with high aspirations—something Bogart could relate to. It would be on these trips back East that their relationship grew into something more intimate.

There were other stark contrasts going on inside of Neil Bogart as well. There was Neil the family man who loved his children and his wife, Beth, and Neil the ego-centric industry man who was living on two coasts and working late nights trying to launch a company. He felt few constraints when it came to living his life. He had had a few flings at Buddah Records, but this latest pairing with Joyce was different. They were seen in numerous New York and Los Angeles hot spots together. Their relationship grew over time into something more serious.

Beth and Joyce had been close friends. Sometimes they and Neil were a trio, even traveling together for business and pleasure from time to time. But something was evolving between Neil and Joyce. Something far more than just friendship and flirtations was brewing. Beth was not blind to some of it. They were public figures who worked together, she understood that, but it was the private moments stolen between the two, when Beth was encouraged not to attend an event, or not to make a trip, that began to upset her. Joyce and Neil were falling in love. Beth sensed this and frustration and trouble quietly began to fester at home. Between his problems with Warner Brothers and Casablanca's early struggles, Neil's duel lives further stressed his already intense life.

"Perception *is* reality" was another of Neil's mantras. He was a promotions man, and he went to great lengths to promote his company and himself. KISS guitarist Ace Frehley described Neil as having a "dementedly fertile mind."[17] Part of Neil's reason for living in excess was to create the impression that things were going his way; he knew that show business was about power, influence, and money—or at least the appearance of such. Neil put forth the facade of power and used borrowed money, which to him was just as good as having his own. In summer 1974 Neil had little to celebrate with KISS's first release struggling so mightily and so much riding on the band. In typical Bogart fashion, he never let on. He rented a beach house in Malibu and threw lavish parties. There was an open summer-long invitation, and any and all Hollywood types were on the list at the door.

Parties would become a way of life for Neil. He had learned from Buddah Records and their late-night gatherings the benefits of keeping everyone close to him, not just in the office but also in casual settings. It's

THE BEGINNING OF CASABLANCA

where business deals were made and relationships were forged. Neil's tendency to take everything to the extreme may have led to some clashes, but it made for a great time. Partying, women, and drugs were part of his life at this time. These extracurricular activities would be the train that drove his moral downfall. "He always wanted to live the fast life," Art Kass told Fredric Dannen. "In New York he was doing marijuana, but out there [in Los Angeles] he could do coke and hang out with movie producers."[18]

The summer of 1974 would throw Neil into a downward spiral. His issues with Warner Brothers would grow exponentially worse, and his affair with Joyce would finally be uncovered. Bogart didn't seem to go out of his way to hide his relationship with Joyce. At one point, *Performance* magazine touted how the couple looked "cozy together" at a concert.

Things came to a head at the beach house in Malibu, where Neil was partying with friends, including Joyce. This was a normal situation, except this time friends of Beth were there. Bogart knew it would all be laid out for his wife; the dots would soon be connected, and Beth would learn of Neil's infidelity. Beth struggled with what to do after finding out, but in the end she was hurt too badly. Losing his wife and his children were terribly difficult for Neil; in fact, he was crushed. He always considered himself a family man. All evidence points to the fact that he loved his children, and he tried his best to convince Beth to stay, but his marriage could not compete with his booming career or the ferocious Bogart persona. Neil also loved Joyce and perhaps her personality was a better fit for Neil's drive and determination. "Joyce was Neil's soul mate. She knew how to handle him," Reingold told us. "Joyce was very smart and savvy. They were more suited for one another." Years later, Neil would publicly joke about his divorce. In a 1980 article in *People* magazine, Neil said this about the end of his nine-year marriage: "That's longer than any of my jobs lasted."[19]

Despite the family issues, Bogart still had to keep up appearances, so he started to date around town. He met Luci Arnaz, Lucille Ball and Desi Arnaz's daughter, at one of the parties in Malibu and had a short-lived fling with her. Luci reminded him of Beth because she came from a family of wealth and name recognition—she wasn't at all like Joyce.

In Joyce, Neil saw himself. Unlike Beth and Luci, Joyce was hungry and in the business. She had her fingers on the pulse of exactly what drove Neil, and she sought success just as much as he did. They were both passionate individuals with a pronounced appetite. In Joyce, Neil would find his other half, a woman who shared the commitment to success. In Neil, Joyce would find her leg up and a man whose hunger and desire to be successful rivaled her own. Joyce said, "He was such a terrific salesman, he really did sell you the Brooklyn Bridge."[20]

Another reaction Bogart had to his failed marriage was to pour himself into his work. He was determined to get Casablanca off the ground. But KISS's second album, *Hotter Than Hell*, released in October 1974, didn't do much better than the first album had done. By this point, Neil's relationship with Joyce provided a clear conflict of interest for Bill Aucoin and KISS. As her relationship with Neil continued to evolve, Joyce was removed as co-manager of KISS.

With little to show on the sales front, Casablanca Records was still struggling; in fact, Warner was barely taking them seriously. Casablanca attempted to expand their artist base in the fall of 1974 with acts like Parliament, Gloria Scott, and T. Rex. No matter what Casablanca wanted to do, they felt Warner was holding them back. And in essence, they were. Warner promotions had their own acts to deal with, and when it came to the pecking order for producing and distributing records, Warner's projects were the priority. Casablanca's artists often took a backseat, and this was infuriating to Neil. He was getting nailed on both ends by Warner promotions and production. First, Casablanca wasn't getting their acts promoted properly, if at all. Also, production—just getting an album made—in the Warner's machine was painstakingly slow. Warner's artists were produced first, and if there was time, Casablanca's records were pressed. This was a slap in the face to Neil Bogart. He had fought hard to stand on his own two feet, and there was no way he was going to get side-pocketed by anybody.

It was too much for Bogart to take. He wanted out of his deal with Warner Brothers, and he went to the head man himself, Mo Ostin. It wasn't hard to convince Ostin. Bogart had proof that Casablanca's product was being held back, so Mo and Neil struck a deal. Neil would pay Warner back every penny and get what he always desired, complete autonomy. Autonomy would come at a tremendous cost though: 1.5 million dollars to be precise.

With Casablanca free from its overlords and now floating on its own, Neil set his sights on making a big splash. With KISS's albums limping along, Neil saw (maybe hallucinated) dollar signs with a Johnny Carson comedy album. The album would be based on Carson's hugely successful late-night television show—Carson had been hosting *The Tonight Show* since 1962—and contain outtakes not seen on TV. Casablanca ramped up a whole arsenal of money and promotion behind the album. The album would be released around Thanksgiving 1974, and Casablanca would have nearly a million records pressed. With expectations to hit platinum status (one million records sold), the Carson album disappointed. When all was said and done, it barely reached five hundred thousand in sales (gold). Gold status was a signature number, but not when you produced platinum—and the Carson album wouldn't reach gold for a while. Casablanca took a bath on the album. Thousands upon thousands of unsold records were returned by stores. It was a nightmare scenario for the young record company. They couldn't give the record away.

"Now that I've taken the biggest possible shot I can imagine taking, I've got to straighten up," Bogart blithely told a reporter. "What else can a guy do after a two-million-dollar roll?"[21] Neil was leveraged to the hilt and headed for a cliff. He had borrowed another million dollars on top of the 1.5 million he had already taken out to pay back Warner Brothers.

KISS's *Dressed to Kill* was released on March 19, 1975. It was the band's third album release and did a little more commercially then its previous two. KISS was sputtering along; three albums released with little success. Neil's magic touch had come up dry, and the company was not finding any major hits. Casablanca and Bogart were headed toward an unceremonious demise. Later on, Neil would joke, "Everything I owned was rented except the clothes I was wearing . . . and those I owed money on."[22]

It had been years since Neil Bogart had tasted this kind of failure. Casablanca Records was supposed to be his mark on the world, and KISS was supposed to be his coming-out party. Bogart went down to Acapulco with Joyce to get away from the business, the stress, and the industry. Neil was at one of the lowest points of his life: He had lost his wife and his kids, and his business was failing. *People* magazine, in a later interview with Bogart, revealed that "Neil considered suicide—one day he cut off his own air supply while scuba diving but quickly changed his mind."[23]

He fantasized about going out in style. As he contemplated how he would end it all, Bogart padded around poolside at a four-hundred-dollar-a-day villa in Acapulco, running up a seven-thousand-dollar tab on his already threatened American Express card.[24] It was a good story from a great storyteller. But really, Neil never truly considered suicide. He did however need some good fortune and fast. Neil told a reporter:

> *I remembered a story someone had told me about a company that called in a consultant and offered him a million dollars if he could turn around its plummeting productivity. After the consultant spent the day at the factory, he returned to the company president and said simply, "Paint the building." They did and within a month productivity was up 100 percent.[25]*

Neil survived Mexico, but finding sanctuary in paradise wasn't enough to sustain him; he had to clean up the mess he had left back home. Specifically, he needed cash. He needed to pay his artists, he needed money for payroll, and he needed money to keep his company and his dream alive. After leveraging everything he owned into Casablanca, he didn't have much money for himself. Amazingly, Neil came to the conclusion that he could only get out of this hole if he *spent more money*. Nobody was going to question him or tell him he was on his last leg—nobody was going to tell Neil Bogart he was broke. He had an everlasting optimism that somehow always seemed to emanate from him, especially to those he owed money to. Los Angeles reporter Anthony Cook tells it like this:

> *When [Bogart] came home after his fateful Acapulco trip, Casablanca was down to its last oasis—and running out of camels. First, to convince himself he wasn't broke, Bogart went out and signed for a few*

lithographs and bought himself a Mercedes on credit—L.A.'s gesture of defiance. He convinced Warner's management to agree to stretch out the repayment of his debt to fifty thousand dollars a month.[26]

Mexico was good for Neil. He knew he had to make some sweeping declarations to get back on track. He became even more aggressive with self-promotion, often using the press to successfully deliver his messages to the masses and the industry. He got his creditors to hold off. The final bit of "paint on the walls" would be the repackaging of KISS's music. Bogart thought about the first time he saw the band perform live. Their energy, their look; it was all so freaking electric. He needed to capture *that* on a record. Bogart realized they weren't a great studio band, and that thing they were missing couldn't be found—or re-created—in production. Neil would resell the first three albums with a new flair to them. The band was going to rerecord their songs live. In an interview years later, Larry Harris said:

> *Nobody at the label ever mentioned it, and I do believe, especially in the early days, they all knew the band could deliver that live perfor-mance that would be so important to garner those die-hard fans that eventually helped break the band. And besides that, we had no choice, as that is what we had to do to break them . . . so we went after it. . . . I would also doubt that other bands would complain, as that would have put them in a very tenuous position to stay on the label. Nega-tivity was something Neil Bogart would not put up with. Besides all that, we spent tons of money on any artist we got a glimmer of success with; some made it, others did not.*[27]

Neil's business and reputation would come down to a single album. Everything changed for Neil with the release of *Alive*. The album was a live version of KISS's best songs to date; more importantly, it captured the dynamic energy that electrified KISS's audiences across the country. Bog-art had his entire staff pour everything into the album, knowing this was a "make or break" moment for his company, his career, and his life. Released on September 10, 1975, *Alive* would not only save Neil and Casablanca from ruins, it would create rock legends.

CHAPTER 9

The Glory Days

To say that the industry laughed at me would be an understatement. [1]
—Neil Bogart

It was an appropriately named album if ever there was one. *Alive* was intended to keep alive the hopes of the band that created it, the man that banked on it, and the company that produced and marketed it. KISS's *Alive* was slated for production in late summer 1975, the fourth album from the freaky band from Queens. The stakes were high, and the consequences of failure were magnified by the huge number of copies Casablanca planned to make available to the public. After the Johnny Carson flop, Casablanca employees held their collective breath, hoping—praying, really—that the album would sell. It would not be an understatement to say that Neil Bogart's livelihood hung in the balance.

Tanned and refreshed from his escape to Acapulco, Bogart knew he needed money to keep Casablanca alive. Reluctant to turn to another studio or label for help, Neil made the decision to turn to the only people who could afford to bet on a flailing company but not interfere with his autonomy: his cohorts in Las Vegas.

Neil Bogart gambled—on his life, relationships, and businesses. He had the brass balls to treat Vegas like his personal bank. So frequent were his visits, it became a second (or third) home to him. He spent countless hours at the tables in various casinos, accruing lines of credit based purely on his reputation and acumen in the business community. Despite his being leveraged to the hilt everywhere else, the casinos treated him like a king.

In 1973 the MGM Grand Hotel was the first new super-resort on the iconic Vegas Strip. Global corporations with their teams of lawyers and zoning and building permits were not yet the norm; Las Vegas was still a relatively small community run by some pretty notorious people. Neil had open lines of credit at several hotels and had relationships with many of them: Dunes, Flamingo, Golden Nugget, Riviera, Sands. His plan was simple: Check in at various hotels for a night and take out his credit while there. Then trek back to LA to make payroll and pay KISS the royalties they were owed.

When the powers that be in a city like Las Vegas give a loan, the expectation to pay is upheld by the receiver. The reputation of a Vegas lender speaks volumes—this is the type of power that keeps organized crime going. Neil got his lines of credit, but the details of how and from whom are sketchy at best, as they're apt to be, given the circumstances. Bogart needed to make payroll. "Neil tried various money sources, but he found no takers," Larry Harris writes. "He ducked into my office, said 'I'm going to Vegas,' and disappeared. Unbeknownst to me, he had a line of credit at one (or more) of the casinos. He cashed in the line and flew back to LA on Friday to pay our salaries."[2]

Indeed, Bogart had more than one line of credit in Las Vegas. He would turn around and use lagging payments from music stores to pay back the casinos as if the money were a short-term interest-free loan. Eventually the hotels began to notice that although credit had been loaned, Neil was not on the floor playing their games. One of those powers got a hold of Bogart and *kindly* asked him to stop. If Neil were another man, he might have ended up buried in the desert. Lucky for him, he was well known, well liked, and respected among this crowd. He managed to pay back each marker, but the Vegas "bank" soon closed up on him.

This was an incredibly risky move. Success was within his sight, and he had a few balls in play. He had banked heavily on KISS, he was about to release a stunningly sexy singer named Donna Summer onto the world, and Parliament was about to release their seminal album. But he put himself, and his future, at enormous risk when he played those casinos for money he didn't yet have. If he'd failed even for a month, he might have gotten himself killed. Instead his enormous gamble paid huge dividends.

Fans of KISS finally could put needle to record and feel that rush so characteristic of the band's live shows. The album was one of the first albums to ever go platinum. It sold over nine million copies and is widely considered the band's greatest accomplishment.

Despite this success, some around the music industry judged Neil harshly. People had lined up to see the charismatic leader fall. He knew his next move had to be the right one. Now that Neil had the money he needed to operate his business his way, he continued to overspend, as he was accustomed to do. This became a huge issue. He was spending more than Casablanca was making, despite dipping into the Vegas fund and borrowing large chunks of money. It was the contradiction that personified Neil Bogart: a man with incredible business sense but, in many ways, a flawed businessman.

In lieu of some of Neil's poor business decisions, September 1975 would be a high-water time for Neil Bogart and Casablanca Records. *Alive* had just gone gold (Casablanca's first) and shot up the charts. But more importantly, the success of that album functioned like a rising tide; the entire KISS catalog started picking up. Their previous three albums started to make some money. Bogart's tireless commitment to KISS paid off in a big way. With every new KISS album, a new audience would be discovered—who would then buy up their whole back catalog. It was a cycle that practically printed money for Casablanca.

KISS was not only on the map, but the band shot to stardom almost overnight. All four of their albums were selling, and Casablanca was seeing substantial returns on its biggest investment. Neil could focus on other acts, in particular, Parliament and Donna Summer. KISS helped the company take a huge step forward. The pieces were now coming together for Casablanca to break through.

In 1975, as Casablanca released KISS's fifth album, *Dressed to Kill*, and the band was screaming "I wanna rock 'n' roll all night and party every day" at the top of their lungs, the funkiest of funky bands from New Jersey, Parliament, with its band leader, the supremely innovative George Clinton, were responding with "We want the funk." With these two refrains, the

1970s had its diverse duo of anthems firmly in place—both courtesy of Neil Bogart.

George Clinton and Parliament were an exceptional and eccentric act that Casablanca wanted to drive hard. Calling Parliament original is like calling Marilyn Monroe attractive—it doesn't begin to cover it. They traveled with a large stage presence that rivaled the theatricality of KISS and featured a smoke-spewing spacecraft lovingly called "the Mothership," Parliament's signature stage prop.*

Parliament added the kind of originality Neil constantly sought. He never required the best singers, the best musicians, or the most talented people—that was of minimal import in his eyes. Success was not driven by a pure voice or pristinely played music but by originality and creativity. Neil constantly searched for this, and he knew he'd found it the moment he heard it. That's why he could sign acts over the phone—he knew all that he needed to know.

KISS and Parliament could not have been more different as far as bands go, but looking at them the way Neil saw them—as bastions of raw energy and originality—the connection becomes apparent. Despite their divergent styles and audiences, Parliament and KISS converged in Neil's mind. They were ensembles—different and original at the same time—but he saw them as pioneers, a fact that gave them value in the marketplace. Parliament released their first two albums, *Up for the Down Stroke* (August 1974) and *Chocolate City* (March 1975), to minor success. They would gain financial success and public notoriety with their third release, *Mothership Connection*, released in December 1975.

Neil believed that in life you make your own luck. As KISS soared and Parliament launched their breakthrough album, another golden opportunity presented itself to him. Just months earlier, a singer unknown to American audiences by the name of Donna Summer had been in a recording studio in Munich, Germany, finalizing a sound that would soon launch Casablanca Records into the stratosphere. Summer was working in the studio with European music producer Georgio Moroder.

---

*As proof of the band's lasting impact, in 2011 the Smithsonian purchased an iteration of the Mothership for display in Washington, DC.

Neil signed Moroder, an Italian-born music producer and songwriter, to a deal with Casablanca to produce music under a subsidiary label called Oasis. Moroder was one of the first "producer-stars" who not only hand-picked band members but also composed and arranged music and lyrics. In some cases, he even displayed pictures of himself on the front of a few of his album covers—something even über-producer and famed egoist Phil Spector would never have done. Moroder supplied the European connection that Neil had been craving, bringing a new kind of sound from abroad to the States. Moroder had a few projects he was working on, but the demo from Summer was the firework. It changed everything.

A package from Moroder fortuitously arrived to the offices before a party Bogart was hosting at his house one night. Neil brought it home and figured he'd test it on the guests to gauge their reaction. It was called "Love to Love You" by an unknown young singer named Donna Summer. Joe Ermilio, Neil's brother-in-law and a future Casablanca mainstay, recalls Neil once joking about his good fortune: "The song just skipped and kept playing. Everybody loved it. They asked for it to be played over and over again."

This was a well-known story that Neil told again and again, and it became part of his lore. But Buck Reingold remembers things quite differently. Buck recalls going to a bank to cash a Casablanca check in 1975 when two female bank associates recognized the company's logo on his check. Excited, they asked about KISS. Buck was more than happy to oblige the young and beautiful women. Neil had just received a demo record from Moroder with a young Donna Summer's voice on the track. Although Neil passed the demo off to Buck to listen to, he had other ideas.

"We had this 'party' house off of Sunset," Reingold remembers. "It was an $1,100 a month five bedroom house with a pool a Jacuzzi." Buck took care of the extras—grabbing grass, cocaine, caviar and Quaaludes per Neil's instructions. Neil and Buck picked up the two curious and beautiful women for a night of fun. The four headed to Casablanca's party house and took to the Jacuzzi. Baring only their skin, they sat back and enjoyed the night, putting the record "Love to Love You" on the player. The record would play to the end and then have to manually be reset back.

Each time the song ended, the girls traded off restarting the song. "These two girls had the most amazing asses," Buck recalls. They did this numerous times. Finally, Neil had an idea. He said to Buck, "At 3:45 seconds this record sucks. At twenty minutes it's a hit!" Neil went to Georgio Moroder and the song was extended out all the way to sixteen minutes and fifty seconds.

Neil loved the song and its melodic, almost hypnotic, tone. Equally, he fell in love with the sound of Donna Summer. There would be no better way to showcase Donna Summer, Neil's handcrafted project, to the world. Give the audience all they could handle, and allow them to enjoy Donna just as he did. This also would enable Neil to do something no one else had done: have a single become an entire album. With this extended version, "Love to Love You Baby" would be like nothing else out there and therefore become the perfect launching pad for the future Disco Queen.

Moroder, however, initially had reservations; he also mentioned to Neil that he was considering replacing Donna Summer and having another singer lay down the track. Neil refused to consider this, insisting it had to be Summer. He'd heard something in the young woman that he knew was special; he just knew the track wouldn't work without her. Neither Moroder nor Donna Summer was exactly sure what Neil had up his sleeve, but they went back and rerecorded the track, extending the original four-minute version to a staggering and unprecedented seventeen minutes. Such an expansive song was unheard of at the time (it's *still* unheard of). Also at Neil's behest, the name of the song was changed to "Love to Love You Baby."

The two versions were sent around within the industry. The rerecorded track later appeared on Donna Summer's second album, which took its name from the song. It was played by DJs at some of the hottest clubs around the country, where the germs of a new disco movement would soon infest the culture. The long version would become one of disco's first extended plays, and the four-minute version would simultaneously hit the radio airwaves—all of Casablanca's bases were covered. The label's next big thing was about to take off.

Neil wanted the seventeen-minute version to hit the airwaves too, an unheard of idea at the time. Neil asked Buck Reingold to fly out to New

York to see what could be done about playing the extended version on the air. Buck visited disc jockey Frankie Crocker at WBLF in New York City. The station had incredible pull. It was the first true test to see if the record had legs. Frankie, knowing Buck well over the years in the business, happily let him into the radio booth with the new extended version of "Love to Love You Baby" in hand. The DJ had no idea what Buck had in mind. He introduced the record having no idea how long it was. WBLF had a requirement—near standard in the industry—that records played during 5–7 p.m. drive time hover around two minutes, believing people didn't have the patience for much more.

Knowing this, the aggressive promo man, who did whatever it took, pulled out a set of handcuffs and locked his friend Frankie to the radiator. For nearly seventeen minutes the song played on air as Frankie Crocker barked angrily at Buck. When Summer's song was over Buck happily unlocked the cuffs. Frankie Crocker and the station manager told Buck never to return. The bridge was worth burning in the short term because Buck believed in Neil and Neil believed in the record.

The next day the station manager called Neil to yell at him and swore off playing any Casablanca music ever again. Certainly, Neil wasn't aware of Buck's extreme tactics but before he could get concerned over the threat, a call came in to order 100,000 copies of "Love to Love You Baby" from Sam "Goody" Gutowitz, the record store mogul. He had heard it driving in New York and was compelled to buy what he thought was the next big thing. Goody came back a few months later with another 150,000 copy order for the record. Buck would make amends with the station by showing up and paying double for all the radio ads during the 5–7 p.m. drive time. It smoothed things over and showed that Casablanca would stop at nothing to be successful. "I didn't fuck around," Reingold says. "Whatever Neil needed I got done."

The press was intrigued by the sultry singer. She infamously claimed to have simulated twenty-two orgasms during the making of the song. Whether this was true or a story fed to Summer by Casablanca promotions was unimportant. The stirring statement made big news. Naturally, several radio stations across the United States and Europe (including the BBC) took issue with the song and refused to play it on the grounds that it was too vulgar. The "sexual sounds" she moaned during her performances were provocative; the sounds and the banning only made the song even more popular in the discotheques and on the street.

After years in Europe, Donna Summer came back home to the United States. Bogart had plans for his new discovery that would help her become not just famous but a "diva." He gave her the red-carpet treatment, even having a four-foot cake made in her likeness flown to her Boston home. Neil wanted only first-class treatment for his budding star; he saw in her what no one else had yet seen and had the foresight to make her feel like a queen. By publicly treating Summer like a star, Neil ensured that she would be viewed as such by others. Neil smartly established Summer's persona *before* people had an opportunity to digest who she was. Long before disco dominated the airwaves, Neil knew he needed someone like Donna Summer. And when he found her, he knew she would be the face and sound of disco. Years before anyone knew that disco would become a gigantic cultural movement, Bogart already had crowned its queen. He and Summer would be perfectly positioned when disco exploded a few short years later.

"Love to Love You Baby" caught fire and began to rise on the charts. It was, in one critic's memorable phrase, "the tuned orgasm that threw disco into a tizzy in 1975."[3] At the same time, Parliament's "funk" was spreading throughout the country with a loyal following and KISS's *Alive* was crushing all the competition. As he looked around at this converging of successful acts, Neil Bogart must've felt pride—but also relief. Casablanca went from the brink of bankruptcy to the stratosphere of success. Rock, funk, disco. And it was only the beginning.

KISS's *Alive* was propelled to #9 on the *Billboard* charts led by its lead single, "Rock and Roll All Nite," which hit #12 and would go on to become a beloved anthem for generations to come, sucked in by its simple and hedonistic chorus. The album succeeded around the world and achieved gold status, exceeding five hundred thousand in sales. Parliament's *Mothership Connection* rocketed to #13 on *Billboard* and #4 on the US R&B charts. The album went platinum in the year it was released. Donna Summer's *Love to Love You Baby* album hit the charts in multiple countries, including #11 in the United States. It hit #2 on the US

Billboard Top 100, #3 on the US R&B charts, and #2 and #4 in Norway and the U.K., respectively.

Casablanca became the hottest thing on the Sunset Strip, but new difficulties emerged as a result of such quick and enormous success. The office was already spread pretty thin when Neil Bogart encountered an odd but enviable problem: They could hardly keep up with demand. More staff was hired to keep pace with the records flying off the shelves and the telephones ringing off the hooks. Production had to be ramped up, and royalties began to increase exponentially.

Neil Bogart began 1975 as a depressed man who faced financial ruin, claimed he had contemplated suicide, and had lost his children after a public divorce. These personal problems were compounded by the fact that his new company was on the brink of imploding. His reputation suffered as Neil did time as an industry punch line due to Casablanca's disastrous start and KISS's odd early appearances. But as 1975 ended and 1976 began, Neil Bogart bounced back in a big way. He purchased a beautiful new house, married Joyce Biawitz, and was on top of the world. Casablanca Records was the talk of the industry, and the future looked grand.

━━◆━━

The train kept rolling, gaining momentum. Casablanca was a behemoth, and it was natural for Neil to see how far he could take things. After all, that's how he had gotten where he was. He had all this money, and he did the typical things people do when they hit a windfall: *Hire a lawyer*, check. *Unnecessary spending*, check. *Extravagant parties*, check. *Spoil his friends and clients*, check. Neil had worked hard and taken huge risks to finally get to the point where he felt a bit of success. The question soon became, "What now?" Neil needed help to figure all this out. Attorney Richard Trugman was conscripted to do just that.

Trugman was an influential player at Casablanca as well as in Neil's life. Bogart had met him prior to releasing the failed Johnny Carson album. The two quickly became friends; Neil sensed a kindred spirit and offered him a job. Trugman would serve as a sort of consigliere at Casablanca Records. In an official sense, he ran the legal department, but more importantly he was Neil's trusted voice when it came to integral business moves. Contracts, financial decisions, and day-to-day operations became a part of Trugman's reach inside the company. And when money starting to come in hand over fist, Neil enlisted Trugman's help to put that money to work.

One of Trugman's more aggressive ideas centered on a real estate deal. He knew a couple of guys looking to invest in a block of real estate on Sunset Boulevard. Neil trusted Trugman and threw money in. Since Casablanca was Neil, and Neil was Casablanca, there was no independent money. Bogart moved his staff and operation into some of the properties. Oddly, though, Neil charged his own company rent—and at a higher premium than the mortgage on the land. Trugman and Bogart both pocketed the difference. "Richard was a powerful force at the office," Chuck Zahler, assistant controller at Casablanca, remembers. "He and Neil arranged the land deal that charged Casablanca rent on the property Richard and Neil owned under a different company name. It technically wasn't illegal, but it was wrong in my opinion."

This kind of "creative" financial decision making didn't end there for Neil. He also used the Casablanca piggybank to fund personal properties. He spent the money on whatever he wanted. Casablanca was in fact Neil's company, but the spending continued into other, more questionable areas. The gambler simply refused to hold back or play it safe.

Neil also secretly used company funds to pay child support to his ex-wife, Beth. He listed her as a promotions manager on the books, which justified her monthly salary. Of course a promotions manager who lives on the East Coast and lacks any day-to-day affiliation with Casablanca probably isn't the best business idea. Unfortunately for Neil, those payments left tracks like a fresh set of tires screeched on asphalt, and they'd cause big problems for him in the future. When asked about the "under the table" payments from Casablanca, Beth told us: "Like a jerk, I decided that I didn't want any alimony. I lost my attorneys over this reckless decision. But I was so angry I didn't want anything from him. The money was for child support. And if it hadn't been for my stepfather, there would have been no money."

Similar to his practices at Buddah Records, Neil actively participated in payola and payoffs to gain radio airplay at Casablanca. With industry watchdogs and the FBI paying closer attention because of previous pay-ola scandals, Casablanca Records instead opted to give out a tremendous amount of "promotional bonuses." These were not bonuses for Casa-blanca employees. They were payoffs—essentially "payola" in everything but name—that went straight to DJs capable of ensuring that Casablanca Records received the airplay they needed for their acts. "The promotions guys would come back and say, 'We need a motorcycle, or a trip, or some cash,'" Chuck Zahler explains. "The various gifts and money went to DJs, and we would catalog them as 'promotional bonuses.'"

While Casablanca used the "promotional bonuses" to help subsidize its share in the market, its influential reach at radio stations across the country knew no bounds. Neil befriended the men who collected the data on song airplay for the industry charts. Casablanca was essentially pay-ing to be in a position where those who owned and operated the charts could help the label and its acts. It was a rigged game. Getting songs played by DJs was a huge advantage, but having the men who decided song chart positions was solid gold (or in some cases, platinum). In *And Party Every Day*, Larry Harris explains how they used relationships to their advantage:

> *[Bill] Wardlow was one of the most important and influential men in the business. As the charts editor for* Billboard, *he held the entire music industry in his hands. Truth be told, if Bill hadn't been in charge of the charts for* Billboard, *we wouldn't have been at Studio 54 with him. The ability to manipulate the* Billboard *charts was a major advantage to Casablanca.*[4]

Casablanca and its magnetic ring leader had officially arrived. Through sheer force of will and savvy, Neil's dreams were finally becom-ing reality. He was the head of a successful record company he had built from the ground up. After years of struggling and being on the verge of bankruptcy and nearing complete failure, Neil and Casablanca rose up from the depths and conquered the industry.

They had everything going for them. They had everything ahead of them. All that could get in their way was themselves.

CHAPTER 10

KISS Takes Off

We had the craziest record-company president around. Neil Bogart was the last Barnum and Bailey of Rock 'N' Roll. He thrived on the spectacular.[1]

—Peter Criss
Makeup to Breakup

One cannot tell the story of Casablanca Records without also telling the story of KISS, who were at the heart of the company in the late 1970s. The band was so intricately intertwined with the label that neither band nor company had a chance at being successful if the other wasn't. Without Casablanca, KISS would never have reached such great heights, while KISS pretty much saved Casablanca from imminent disaster. But it took a little bit of luck, a lot of patience, and some visionary thinking to get the act off the ground in the first place.

The boys from Queens decided to hitch their wagon to the kid from Brooklyn—and the unlikely partnership ended up making music history. From 1974 to 1979 Casablanca and KISS created some of the most enduring sounds from an era defined by its flourishing and experimental creativity. It was not smooth, and there were contentious moments, but KISS and Casablanca reached a place that neither, boldly confident as they were, could have predicted.

Some critics would brand KISS's music as too simplistic; others dismissed them as a novelty act. KISS had heard it all—and they didn't care. With every indignity, the band simply added a few more giant speakers and cranked up the power a little more until the critics became white noise behind KISS's blazing guitars, driving drum beats, wiggling tongues, and impassioned lyrics.

KISS's sound was something of an enigma. Was it hard rock or heavy metal? It wasn't glam, though their look confused a lot of people. Over the years, the band has been labeled a few different things. Their noise level prompted some to refer to KISS as "thunder rockers." Whatever their genre was, they helped blaze a trail the likes of which few bands have matched since. Bogart and the rest of the Casablanca team eventually figured out exactly how to brand and sell the band, and the growing legions of fans ate the act up. In fact, in Tokyo in 1977, KISS broke the attendance record at Budokan Hall set by the standard bearers of popularity—the Beatles. *Rolling Stone* fawned that they were "an American Black Sabbath."[2] The iconic magazine also wrote, "Kiss spews forth a deceptively controlled type of thunderous hysteria, closely akin to the sound once popularized by the German Panzer tank division."[3]

In the beginning, nobody was sure what KISS had that was so special, but industry insiders knew that if Neil Bogart was involved, something was up. It did, however, take time for Casablanca promotions to nail down how to sell them. *How do you get the public to accept guys that looked and sounded like this?* Neil himself wasn't entirely sold on KISS at first; for one thing, he wasn't into their "glam" look at all. The face paint and outfits were a growing concern to Bogart. A man of his time, he felt their makeup and costumes created a less than heterosexual impression of the band—and this was rock and roll, he reasoned. KISS would stand their ground on this issue (and many others), feeling that their identity would remain *theirs*, even though each member's identity was a comic book–inspired persona: the Demon (Simmons), Starchild (Stanley), Spaceman (Frehley), and Catman (Criss).

KISS was happy to gain a record deal, but Gene Simmons sensed Bogart's reservation about the band and, predictably, had some thoughts of his own. In his autobiography, *Kiss and Make-Up*, Simmons was pretty harsh about Bogart's musical pedigree: "Neil came from a hit singles background and, more specifically, from a show business mentality. He wasn't qualified to make musical decisions—for all intents and purposes, he might have been tone deaf, and he was never a pure music guy."[4]

However, years later, in 2013, Neil's daughter, Jylle, remembers Gene Simmons coming up to her and saying, "Your dad was right, huh?" After decades of success, Gene Simmons realized what Neil Bogart had done.

Simmons's strong opinions of Neil Bogart at the time and his talents were not shared by most in the industry. However, his words certainly indicate the underlying issues that would plague the band's relationship with both Casablanca and Bogart. Neil never saw KISS as musical virtuosos or singers blessed with melodic voices. They were good enough musically, but he also knew they were a fantastic gimmick, and Neil was great at selling gimmicks. At first it was a typical "creative" versus "suit" relationship, but it evolved into something much more complicated as KISS got bigger.

As KISS worked on their style, their sound, and their performance (part Alice Cooper, part the Who), Neil hit the pavement promoting the group. At numerous meetings Neil even went into executive offices, announced that "KISS is magic," and then blew a puff of smoke from his open hands. Bogart knew that part of revealing KISS to the public would be to create a shroud of mystery around the band. And the natural salesman obliged.

Once Neil had committed financially and mentally to KISS, he knew he was on his own. In 1974 the Warner Brothers' team was out to do the bare minimum on KISS's first release. The company took a standard "wait and see" approach with the untested band, which is why it was so hard to break new groups in the first place (it still is). Bogart was mostly alone on his own island in promoting KISS.

The biggest problem was that the Warner promotional department didn't believe in the band's potential, certainly not enough to invest time and money into them. Another component that didn't sit well with Warner was Bogart's spontaneous nature when it came to decision making. Bogart worked on instinct, often impulsively, which is not something a corporate behemoth like Warner Brothers ever wants to do. Bogart's gut would always be his guide and he decided to press forward with the made-up newcomers based on nothing but this instinct.

Released on February 18, 1974, KISS's self-titled debut album was quite a disappointment. It struggled mightily to stir up any sales. It hit stores with a whimper—and just got quieter from there

When it was obvious that KISS's debut album was not selling, Bogart concocted a promotional strategy to help complement the band's initial release. He needed people to know who KISS was. At this point, the band was gimmicky at best. Neil needed to get them into the public consciousness and felt that using their name was a good start.

He arranged a contest to spur excitement for the band and turned to Bobby Rydell's hit "Kissin' Time" to do just that. The pairing of KISS and Bobby Rydell's hit song hardly seemed a wise match, except marketing-wise, that is. Neil was interested in the promotional possibilities with covering the song, not the artistic logic to it. He created a kissing contest and got radio stations to play along, hoping to garner the kind of chart ratings Rydell got when "Kissin' Time" had launched him to teen-idol stardom fifteen years earlier.

However, the venture would have to be sold to KISS, the band that had little interest in remaking a pop song, much less one from a more innocent time. In *KISS: Behind the Mask: The Official Authorized Biography*, David Leaf and Ken Sharp tell the story:

> *[Bogart] knew that a catchy single could save the album and ordered the band to record "Kissin' Time."* . . . *It first had to be drastically reworked because of the lines like "They're smoochin' all over, even in St. Louis." A song with lyrics like the original ones wouldn't fit KISS's leather-clad style.*
>
> *Kenny Kerner, one of the album producers, said about the reworking of the song: "We sat there, we all had pads and pencils, and we just went around the board. And we went, 'Alright, well . . . they're Kissin' in' . . . and somebody would go, 'Detroit!' And we'd go, 'Alright, they're kissin' in Detroit.' And that's how it went. We rewrote the song in like twenty minutes." The band wasn't thrilled with the decision of the record company about recording the song and the later inclusion of the song to the album in July 1974 but were pressured into doing it.* [5]

To get them to go along with the idea, Neil promised KISS *not* to use the song on any album. On May 10, 1974, KISS's version of "Kissin' Time" was released, with the kissing contest promotion running concurrently. "Kissin' Time" would hit only #83 on the US charts, so Neil was in a bind. He felt he *had to* add the song to KISS's debut album to aid the struggling sales. Desperate for any kind of forward momentum, Neil reneged on his promise to KISS and added the song to their first album as a July addition. This desperate act, a pretty clear betrayal no matter how you sell it, showed the enormous stress Neil was under to increase album sales. The band would be bitter over the decision, and it would widen the gap between Neil Bogart and KISS.

In Neil's mind, his priority was to make Casablanca Records work, not fulfill a promise to a group of musicians. He justified it by recognizing that his entire company was in trouble and he needed to keep Casablanca afloat any way possible. Paul Stanley was diplomatic about it, to a degree: "Neil, bless his soul, if he could get you a hit today and ruin your career, that was well worth it 'cause you'd have had a hit. So that's just a different way of looking at things."[6]

Neil had a small but strong core of promotions men working around the clock to get KISS's records played. No matter how hard the Casablanca team tried, 1974 would feature dismal levels of success. Not only was Casablanca struggling with sales but their parent company, Warner Brothers, refused to support KISS albums in a timely manner. Casablanca's promotional team knew they needed to showcase KISS, not just for the band's success but for the company's as well.

The established business model for promoting music in the 1970s relied heavily on support from a limited number of gatekeepers. Unlike in the twenty-first century, there was little in the way of grassroots or digital platforms that bands could utilize to promote themselves. It was a one-way channel; companies promoted their artists leading up to and after the record's release. Because of this, timing was king: Publicity and advertising needed to be in place when records were in stores or it was pointless. This coordination was the bare minimum of what an album needed to break out. However, the promotional group at Casablanca was repeatedly stymied by Warner, which meant that

Casablanca and Neil Bogart's entire business model would collapse if something didn't give.

⸻

In October 1974, KISS's second album, *Hotter than Hell*, came and went in similarly inauspicious fashion. Despite the concerts and publicity tours, KISS's initial sales barely hit seventy-five thousand. *Hotter than Hell* had stalled at #100 on the charts, and the only single that was released, "Let Me Go, Rock 'n' Roll," failed to chart at all. It was at this point that Neil felt the band needed a hook, an anthem, something that the public could latch onto and associate with KISS. He advised the band to create a signature song—one that would be instantly recognizable as theirs. The band went to work.

On March 19, 1975, KISS's third album, *Dressed to Kill*, was released. Although the album fared better than its predecessors, it again failed to hit. *Dressed to Kill* did, however, deliver a crucial piece of KISS's future success—the song "Rock and Roll All Nite." The eventual anthem was on the album, although this version did little to raise any eyebrows at the time. But that wouldn't be the case for long.

After three albums, there was little sales growth for KISS and not a lot of promising signs. Casablanca was clearly frustrated. Bogart knew that, at the very worst, KISS was an original and a special entity. The band *should* have commanded greater attention, but Warner Brothers refused to give it to them. Warner saw the bottom line—dismal album sales—and that's it. However, Bogart knew there was so much more to the band than what Warner Brother's could see in their books. And he was about to let the bosses at Warner, and the world, know about it.

Bogart knew that looking at just the bottom line was missing the big picture. Despite low album sales, something interesting was happening to KISS. As a live act, they were becoming something of a smash. In fact, KISS was so successful in concert that many groups and artists refused to have them open because audiences were leaving after KISS left the stage. These opening-act performances led to a grassroots following that started to build. The band was blowing fire, spitting blood, just giving people incredible shows; the fan base grew with every concert they gave. And the guys noticed. Peter Criss wrote, "Most of the time we would blow away the headliners, and sometimes the reaction was so great that we'd get booted from the tour. Aerosmith booted us after two dates. Argent got rid of us. We opened for Foghat, ZZ Top, and REO Speedwagon, and they all were threatened by the reception of the crowd."[7]

Bogart's job was to figure out how to translate this live performance excitement into album sales—which is what Warner needed. But despite Casablanca's hard promotions work, things just weren't happening. If only he could bottle what the band gave in their live shows and sell it in stores. Pretty soon, he would.

Meanwhile, Casablanca was still struggling, and Warner was barely taking them seriously. Warner was the biggest record company in the world at the time and the blueprint for the "artist-friendly" company, creating an impression that it was a no-brainer for top musicians. No matter what Casablanca wanted to do, Warner appeared to be holding them back. Bogart would eventually have the proof that he was right.

Casablanca attempted to expand their artist base in the fall of 1974 with acts like Parliament, Gloria Scott, and T. Rex. Warner's promotional team had their own acts to focus on, and when it came to the pecking order for promoting and distributing records, their projects had priority. It was clear to Casablanca Records' brass that Warner had little interest in promoting their acts.

KISS was a big part of the problem. Warner did not share Casablanca's assessment of KISS's potential. Their lack of enthusiasm for the band was clear to everyone, which infuriated Bogart. In addition, they were constantly being stymied by Warner promotions people, who not only ignored Casablanca's request to help push KISS but were backlogging production of KISS albums in favor of Warner Brother artists. This was fatal to KISS's momentum. KISS's and Neil Bogart's futures were being crushed from both ends by both Warner promotions *and* production.

In this context, it's easy to see why Bogart wanted out of his deal with Warner Brothers. With few other options, he went directly to the head of Warner Brothers' music, Mo Ostin. At first Ostin claimed ignorance at the imbalance in promotion and lack of attention being given to Casablanca or any of the other subsidiary companies. But over the period of a few weeks in 1974, Neil came prepared with proof that Casablanca's product was being held back.

Warner manufactured and distributed albums for its own acts, as well as all its subsidiary labels. Both Casablanca and Warner handled promotion for Casablanca artists. However, Warner began experiencing manufacturing problems; the Warner plants simply could not keep up with its own pressings, its other subsidiaries' pressings, and the amount of album pressing Casablanca was requesting. Bogart considered this an unfair hardship and a reneging of their contract. In his mind, the relationship between the two companies was unsustainable and thus needed to dissolve.

Ostin was a rational businessman and never felt strongly either way about the Casablanca partnership. He decided to handle the situation by putting it to Neil for a conclusion. Ostin and Bogart struck a deal. Neil got what he always desired: complete autonomy. Neil chose to take Casablanca out on his own, completely breaking the company away from Warner, and giving himself complete ownership of the label. Essentially Casablanca became an independent label. Autonomy would come at a tremendous cost though: 1.5 million dollars to be exact. But since Bogart was paying for the manufacture of his albums and taking second seat in the terms of distribution dollars, the enormous cost proved beneficial over time. In fact, the decision was an easy one.

Bogart was thrilled at the opportunity to own Casablanca outright and be able to make all the decisions, but he did insist on paying Warner back in installments—as opposed to taking the matter to court for breach of contract. Now that Casablanca could not rely on any distribution help from Warner, Neil was left with a company with only modest success with its releases because it never had to set up a fully functioning distribution center.

Neil felt as though he wasn't on that island alone anymore battling Warner by himself. Now he had KISS right along with him. But as KISS sales continued to falter, Casablanca Records stared into the face of bankruptcy. Bogart and Casablanca Records would have little time to turn things around.

❧

To make matters even trickier, personal relationships around Casablanca were becoming a bit too incestuous; the professional atmosphere was fading. Roles were not clearly defined between management and talent, which caused much of the dissention and infighting. Bill Aucoin and the members of KISS were tired of Joyce Biawitz's "conflict of interest." They felt (perhaps fairly), that as their comanager who was carrying on an affair with the president of their record label, her impartiality and loyalty were compromised.

As far as they were concerned, Joyce was no longer on KISS's team but rather another one of Neil Bogart's toys, easily manipulated to get Neil what he wanted. But in other ways that were maybe not clear to outsiders, she was Bogart's inspiration and partner in fostering ideas. Joyce did whatever it took to get what she wanted, and Bogart was the same way. Carrying on a cross-country affair with her friend's husband, who was also the father of three children, was only one example of her drive and tenacity, though not necessarily an ethical one.

The Joyce situation left KISS in a difficult spot. As Joyce's relationship with Neil grew, all parties decided it was best for her to part ways with the band. To make matters worse, Casablanca was way behind on their royalty payments to KISS (which they would sue Bogart for) and Bill Aucoin was continuing to do all he could to keep the band on the road. The relationship between the band and Neil was starting to fray. On top of this, without Warner Brothers and the backing they provided, Bogart had to mortgage his house to keep Casablanca from folding.

It was in this contentious and somewhat desperate atmosphere that KISS's fourth album, *Alive!*, exploded into the world on September 10, 1975. And *exploded* was the right word. Unlike all the band's previous records, this one focused on the live shows that had built KISS such a dedicated following. The double live album harnessed much of the excitement the band displayed in concert; Bogart had indeed found a way to bottle it. Additional audience noise was layered into the background of all the songs to add to the experience.

On the momentum of the live album, the band took off. They had their first Top 40 single with the live version of "Rock and Roll All Nite," a song off *Dressed to Kill* that had gone mostly unnoticed in its studio incarnation. This is particularly amazing, considering that the song would become a definitive anthem, still on the radio and in the head of every rock and roll fan decades later. The live version of "Rock and Roll All Nite," which added a driving guitar solo, was enormous—more than one million singles sold. On the strength of the live album and its monster single, the entire KISS catalog began selling off the shelves. It was a classic story: Fans bought *Alive!*, discovered the band, and started buying its back catalog. The long, hard struggle had finally paid off. The live album release not only launched KISS into superstardom but also provided the seed money for Casablanca to expand. KISS and Bogart had gambled, and now both parties were reaping the rewards.

KISS, already a must-see act on the road, now had a hit album under their belts. *Alive!* spurred sales of all three previous KISS albums into hyperdrive. Casablanca could barely keep up distributing the albums. The cost of pressing all the albums combined with KISS's massive road show was also adding up. Fortunately, KISS was suddenly a chart darling and the money finally rolled into Casablanca. Unfortunately, so did a lot of other things.

Neil's parents (Ruth and Al Bogart) dress him up to get an early start on his modeling career.

Even at a young age, Neil was the constant showman.

Neil Bogart and his father Al at Neil's bar mitztvah, 1954.

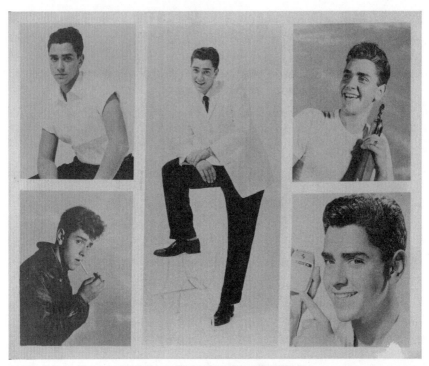

At age 15, Neil takes modeling photos for magazine ads.

Neil showing some attitude.

Neil and his sister, Bonnie, dancing at the Laurel in the Pines Hotel in Lakewood, NJ.

A young Neil Bogart looks dapper in his tuxedo. BOB GRUEN

Neil and Ermine McNulty.

Neil joins the Army National Guard.

Neil as a proud father.

Neil Bogart.

Spiderman Breakfast in NYC, 1972
BOB GRUEN

Neil gazes over his son Evan.

Neil Bogart with Buddah employees and a naked woman on his birthday at Buddah Records, February 3, 1972 BOB GRUEN

From left to right: Peter Criss, Paul Stanley, Neil Bogart, Gene Simmons and Ace Frehley of KISS. December 26, 1973. BOB GRUEN

The "Cousin's Club"—Beth, Neil, Ruth, and Al.

Ruth Bogart (right) with Neil Diamond.

Al Bogart with Donna Summer at the Bogart home.

Neil on a casual day away from the office as his son, Timothy, plays in the background (c. 1979).

Neil and his Aunt Dottie (c. 1980), who protected him and Bonnie during their darkest hours as children.

Neil Bogart's fundraiser held for President Gerald Ford, 1978. From left to right: Neil Bogart, Al Bogart, Ruth Bogart, Bonnie Ermilio, President Gerald Ford, Joseph Ermilio.

Neil and his daughter Jylle (c. 1981).

CHAPTER 11

The KISS Explosion

They knew we might be sitting in our hotel room drunk and we might look around and say, "fuck it," and then the TV was going out the window. We thought that was hilarious.[1]

—PETER CRISS
MAKEUP TO BREAKUP

After the monstrous success of KISS's live album *Alive!*, the band's days as an opening act abruptly ended. They became in-demand headliners, with mountains of fan letters from people all over the country eager to touch base with their favorite KISS characters. They were bona fide rock stars now, with concert schedules that had them traveling fifty-one weeks out of the year. Every venue in the country wanted an appearance, which in turn meant more money coming in and the freedom to do the types of large-scale shows they thrived on. *Alive!* ushered in a sea change that couldn't have come at a better time for KISS and Casablanca.

While touring, KISS found time to work on the next album. They started working with super-producer Bob Ezrin—of Alice Cooper fame—on *Destroyer*. Released in March 1976, the studio album was by far their most ambitious to date. An orchestra, a choir, and numerous studio effects highlighted a distinctly different approach from KISS's raw, unpolished sound. *Destroyer* featured another smash hit—though one that shifted considerably from KISS's signature sound: "Beth."

Originally placed on the B-side of the "Detroit Rock City" single, "Beth" cracked the Top 10 on the charts and helped drive record sales for *Destroyer*. The song was a departure from the band's more upbeat, rock music. Its success was a surprise to everyone, including the band. Nobody in KISS really had faith in "Beth" becoming a hit. Gene Simmons and Paul Stanley believed it to be too "soft sounding" for the album.

Peter Criss claims to have written the song in the early 1970s while in a band called Chelsea, long before he joined KISS. That it even got on the album—it was a last-minute addition to *Destroyer*—is a testament to the blind luck involved in producing music and creating hits. "Beth," named for a former band member's wife (*not* Neil Bogart's first wife), provided Peter Criss with much-deserved accolades for his left-field effort. But Gene Simmons and Paul Stanley weren't impressed with the song, which widened a growing rift in the band.

Despite the band's claim of being four equal parts, Simmons and Stanley were the standout leaders of KISS. Criss and Ace Frehley tended to migrate toward drugs and large amounts of alcohol, whereas Gene and Paul remained more "level-headed," were more vocal, and tended to impose their will on the other two. As Criss described it, "[Gene and Paul] were master manipulators. Ace and I weren't. Gene admits now that if he and Paul wanted to do something and Ace and I didn't, they would 'emotionally batter' us."[2]

When the single was released, people responded better to "Beth" than to "Detroit Rock City"; surprisingly, "Beth" eventually became the band's most successful song in the United States, reaching #7 on *Billboard*'s Hot 100, going gold as a single in the United States. The underdog song proved so powerful that Bogart had to flip the record around; Casablanca reshipped the single with "Beth" on the A-side and "Detroit Rock City" pushed back to the B-side.

On a personal level for Peter Criss, it was a seminal moment. At each concert, "Catman" was given his moment on stage, singing the ballad and garnering rare attention for his voice. Criss could be muted at times (at least compared to Frehley), and as the drummer, he was relegated to the back during performances. However, with "Beth," Criss was given his moment in the spotlight—he was the star.

Hitting the charts with a low-key ballad was unexpected, but KISS had never been just one thing. In fact, the band endured a great deal of change over the years. Even their onstage personas went through some flux. (They would even famously go without makeup for a time in the 1980s.) But the hair and face paint were synonymous with the band by then, and their characters had become stuff of legend. In fact, their characters were dictated in some ways by the fans themselves.

They took on the personas of their characters because their fans had written in expressing their opinions on face paint. Stanley became the "Starchild" because of his tendency to be referred to as the "starry-eyed lover." The "Demon" makeup reflected Simmons's cynicism and humor, as well as his affection for comic books. Frehley's "Spaceman" makeup was a reflection of his fondness for science fiction but was also because he was considered something of a space cadet (perhaps because of all the drugs). Criss was "Catman," a nickname he earned from his Brooklyn days when survival in the music industry—and perhaps in Brooklyn—wasn't assured.

Destroyer further cemented KISS as a music superpower. Casablanca worked tirelessly to promote the band and had the group touring constantly. They loved the road and perfected their performance on it. "It cost us a bloody fortune to keep KISS on the road," says Joseph Ermilio. Ermilio remembers Bogart crowing on about "Their stage setup and their shows [being] hugely expensive costs."

Casablanca cringed when KISS was on tour. It was a double-edged sword, as the band's success was in large part due to touring. The Casablanca team had a constant dilemma: how to keep KISS album sales up while limiting the company's financial exposure for the band's touring. Expensive guitars that were routinely smashed, a drum lift, massive amounts of pyrotechnics—the KISS tour was a lavish operation. The band also made a meal out of hotel rooms, eating them up and shitting them out. "They knew we might be sitting in our hotel room drunk and we might look around and say, 'fuck it,' and then the TV was going out the window. We thought that was hilarious,"[3] Criss remembers.

Typical for rock musicians who get a taste of success and power, KISS thought they could do anything they wanted. And they did. The expense of having them on the road, destroying hotels like drunken teenagers, and the multi-million-dollar traveling road show cost Casablanca, which sorely upset Bogart. Any money they made in record sales was offset by the monstrous expense of their tours.

Joseph Ermilio, who joined Casablanca in 1978, saw KISS in the same way Bogart did: "KISS weren't studio musicians. They weren't that good. . . . It was the visual theatrics and energy live that made KISS special." Transferring that into a package fans could buy is what Bogart knew he had to do. Ermilio adds, "The experience in concert was what got the fans all excited. Putting that experience to vinyl is what got the fans motivated to purchase the albums."

KISS were road warriors; they absolutely loved touring, the energy from the audience, the spectacle of performance, the grassroots following. However, their multi-million-dollar tour was plagued by massive overhead. To combat the overhead, Bogart helped turn KISS into not just a band, but a *brand*. He initiated an aggressive merchandising campaign selling KISS dolls, posters, and other promotional items—he even got the band involved in movies.

Bogart needed to find new ways of generating money to help pay for the band's expensive traveling costs. As the band got bigger and bigger and partied more and more, an issue was quickly bubbling to the surface. Peter Criss and Ace Frehley were becoming problems. Gene Simmons, in typical brutally honest fashion, wrote, "Recording was smooth, more or less, although Peter and Ace were a handful. Ace has his usual problems showing up on time, and Peter was, as Peter has always been, deeply insecure about his role in the process."[4]

Bogart wasn't one to help the situation. Instead of being a problem solver and mediating some of the band's issues, he was the constant facilitator of the party. According to Criss, Bogart would send a basket of fruit, wine, coke, and Quaaludes as a welcome package when the band got to LA. The note would read: *Welcome to LA, Love You, Neil, Casablanca Records.*[5]

Tensions were starting to swell on tour due to Frehley's and Criss's excessive partying and drug addiction. The band could tear through hotel rooms with the best of them, but their issues went far beyond adolescent binges. Their problems were starting to leak into stage performances. Simmons wrote: "The problems kept surfacing. Most of them originated with Ace, who kept shooting himself in the foot, and Peter kept following right along. At one point Ace started saying, 'That's it, I'm leaving. I'm going to do my own solo record.' So Bill Aucoin said, 'Look, don't leave the band. Let's all do solo records.' Everyone agreed."[6]

To try and ease some of the tensions within the band, Casablanca and KISS agreed to allow each member to record his own solo album—an unprecedented move at the time (and really, at any time). Naturally, Neil saw dollar signs on the compromise, excited at the proposition of getting his hands on not one but *four* solo releases. The results were mixed, to say the least.

Bogart didn't have the foresight to realize he wouldn't be getting four KISS albums at once. Each album ended up being vastly different. Stanley's and Frehley's albums were pretty consistent with the hard rock sound KISS was known for. Criss's album was layered with R&B sounds and additional rock ballads. Gene Simmons offered a far more expansive display of music, including rock, ballads, pop, and even a cover of "When You Wish Upon a Star" from the film *Pinocchio*. Simmons, the clear celebrity of the group, also had collaborations with Bob Seger, Cher, and Donna Summer, along with members of Cheap Trick, Aerosmith, and the Doobie Brothers, laying their voices down on tracks.

All four albums were famously released on the same day: September 18, 1978. The marketing campaign was nothing short of epic. Casablanca spent well over 2.5 million dollars marketing *each* record. The record company matched their massive marketing campaign by announcing it was shipping five million copies of the albums to stores, virtually guaranteeing each album would achieve platinum status at release. This was a self-inflicting kind of pressure for Casablanca, and not everyone involved was sold on such a massive campaign.

Peter Guber told us: "When [Neil] decided to release the four individual KISS albums, I urged him not to put all 'our' money into the venture. I said, 'Neil, we have successful movies and albums, we have money coming in from all our ventures, why don't you do big advertising about the four albums but only press and release one.' To which Neil replied, 'I can't do that. I'm the kind of guy who has to be "all in." So the four albums were released and we lost a ton of money. But I respected him for who he was."

Almost not surprisingly, considering the expense, Casablanca took a bath on the albums. All the albums charted in the *Billboard* Top 50, but this was not the kind of success KISS or Bogart had hoped for. The solo releases proved one thing: The band was clearly more than the sum of its parts.

The four solo KISS albums were another example of Neil Bogart getting caught up in the possibilities, flying too close to the sun. In *Hit Men: Power Brokers and Fast Money Inside the Music Business*, Fredric Dannen interviewed a former PolyGram executive, who said:

> *Neil ended up selling 600,000 or 700,000 of each guy, which would have been enormous, but he pressed so many that we were getting killed on the returns. We were already way behind in September, yet Neil persuaded everyone that Christmas would take care of it. So he pressed another quarter million and lost even more!*[7]

Manager Bill Aucoin wanted even more for KISS; he wanted to turn them into "superheroes." So Aucoin looked for an opportunity to get the band into movies. Neil was always enamored with filmmaking and the ability to cross-promote music artists in films. *Saturday Night Fever* (1977) and *Grease* (1978) were the models for this, both enormous successes for RSO Records. So the band filmed a movie that would arrive just after the KISS solo albums were released.

KISS Meets the Phantom of the Park premiered on NBC in 1978. The movie was Aucoin's idea. The band was not impressed. They were taken off the road—a place they loved—to film the movie, which by all accounts was a miserable experience. Their patience with film production was limited, and they had little interest in the project. Ace Frehley and Peter Criss both struggled through the long drawn out process of filmmaking. It was one thing to play the same two hours of music every night while high; it was quite another to sit around a movie set, remember lines, and hit your marks. Ace and Peter were battling serious drug issues during production, and it was creating a big problem among the band members. Gene Simmons and Paul Stanley began to lose patience. Simmons wrote:

> *Paul would get slightly angry because he perceived that I was dominating the band too much, or vice versa. But the ads for the movie, and particularly those in* TV Guide, *really bothered Ace and Peter.*

Even the simple matter of getting Peter and Ace in front of the camera didn't always work out. Sometimes they went missing. They just didn't come on set.[8]

Criss doesn't offer much rebuttal on the matter: "[Ace and I] would get so fucked up that when we finally got the call, we'd stumble out of the trailer slurring our words and hitting the walls and knocking props over."[9]

The movie was a disastrous process, highlighted by so much absence on Frehley's and Criss's parts that stunt doubles had to pose as them in numerous scenes—including ones where they were required to just stand there. Their addictions were spilling more and more into their work, and the band was becoming deeply divided. "The headaches with [Peter and Ace] continued. Peter was depressed, Ace was infuriating as ever, and both of them were increasingly controlled by substances,"[10] Simmons wrote in his memoir.

The long and short of it was that KISS was becoming overexposed: A movie that embarrassed the band, dolls in their likeness, worldwide merchandising, constant touring, and four dismal solo albums all proved to be too much for the band's reputation. Things started to cave in.

Today we have the luxury (and confusion) of four competing memoirs from four individual members recounting four different versions of events. In his own memoir, Criss notes, "It was really over by then. Even Gene and Paul knew it. They had enough of my and Ace's crap, and we certainly had had enough of theirs. We weren't a band anymore. All of us were ultimately embarrassed by doing that movie. The reviews were uniformly horrible. The *Los Angeles Times* called it a 'four-star abomination.'"[11]

Bill Aucoin, the man largely applauded for discovering KISS and getting their first record deal, was on the hot seat. The movie made them look like clowns rather than the superheroes he had envisioned; this ultimately led to a rift between band and manager that didn't just go away. With the overextension of the band, its internal problems, and the film, KISS was headed toward certain demise. On top of all of this, there was no plan to bring the band forward into the 1980s.

KISS released *Dynasty* on May 22, 1979, their first album of all-new material in nearly two years. The album went platinum, and the disco song "I Was Made for Lovin' You" became one of the band's biggest hit singles to date. However, the tour billed as "The Return of KISS" failed to match the success of previous concert tours. It seemed as though the public had had enough of KISS. In some ways, it seemed as though even *KISS* had had enough of KISS. Peter Criss played drums for the last time on December 16, 1979, ostensibly the end of the *Dynasty* tour. He had become despondent by the end. The band's demise was already well on its way.

Casablanca left KISS on autopilot after the failed solo albums and feature film. Neil Bogart's detachment from the group was evident, given the lack of creative guidance (which they clearly needed) KISS received during this period. What had once been a successful journey for Neil Bogart and KISS had run its course. Neil had little time for a band that was becoming overexposed in the public, and he knew it. The sad truth was that Neil focused on what was hot, and KISS was no longer hot. Bill Aucoin was too distracted with other projects, and the band members were growing frustrated. Peter Criss admitted: "We were jealous that [Bill] was spending a lot of time with his other clients, especially since we were probably the only ones to generate income for him then."[12]

With Aucoin and Bogart distracted by other things, no one was really pushing KISS hard at Casablanca Records. Equally, Casablanca had its own hands full with all kinds of financial issues. Near the end of Bogart's run with KISS, both parties were disintegrating before the public's eyes. In a commentary on the cycles of fame, their implosions coincided in the same way their successes had.

Although the group and Neil were never personally close, they needed each other for a time, and they all knew it. KISS needed a fearless promotional leader who would have their backs; Neil needed a breakout core group on which to hang his reputation. For a time, both got what they needed. But like a lot of things in the 1970s, it couldn't hold up under the excess.

There's an irony in the story of KISS's rise. One of the least-recognized legacies of the band was the rise of disco. Casablanca's financial windfall from *Alive!* almost single-handedly bankrolled the disco phenomenon in the late 1970s. If Casablanca had fallen or KISS had failed to find success, would disco have ever found such a wide audience or been as popular? There's no way to know, but it's strange that KISS, of all bands, should be thanked (or cursed) for disco's dominance at the end of the decade.

Despite KISS's fragmenting and its members parting ways, the KISS name continues—impressive for a band formed forty years ago. A reunion tour brought the original members back together in 1996 and once again made the power-rock icons relevant. MTV and VH1 took notice and not only showcased the band's live performance but also nominated the group for numerous "Top" lists. Inducted into the Rock and Roll Hall of Fame in 2014, the band is widely seen as one of the greatest American rock bands of all time.

And then there's the other side of KISS—the brand. As CNN reported in 2011:

> *Simmons . . . believes the KISS brand is worth between one billion and five billion dollars. "We've made no compromises to anyone," Simmons says. "We're stubborn, we're mule-headed. We've completely ignored fashion and fads and marched to the beat of our own drummer, if you will. By some estimates, KISS are the four most recognized faces on planet Earth. I'll prove it to you. Do you know what the king of Sweden looks like? That's funny, because everybody in Sweden knows what KISS looks like."*[13]

The band has so entered the American cultural landscape that they have even leaked into comic books. In 1977 they made an appearance in Marvel Comics, *Howard the Duck* issue #12. Another testament to their longevity came in October 2012, when Simmons and Stanley, with Tommy Thayer and Eric Singer on guitar and drums, respectively, released *Monster*, a twelve-track rock album that reached #3 on the US charts and remained there for several months. IDW Publishing recently published a four-issue comic series starring the Demon, the Starchild, the Catman, and the Spaceman,[14] as well as KISS kids comic. Into their fifth decade, the band still stands—a testimony to their lasting effect on our popular culture.

"Rock and Roll All Nite," which has stood the test of time as a rock and youth anthem, is a small sample of the kind of magic Neil Bogart created with his artists. He knew how to develop the talent; but more than anything, he knew how to promote the heck out of it, to get it heard on a mass level. Though KISS is one of the most recognized bands in the world now, back then this was by no means inevitable—especially in KISS's case. KISS was the kind of band that needed a monster following; they almost didn't make sense any other way.

Though KISS and Neil Bogart went their separate ways, Bogart must be credited for having a vision for KISS and taking a shot on them. He was the one who first sat in front of those rockers from Queens in the scary makeup; he watched them blow the room away and knew that he saw something there. In essence, what he saw in KISS was the future.

CHAPTER 12

Summer Days

Easing her full-throttle delivery down to a shivery whisper, she moaned over and over into the microphone, "Ooooh, aaaah, love to love you, bay-bee . . ." Summer would later boast of simulating 22 orgasms, but whatever she did, it worked.

—"THE LONG HOT SUMMER," *NEWSWEEK*, APRIL 2, 1979

Way back in the archaic world of the 1970s, before the dawn of the Internet, it took significantly longer to "break" musical artists. A band or singer could have only so much impact in a short span of time. Donna Summer's dramatic and nearly instantaneous rise in the latter part of the 1970s was a rare phenomenon. Summer was an enormous talent, no doubt, but she also began as the vision of Neil Bogart, who saw her potential. From the start, Bogart saw Donna as a "diva," a queen and a sex symbol, a star to be catered to, to be cultivated. He saw her as a disco icon before anyone even knew who she was and he set out to treat her as such from the moment they met. Summer would be welcomed into Neil's family, his company, his inner circle, even his parents' home. She became extremely close with Neil, who treated her far differently from the other artists at Casablanca. He genuinely loved her—their bond was something only they would truly know and understand. To her dying day in 2012, Summer had trouble speaking about it.

Donna Summer was born LaDonna Adrian Gaines on December 31, 1948, to devout Christian parents in Dorchester, Massachusetts, just outside Boston. She honed her skills singing inside the hallowed walls of local churches. Her dream as a little girl was to be a famous singer, which led to her becoming somewhat of the black sheep of her family. A life in the music business was a far cry from the Christian morals and values on which she was reared. Donna had bigger aspirations for herself and a healthy ego—and the talent to back them both up. "I knew I would be great," she confidently told *Newsweek* in a 1979 cover story called "Disco Takes Over."[1]

In 1968, after moving to New York, Summer auditioned for a role in the Broadway musical *Hair*. She didn't get the part, but when the musical moved to Europe, she received an offer to perform in the touring version of the play and ended up in West Germany. While in Germany, Summer decided to chase her dream of being a professional singer and spent several years during the early 1970s singing background vocals on albums and appearing in various musicals. To make ends meet, she worked as a file clerk and took opportunities to sing as they came along. While singing backup vocals in the studio, Donna Summer met Georgio Moroder. Upon hearing her sing for the first time, Moroder immediately spotted her potential.

Moroder had just inked a deal with Casablanca, so he decided to make Summer one of his pet projects. Moroder and producer Pete Bellotte worked together with Summer. The result was the 1974 album *Lady of the Night*, which had some modest success in a few European countries.

In 1975 Moroder was in a studio in Germany working with various other singers when that skinny girl from New England, who was just a backup singer in the show Moroder was working on, showed up to record her song, "Love to Love You." Moroder took a look at the lyrics and was impressed. But when he listened to her lay down the track, he didn't think her voice was lead-singer quality. At first Moroder pictured someone else singing the song, so he asked Summer to demo the track for another singer. When Summer attempted the song again, she seemed uncomfortable and struggled to develop a sound. While her voice may have been off, her body movement was alluring; Moroder couldn't deny that sexiness just oozed from her. This gave the producer an idea. He decided to give her another chance, only this time he removed everyone from the studio and turned down the lights. Summer made herself comfortable. On her third try, she nailed it. "Love to Love You" would be the catalyst for so much more than anyone expected.

~—~

The newly formed team pressed forward and recorded Summer's US debut album. Although most of the album was considered raw, "Love to Love You" caught Neil Bogart's interest. Neil visited Donna Summer in Germany and was immediately taken with her. He saw something in Summer: an attractive woman with mass appeal who could bring large numbers of people together from varying walks of life. Plainly, Neil Bogart saw Donna Summer as a game-changer long before anyone else saw much in her. He was drawn to her innocence and purity and thought melding those qualities with her natural sexual appeal would make her a star. Summer looked up to Bogart, and they developed a sacred bond very quickly.

Bogart then had his unprecedented idea to extend "Love to Love You" to a full side of the album. Whether his skipped record tale or Buck Reingold's Jacuzzi story is the true reason, Moroder and Summer re-recorded the version.

After receiving the extended version—now "Love to Love You Baby"—Neil knew he had something different, something to help sell the whole album as well as something to get the song played in the increasingly influential discotheques. He invited Donna to leave Germany and come back to the United States. Though Neil was sold, as with KISS a few years earlier, not everyone at Casablanca saw in her what Neil had seen. Larry Harris noted that "[her album] was unimpressive . . . she was nothing more than a well-trained session musician."[2]

Harris may have thought Summer was just average; throughout her career, that was exactly what she heard from a lot of critics. But Bogart saw her as much more than the studio voice that Moroder and Harris saw. The first time he heard her sing, her voice hit something deep inside of him. He saw it in her smile. Bogart viewed Summer as bottled-up dynamite just waiting to be uncorked. For him she was a reservoir of untapped potential. He had a gut feeling that the magnetism he felt with her would carry over to an audience.

Bogart purchased a first-class airplane ticket for Summer to come back to the States and made preparations for a four-foot cake to be made in her likeness. The cake was waiting for her when she arrived at her hotel in New York. It was going to be all first-class and red-carpet treatment for Donna Summer from that point forward. Of course she was seduced by this treatment. Before she had made any impact, Neil wanted her to feel like a superstar. From day one, he wanted her to believe she could take the disco world by storm and turn her sound into a worldwide phenomenon.

Summer arrived in New York for a promotional tour to support the release of the *Love to Love You Baby* album. Neil sought to get Summer a comanager, someone who would help foster his vision more locally and be more hands-on than Moroder could be. Joyce Biawitz, with whom Neil was partnered both personally and professionally at this point, was brought in. Moroder was Summer's producer and wrote much of the music, but he was living in Germany. The opportunity to pair Joyce with Summer was a tactical move by Neil, and it would pay dividends for all parties involved. Bogart and Joyce began implementing a plan to bring Donna Summer to the forefront of the disco movement. It would take incredible patience by management, but even more diligence from the artist, to perfect the plan. Larry Harris hypothesized that Neil brought Joyce in as a proxy for himself; through his partner (and girlfriend) Neil was able to control Summer outside of Moroder's purview.

The first step Neil and Joyce took was asking Summer to prep for an immediate kickoff concert in New York City. There would be a subsequent industry bash to build name recognition. They soon found out how raw her talents were. The show lacked the pizzazz, the pop—qualities Summer would become known for in the future. Also, Summer was not crazy about touring. Unlike the members of KISS, who were touring machines, Summer did not relish life on the road. Even getting her to do interviews was difficult at times.

Donna Summer was a small-town girl, not used to being in the spotlight. Neil thrust her right into the glaring lights of fame and the noise of show business and insisted that people pay attention to her. He instinctively felt that once the public saw what *he* saw in her, they would have no choice but be as taken as he was. This is where Joyce's involvement paid off. She ensured that Casablanca's needs were met while at the same time educating Summer on how the industry worked.

After the New York event, Summer worked with Joyce and others to polish her act and performance. They spent long hours in the studio perfecting every aspect of it. It all began to click for the singer soon thereafter. Neil created Donna Summer out of what appeared to be thin air. From the beginning, he established a look. He pushed the image of a sexy, sassy woman. Despite being religious at heart, Summer was able to split herself into two personalities to generate "the performer" versus the low-key kind of woman she was in real life. Neil and Joyce helped develop Donna's onstage persona as well. Everything about her had to be choreographed perfectly to ensure that the "product" would be exactly what Neil wanted to promote.

Further evidence of Summer's two selves would come out in her carefully crafted photographs. She was uncomfortable in some of her sexier outfits but quickly learned to deal with it in order to satisfy the business demands on her. Her hair, however, was another story. Larry Harris recalls his first meeting with Donna Summer:

> She was very pretty, but she looked a bit heavier than she had in the picture, and her hair was not the flowing mane of her album covers and press photos. It was very, very short, and not at all keeping with the diva status that she was pursuing. This is why Donna would always be photographed in a wig.[3]

Disco was about to explode, and if Neil Bogart had his way, Donna Summer was going to be its white-hot center. Summer's producer, Georgio Moroder, understood the performer's role quite differently. He had his own opinions about disco and the importance of the artist: "Everybody in a rock group gives some input, but in disco the producer is the dictator."[4] Moroder developed the sound. Neil and Joyce developed and packaged the look. Ultimately Summer's voice and personality would have to shine through, or no packaging would matter. She had to sell it. Bogart had some vision for her record though. He told *Rolling Stone* in 1978: "You know what I used to tell people in the beginning? Take

Donna home and make love to her—the album that is. It'll become part of your family."[5]

Due to the underground success of the extended version of "Love to Love You Baby," combined with album sales and the rise on US charts, Donna Summer quickly became noticed for the first time in her life. In the US, the single "Love to Love You Baby" hit #2 on the US *Billboard* Hot 100 and #3 on the R&B charts. In Norway the song hit #2. In the U.K. it topped out at #4. Summer was an instant star. Despite the song being labeled as "graphic" and deemed "too sexy" by certain radio executives, "Love to Love You Baby" let the masses do the speaking. One journalist would memorably call the title track, "16 minutes and 48 seconds of arousal and refill. . . . Hunger without recourse; essential disco."[6] The album would be certified gold, and Donna Summer fever took over the world.

After *Love to Love You Baby,* Summer wanted to go back to work, proving herself to be not only talented but also a committed and dedicated artist. However, stepping forward wasn't nearly so easy. Sales of the first album with Casablanca were driven by a single song: "Love to Love You Baby" *was* the entire album. The rest of the album was ignored. Summer's subsequent albums, *A Love Trilogy* and *Four Seasons of Love,* both released in 1976, failed to live up to the extraordinary hype created by her major label debut. While both albums did achieve gold status, there just wasn't the same overall excitement. However, the Casablanca promotions machine had worked. Despite not having one song soar off the two subsequent albums, Summer became a bona fide star.

Neil Bogart typically drove the production of albums at a near-feverish pace. He was a strike-while-the-iron-is-hot kind of guy. He truly believed in flooding the market with whatever was selling; once Donna Summer broke through, he drove her hard to pump out album after album. By this time, however, Summer needed a big hit before the iron went cold. The added stress drove her hard, and she turned to prescription drugs to help.

On May 13, 1977, Casablanca released Summer's fifth album, *I Remember Yesterday.* The album hit #3 in the U.K. and #5 in Norway, proving her staying power overseas. But the real score was the single, "I Feel Love." It was embraced by a mass audience and finally gave Summer a big follow-up to "Love to Love You Baby" in the United States. "I

Feel Love" hit #6 on the US *Billboard* Hot 100, and go to #1 in the U.K. The album went platinum. The song would become synonymous with the disco era.

Bogart continued to sell her. He began to float the moniker "First Lady of Love" to the press. It was a shrewd move and part of his plan. The "First Lady of Love" label gave Bogart exactly what he had envisioned when he brought her back to the United States. Summer wasn't just a hit artist anymore. She was a symbol for the time, for the era. Donna Summer was the poster child for disco.

On October 25, 1977, Donna Summer released her next album, *Once Upon a Time.* The concept for the album was based on an original short story written by Al Bogatz, Neil's father. The double-album depicts a feel-good "rags to riches" story of a woman ultimately finding love. The work was so personal to many of the people involved that it came together within days of the concept's being kicked around at Casablanca.[7] The *New York Times* was impressed, calling *Once Upon a Time* "artful . . . a fanfare announcing disco's artistic coming of age."

Unfortunately, Donna Summer would be hospitalized after working tirelessly to develop the tracks for the album with Giorgio Moroder and his right-hand man, Pete Bellotte. The combination of Summer's tireless touring schedule and her prescription drug abuse was beginning to overwhelm the reigning Queen of Disco. Depression and anxiety combined and fed off each other to trigger Summer's mental slide. She turned to drugs to ease these conditions, but she started to spin out of control. She needed and got help for her exhaustion and the various issues that would follow—and that eventually would break her away from Bogart permanently.

But at the time, it was marriage that would vault Summer and Casablanca Records into another stratosphere. Neil always had a deep desire to merge the mediums of music and film. An old friend would come knocking and Casablanca Records was about to get bigger.

CHAPTER 13

The Filmworks Marriage

You walked into Casablanca and the size of the speakers just assaulted your senses, and there was cocaine on people's desks, and getting loaded. And by the time we got down to business, it was almost irrelevant.[1]
—JEFF WALD, DONNA SUMMER'S MANAGER

By the mid 1970s Casablanca Records was turning into a regular fraternity house. The executive staff had a drug runner on salary and served a menu of marijuana, cocaine, and Quaaludes. The drug runner would take orders from the staff as though he were grabbing sandwiches for lunch. Danny Davis was the national pop promotion director at Motown before he came to Casablanca in 1979. His experience differs from that of men who were easily coerced into the frat-like atmosphere. For starters, he didn't do drugs. In *Hit Men*, Davis told Fredric Dannen:

Twelve minutes after I started at Casablanca . . . I called my wife and told her I had made the biggest mistake of my life. It's a true story. And I surely wanted to do good. First of all, I was getting more money [at Casablanca]. Second of all, they had given me a Mercedes 450 SEL. At three o'clock in the afternoon, an adorable little girl would come up and take your order for the following day's drug supply. On a Monday or Tuesday, I'd be looking for a secretary; I'd be calling her name. I'd look all over, and there she would be with a credit card in her hand, chopping, chopping the coke on the table. I would go into a meeting, and there on the desk would be maybe a gram and a half of a controlled substance. An executive would look at me and say, "This shit isn't going to bother you, is it?"[2]

Welcome to Casablanca, Danny Davis. Baggies, vials, and satchels were kept in drawers and pulled out when necessary; which was often more than daily. Things were hot, loose, and brazen, although a lot of work got done as well. But the combination of blasting music, sex, and drug use compounded Casablanca's problems. It would also change the narrative from the little company that could into a mythical story about a hedonistic company that tried to make history on the Sunset Strip off a 24/7 coke high. The party atmosphere had been in full swing since 1975 and continued through the rest of the 1970s.

Despite the free-for-all at Casablanca, some semblance of business order remained. Attempts were made to keep the train on the tracks. After all, the company kept making many good decisions. Despite the easy temptation, they were a highly productive bunch.

However, some tension was simply unavoidable. Larry Harris and Buck Reingold were not the best of friends. Buck saw Larry as a big problem, a man who abused drugs terribly in the halls of Casablanca. "Larry supplied the 'Ludes.' Neil's downfall was he lost his edge. You lose something on those drugs. They even could have caused his cancer." (Buck Reingold).

Larry Harris goes even further, writing:

> *We were all tiring of his [Buck's] shit, his boorish behavior, and the constant parade of sex partners he would bring into the building. He was loud and pushy and determined, but he dressed like a redheaded, white pimp, and it was clear to everyone that he was a huckster with no real passion for, or understanding of, the business. Some radio station people liked him a lot because he supplied them with women and drugs and (possibly) money, but just as many would call Neil and ask him to ensure that they never saw Buck again.*[3]

It was time for Buck to move on. The non-stop party was simply unsustainable. What started out as a three-month experiment had turned into a nine-year run. But he had a falling out with Neil over a matter he did not care to divulge on. One thing is for sure, he loved Neil with all his heart. His relationships inside the Casablanca walls had frayed. He felt it was best to move on and the feeling around the office was mutual. As Reingold departed, a new man arrived, Bruce Bird. Neil had previously used Bruce to help with airplay in the Midwest. Bruce made a profound impact on Casablanca, joining the team as head of the promotions department. In an ironic twist, he too had a past with Beth's twin sister, Nancy, having dated her some years back. It was an odd coincidence, and many in the office felt weary of the dynamic between Buck, Nancy, and Neil and now Bruce, Nancy, and Neil. It didn't seem to bother Neil, who made room for Bruce; it also helped keep Nancy in Los Angeles, which was important to Neil. Bogart's relationship with Nancy was always difficult to gauge. She was a friend, a confidant, and, more importantly, a key connection between him and his ex-wife and children. Neil always seemed to have more in common with Nancy than with Beth. Although Nancy and Beth were twins, they had entirely different personalities. Neil was always close with the free-spirited Nancy, which led many to believe that Neil had married the wrong sister. Neil and Nancy had a special connection, and if she left town, he would suffer another personal setback. Bruce helped mend that fence and kept Nancy grounded in Los Angeles.

Bruce was a strong force who, along with Richard Trugman, helped run day-to-day operations at Casablanca and steer the chaotic ship. He took helm of the promotions department and is credited with being a driving force in ensuring that Casablanca artists got on the airwaves and rocketed up the various charts. Trugman took care of the contracts and protected Casablanca legally. There were numerous lawsuits coming at Casablanca from its own artists, many of whom were upset that they weren't seeing royalty payments.

With so many moving parts, working in the legal department at Casablanca Records was an around-the-clock job. Additionally, Trugman was Neil's financial confidante, an advisor he trusted and believed in. Combined, Bird and Trugman allowed Bogart to utilize his natural gift: mingling with the world. Neil had his lieutenants in place so that he could make snap decisions, travel, and conduct his role as Casablanca's leader.

Never shy to jump in on a business opportunity, Neil Bogart had a big one coming his way in 1976. It arrived by way of an old friend, Peter Guber, who he had met on a double date with Beth and her friend years earlier in New York, when Bogart was still in college. Like all hungry young men wise enough never to lose a contact, they spoke about working together in the future. But the timing or opportunity hadn't yet presented itself. For years Bogart had dreamed of being a bigger player in the film industry; in fact, it was a dream he had had since he was a young boy. With his reputation and track record in the music business in Los Angeles at an all-time high, Neil found the opportunity to make his first legitimate foray into film.

Peter Guber enjoyed a meteoric rise in the film industry that paralleled Bogart's own ascent in the music world. After joining Columbia Pictures in 1968, Guber rose quickly, only to be unceremoniously fired in 1973 from his position as vice president of worldwide production. Guber was quick to sign actors and directors to long-term deals, a practice that lost him his job at Columbia, because many of his decisions were considered reactionary by the leadership. Others were jealous and intimidated by Guber's quick ascent into the business. He was confident, strong, and smart and clearly on the rise. Even when he was starting out, Guber did things *his* way. That combination led to clashes with certain members of Columbia's executive team and his ultimate demise there. Guber then did what any young, flashy executive with a lot of chutzpa would do—he started his own film company. He called it Filmworks.

In 1976 Filmworks was having difficulty completing the film *The Deep*, a big-budget action film based on a novel by Peter Benchley, who was coming off the gigantic success of *Jaws* the previous summer. *The Deep* was about a couple on vacation in Bermuda who uncover a shipwreck and become involved in a cat-and-mouse game with a group of dangerous treasure hunters.

After successfully leveraging Columbia Pictures and getting them to jump in on the project, Guber found himself in the enviable position of green-lighting his first, albeit ambitious, movie. Ironically, he wasn't in love with the story. "I wasn't crazy about the book," he admitted, "but I was crazy about the opportunity it presented. In the movie business, if you buy an important property with market awareness, that becomes a star of your film."[4] Despite not being impressed by the book and not having a budget actually in hand, Guber pushed on.

The film proved a massive undertaking. For starters, with a big cast featuring the likes of Jacqueline Bisset, Nick Nolte, and, fresh off his captivating performance in *Jaws*, Robert Shaw, the cast alone cost a hefty sum. The budget for the film would end up being nine million dollars (an estimated forty million today, adjusting for inflation). Today that would be a drop in the bucket; in the mid 1970s, it was sizable. Around the same time, the hugely successful *Annie Hall* cost four million dollars to make, and the first *Star Wars* film had a budget of eleven million. At nine million dollars, *The Deep* was enough to make any company nervous; Guber would need to deliver.

Filming issues would arise almost immediately and cause the budget on the film to soar. First off, nearly a staggering *40 percent* of the scenes would need to be shot underwater. On paper, the underwater adventure seemed like an exciting idea. In reality, filming underwater, especially back then, posed a litany of challenges. Some of the film was shot using a real ship wrecked in 1867 off the British Virgin Islands—an exorbitant cost that added to the already expensive on-location shooting in Bermuda.

The crew would also be at the mercy of Mother Nature, with the weather and the ocean posing its own set of challenges.

About the shoot, Guber said:

> If I'd actually had first-hand experience of any water-based productions at the time, I probably wouldn't have touched The Deep. Weather is . . . a particularly agonizing ingredient when millions of dollars are staked on it. But the worst, the very worst of all the taboos, is water. . . . The warning flags were at full mast."[5]

As the budget swelled, Guber realized he needed help. He contacted an old friend, Neil Bogart.

Bogart was salivating at the opportunity to get involved in movies and developing a springboard for cross-promoting his musical artists, so he immediately agreed to team up. Bogart would come through and provide Guber with the money needed to finish *The Deep*.

Guber merged with Casablanca to form Casablanca Records and Filmworks, fulfilling the needs of both industry giants. Guber gained a 20 percent stake with full share of ownership in Casablanca Records, which provided big hits with its three top acts: KISS, Parliament, and Donna Summer. The deal worked for Bogart as well, as it ensured the cross-business appeal (today they'd call it synergy) of merging music artists with films—something that would become enormously popular in the late 1970s, when *Saturday Night Fever* and *Grease*—and their soundtracks—became absolute juggernauts. Soundtracks were a lucrative outlet, as was promoting artists by putting them in films themselves. As the first act of their new partnership, Bogart helped Peter Guber complete *The Deep* with funding from Casablanca.

Despite the commonalities in the way they conducted business, the two men were stark personality contrasts. Like Bogart, Guber understood the importance of the occasional glass of celebratory champagne or congratulatory cigar, but unlike Neil, he usually left it at that. Guber was far more conservative, understanding the importance of maintaining composure at work. Guber's Filmworks department would be run as a business. They maintained a corporate environment, residing in the building next to Casablanca Records. Of course, Filmworks' suit and tie atmosphere differed greatly to that of Casablanca's. Despite these differences, their goals coincided beautifully—at least for a time. The unlikely pairing of music titan Casablanca Records and Guber's upstart Filmworks would lead to three Academy Award–winning films: *The Deep, Midnight Express,* and *Thank God It's Friday.* Guber and Bogart would start auspiciously, with sudden success—though the partnership would end with unfulfilled promise.

Bogart and Guber always had one concise goal: to make as much money as possible. With Neil as a partner, Guber would have the greatest gambler in the business at his side. Peter Guber told us: "Neil was like a riverboat gambler. He was always all in."

Casting also proved vital in the success of the *The Deep*. Rarely had one actress, and one scene in particular, driven sales for a film so much as in *The Deep*. Jacqueline Bisset's famous wet T-shirt scene showed substantial potential—everyone flipped over the dailies.

Guber conceived the vertical poster design: tall and narrow, with bubbles rising and the logo on top, reminiscent of *Jaws*. He made good use of the images of Bisset in her revealing T-shirt, sensing they would cause a stir. Guber knew he had hit pay dirt when he screened the first ten minutes of the film for exhibitors. "Well, the exhibitors went out of their minds when they saw Jackie," he exulted. "That T-shirt made me a rich man."[6]

—◦—

Neil Bogart knew that Casablanca, despite all it had going for it in 1977, was still cash-strapped. Parliament and KISS were selling exceptionally well, but their elaborate sets and theatrical show setups required huge touring budgets. The shows sold the acts, so Neil, being more focused on promotions than he was on the company's bottom line, swallowed the high touring expense costs. He was able to rationalize the large touring costs because they helped drive up sales and the popularity of his acts. Pennies just couldn't be pinched there—the fans would know, and then everything would bottom out. Bogart had no choice; he had to find other ways to bring in cash. He soon had an idea to approach his partners with the goal of selling off a piece of the company. Adding a larger distributor with deep pockets and wide reach would only benefit the company financially, he reasoned. And Casablanca would soon land a big fish on its hook: PolyGram.

PolyGram was a big European conglomerate that wanted a piece of the US music market. It gobbled up Polydor, Mercury, MGM, RSO, and then Casablanca in 1977—the last two being the disco drivers of the 1970s. RSO survived on the backs of two massive successes, *Saturday Night Fever* and *Grease*. The two movies and their accompanying soundtracks were behemoths, drawing RSO huge amounts of cash and clout.

PolyGram wanted to sink a big chunk of money into Casablanca. But before they could do so, they wanted to see the books, which were a disaster. The money coming in and out was extraordinary, but there was little in the way of a paper trail to define the profits and expenses. It was a mishmash of bookkeeping. Chuck Zahler, assistant controller at Casablanca (an unenviable role, to say the least), told us: "Everything was bullshitted. The purchase orders—all of it. And when PolyGram wanted to look the books over, Neil brought in a friend, I'm pretty sure his name was Arnold

Feldman, an accountant to BS the entire audit. PolyGram believed the audit, and the rest is history."

Arnold Feldman was a friend of Bogart's from New York who came out to Los Angeles, took Casablanca's numbers, and turned them upside down. He created a picture for PolyGram of a functional company, establishing a paper trail where none had previously existed. When PolyGram management looked at the numbers, they didn't see the massive amounts of wasteful spending. If they had, they probably never would have invested millions into the endless dark well that was Casablanca Records. Feldman ensured that everything was on the up-and-up. He did what Neil asked him to do—establish fact where there was none and exaggerate where necessary to make sure the sale went through.

PolyGram saw similar opportunities with Casablanca as it had with RSO and believed the company was making money. The reality was that, despite their perceived success, Casablanca was hemorrhaging money at an alarming pace for a variety of reasons. KISS's and Parliament's success was tied to the fact that they cost a fortune on the road. Huge trucks had to transport their stages from city to city. Their shows were elaborate, spectacular, and costly.

Neil also loved to find and sign the next big act. He would go to the wall with an act, spending thousands even if the act ended up busting. He pushed and pushed and signed and signed. This was exorbitant, especially for the many acts that didn't hit at the company. Finally, Casablanca failed to keep track of money coming in and out. There was poor recordkeeping and virtually no accountability regarding how much money was flowing back and forth. Payouts and payoffs weren't tracked for obvious legal reasons. Those "costs of doing business" were masked by whatever recordkeeping there was. A line item on an expense report might read "Artists Development," which could stand for anything, including drug purchases. Since there was no central system for keeping track, loose pieces of paper atop desks accounted for the major paper trail issues at Casablanca. All items were handwritten and regularly misplaced.

To make matters worse, employees notoriously took products such as furniture or home sound systems and high-quality speakers home for their own personal use. There was only one person responsible for gathering purchase orders and receipts, and ironically he was the same man put in charge of Human Resources—Stan Lenarkski. Assistant Controller Chuck Zahler remembers Stan well. "[Stan] was a regular crook," Chuck told us. "He ripped Neil off. He'd fill his house with furniture and then write it off as purchase orders for the office. He was terrible."

Casablanca was not set up technologically, and the accounting department struggled to get information. Because Casablanca had no computer system operations at the time, all of their accounting was outsourced. They used a separate firm to run the numbers called Statistical Tabulating Service, "Stat Tab" for short. Stat Tab was responsible for much of the accounting pre-computer age at Casablanca. The outsourcing caused a two- to three-week delay on financial reports and a whole lot of confusion. This drove Neil and the accounting department crazy. Also, Casablanca used the numbers of records sales being distributed but never accounted for returns in the audits. The numbers came in at a snail's pace from the outsourced firm, and the actual results just weren't accurate. This gave the impression that far more money was actually being made; it's also why record returns and tour expenses did in fact cripple the bottom line. Casablanca was going for the appearance of raking it in, especially Neil, which was part of his image, but profits were a mirage. So much money was coming in, but even more was going out.

PolyGram, which did little due diligence, bought the phony audit. In 1977 they stepped in to purchase 50 percent of the company for fifteen million dollars. Bogart, Peter Guber, Larry Harris, Cecil Holmes, and Richard Trugman all reaped the rewards of the huge deal. They not only received a big personal injection of cash but now had a blank check to keep them ahead of the industry curve. PolyGram loved the potential Neil and Peter brought to the table, thinking that the music and movie geniuses were a golden combination who, along with RSO, had cornered the exploding disco market. In their book *Hit and Run*, which focuses on Peter Guber's later years in the movie business, Nancy Griffin and Kim Masters note:

> *Bogart wasted no time spending PolyGram's cash. Casablanca quickly grew from fourteen to two hundred employees. Casablanca employees*

were awarded such perks as Mercedes 450 SELs. Even in a decade marked by excess, Casablanca was notorious. The host of the twenty-four-hour-a-day party was Neil Bogart, whose high spirits and paternal manner made him a beloved boss. Bogart openly indulged his sybaritic appetites on the premises and encouraged other to do the same.[7]

To celebrate the deal, Casablanca expanded its promotional department and added expenses for leased Mercedes Benzes for all promo men. The higher-ups also each received his own Rolls Royce. The company paid for the cars, as well as the accompanying insurance.

Chuck Zahler told us, "The cost of the cars, you have to remember—there were over seventy promo guys who got Mercedes and car insurance paid for—was huge. Also, Neil wanted to get everyone new monogrammed jackets with their names on them. Instead of shopping around, he ended up spending five thousand dollars on jackets that shouldn't have cost more than five hundred. We just spent so much money."

Hoping to keep a close eye on Casablanca and its questionable expense practices, PolyGram sent a young accountant from New York by the name of David Shein out west. Shein was paid by PolyGram to keep a close eye on everything. David would work hand in hand with Joseph Ermilio, who ran the computer system at Casablanca, to revolutionize the tracking system for sales. Unfortunately for PolyGram, that's where the benefits of Shein's presence in Los Angeles ended. "David was always a big partier," Ermilio remembers. "He was probably the worst guy to send out."

Shein was given the Casablanca treatment. He was handed a Mercedes and became another indoctrinated member of the team. Once Shein joined the "Casablanca Program," PolyGram lost their man on the inside to the vortex. While Shein was ordered by PolyGram to oversee and ensure legitimate accounting practices, he ended up doing the complete opposite, slipping easily into the culture at Casablanca and only multiplying the excess. Seemingly everyone on Sunset had been easily charmed into the glorious glut at Casablanca, including David Shein.

Shein was just one example of how the ethos at Casablanca was drowning out any good sense or business practices. Casablanca continued to run amok. It was only a matter of time before PolyGram's bottom line was going to feel the financial crush. The problem was that in 1977, things were going so well for PolyGram that they couldn't see the truth. They actually wouldn't find out how bad it had gotten until the dust started to settle on the disco era at the end of the 1970s. Until then, they remained in the dark.

Who would have thought an innocuous double date many years earlier would so fortuitously marry one man's childhood dream with another's desperate need for a partner? With a 20 percent stake in Casablanca Records, Peter Guber inherited a fantastic opportunity. Casablanca was lighting up the Sunset Strip at the time with its blazing inferno of disco hits and the power rock of KISS. Neil got a 5 percent stake in *The Deep*; more importantly, he gained an important ally. Guber would provide Neil with a foot in the world he'd always dreamt about: Hollywood. Casablanca Filmworks was born.

For Bogart's part, he would inject a massive amount of life into the soundtrack for *The Deep*, placing Donna Summer and her molten-hot voice as the soundtrack's lead song. British composer John Barry provided the music, with Summer penning the lyrics. The song, "Deep Down Inside," would become a huge hit, charting in the United States, the U.K., and Netherlands, and would help the soundtrack hit double platinum. The Guber/Bogart partnership paid off huge: *The Deep* grossed over fifty million dollars (over 216 million in today's dollars).

However, with the success of their partnership came added pressure. They had a company capable of driving projects through production and an army of staff to help keep the daily workload in motion. This allowed Neil and Peter Guber to think large scale in terms of best strategies to merge music and movies together, essentially creating one powerful studio that they alone controlled. The two were driven, and both were determined to turn Casablanca Filmworks into both a large thriving music studio and a moviemaking monster. They had visions of becoming entertainment industry giants. "It was like Camelot," recalls Joyce Biawitz, Bogart's second wife.

Their goal was to buy or start their own studio. That way Casablanca Filmworks would not require a larger partner, who could simply cut them out of the gross sales figures by claiming there were no net profits. *The Deep* made millions, but Bogart expected to see more from it. He was frustrated when the returns came in and Columbia pictures wrote off everything under the sun. After everything was said and done, it left Casablanca with almost no money. Neil wanted to own a studio. He didn't want to be beholden to a studio that he suspected would cook the books. He wanted to own the movies and insert his music artists into those films, making money on both ends.

Certainly it made sense from a business standpoint. If Casablanca Filmworks could develop projects with Guber's guidance, use their studio to produce the films, and then have the music department led by Neil produce the soundtrack, it truly would be "Camelot." Despite the optimism and the opportunities for success before them, there were still issues to hash out. There was some disharmony as Guber and Bogart combined their companies. Sue Barton, publicist on *The Deep*, recalls, "I had a hard time when they [Casablanca] couldn't figure out why I wouldn't send a dancing girl and balloons to see the *New York Times* film critic Vincent Canby. I would keep saying, 'You can't do that with film critics!'"[8]

Casablanca Filmworks had separate offices from Casablanca Records, an entirely different office decor, and, understandably, a much different environment. Filmworks was more businesslike, and often the staff was working tirelessly on film projects. In contrast, the party never stopped at Casablanca. While 1970s Hollywood had its share of excess and partying, it could never hold a candle to the music business. The disconnect between Casablanca's music staff and Filmworks' film department was wide. The potential, however, was endless.

With the success of *The Deep* under their belt, it was time to create the next vehicle for the duo.

Bogart was focused on turning Donna Summer into a movie star. With the singer already rocketing up the charts with both critical acclaim and commercial success, and her hit song on the soundtrack to *The Deep*, Neil and Guber concocted another vehicle for Donna Summer—this time, a movie to star in. The movie would feature an onslaught of disco music and provide Casablanca Filmworks with an ideal product to pursue revenue on both the film and music sides. It was the perfect scenario for the new team.

The Filmworks division at Casablanca gave Bogart the opportunity to move his musical artist into the movies. The time was ripe; Casablanca Filmworks was firing on all cylinders. With multiple successful feature films thriving in theaters, the duo turned their attention to creating a true "disco" movie. Neil pitched it as the *American Graffiti* for the late 1970s, and *Thank God It's Friday* was born. The idea was to place Donna Summer in the movie as an actress and have her dominate the soundtrack as well. By casting her in the movie, Casablanca would garner a national stage to cross-promote the music and the movement. It would be a coup for the label.

Neil Bogart was never shy about over-promoting and likely never believed there was such a thing as overexposure. He threw everything at the wall to see what would stick. This tactic was reminiscent of Neil's approach to the bubblegum music craze. However, many in the industry scoffed at the idea of the film and cynically saw it as an excuse to promote Donna Summer and disco. This wasn't entirely untrue.

Thank God It's Friday almost never came to fruition. Guber's Filmworks division had a distribution deal with Columbia. His good friend Bill Tennant was an executive at Columbia at the time and had just signed on to do a deal for a film entitled *Disco*. Guber called Bill Tennant and told him what Neil and he were brewing over at Casablanca Filmworks, so Tennant killed the deal for *Disco*. It took a lot of negotiating and phone calls and coordination, but finally a deal was done. Despite not having a script or a cohesive story, Tennant always went to bat for Guber. Although the *Disco* project appeared to have little life left in it, there was still a deal to be made. In *Hit and Run (How Jon Peters and Peter Guber Took Sony for a Ride in Hollywood)*, Nancy Griffin and Kim Masters tell the memorable story:

> *Rob Cohen, head of the movie division at Motown, was under the impression that he was making a project called* Disco *for the studio. Determined to save his project, Cohen picked up the phone and called Guber. "I don't think you have a script," he began. "I have a script and*

you have a studio—we can merge." Cohen had struck a chord. "In less than fifteen minutes, Peter and Neil Bogart were in my office here at Universal," he remembers. Bogart strode in wearing a black leather jacket, a silk shirt, and gold chains; Peter was well groomed in a handsome knit sweater. The three quickly shook hands on a deal whereby Motown and Casablanca would go fifty-fifty on the film. "Peter cut his teeth on the TGIF *deal in terms of how to jump in on the action," says Cohen. This was the beginning, he says, of "a pattern of parasitic action."*

Though Bogart and Guber may have had different ways of getting things done, both knew how to achieve their goals. They turned the *Disco* movie deal into *Thank God It's Friday*.

At the time it seemed like a slam dunk. Disco was on the threshold of exploding. Donna Summer's "Love to Love You Baby" had set her atop the disco world as its Queen.

Donna Summer would be the vehicle for Neil's brainchild, *Thank God It's Friday*—a film he would lay his fingerprints all over, from start to finish. Larry Harris called the film "an expensive and lengthy commercial for Casablanca."[9]

That Columbia Pictures modified their deal with Motown on *Disco* meant Neil and Guber got immediate funding for *TGIF*. Casablanca would head the project funded by Columbia Pictures, and Motown would get a smaller cut but still be able to use their artists on the soundtrack. It wasn't a complete coup for Casablanca, but it was as close to complete control as they could have hoped for. Neil knew the potential in doing a disco movie just as the music craze was about to reach its peak. He was always a man of impeccable timing, and the timing for this movie couldn't have been better.

Thank God It's Friday was also a catapult of sorts for its young stars, Jeff Goldblum and Debra Winger. "It was a delightful experience," Goldblum told us. "It wasn't my habit to frequent discos at the time. It was a crazy little movie!"

Despite having the Casablanca name on the production, the film process was professional. The set was lively with disco music playing and everyone had a good time. Its big star Donna Summer had never starred in a movie but handled the experience well. "Donna was terrific, fantastic," Goldblum says.

While Casablanca toiled with their own version of a disco movie, RSO was producing their own disco film: *Saturday Night Fever*. Disco was just emerging, but the combination of *Saturday Night Fever* and *TGIF*, along with their accompanying soundtracks, would make both RSO and Casablanca—already entrenched in the music industry—huge potential players in the movie markets as well. Both projects would also send PolyGram's executives, the parent company to both records companies, into a celebratory frenzy.

With a firm hold of the script for *Thank God It's Friday*, the Casablanca team began to focus in on making *TGIF* a smash. In *And Party Every Day*, Larry Harris writes:

> *The marketing campaign had to be nothing less than spectacular. The title song, performed by Love and Kisses, had to be huge. Cost was no barrier. The song had to be a hit before the movie was released; it needed to be big enough to get people interested in the movie. We spent two million dollars promoting the movie and the soundtrack—almost double what it cost to produce the film itself.*[10]

Casablanca created a massive promotional scheme to launch *Thank God It's Friday*. With millions spent on advertising the film and establishing the soundtrack as a "must-buy" item with artists like the Commodores, Patti Brooks, Diana Ross, and Donna Summer, the money poured into the project would pay off. Neil's move to buy out Motown from having a take in the soundtrack also would pay huge dividends. The soundtrack for *TGIF* raked in huge sales, going platinum.

In the end the box office take for *Thank God It's Friday* was twenty million dollars, far exceeding the two million it cost to make. Casablanca, well versed in how things were done after making almost no money out of *The Deep* from Columbia Pictures, split the pie with Universal and turned the tables on Motown, claiming a net loss and essentially cutting them out. They could do this because Motown didn't get on the front side of the money, relying instead on back-end profits. Their deal was constructed poorly, and they were not able to lay claim to gross gains, only net profit. The difference between gross and net was worth millions.

"They declared it as six million dollars in the hole," [producer Rob Cohen] says. "They said they spent three million dollars on advertising. There are so many ways to pad it. . . . There was no way to prove they didn't spend it."[11]

Neil's first run at feature films was exactly what he had wanted. He had a crossover promotional feature film that highlighted both his music artists and his new film division. The venture into movies was a personal dream come true for Neil Bogart, who always was fascinated by the cinematic world.

There was only one problem, and it was a big one: *Saturday Night Fever*. Released in December 1977, *Saturday Night Fever* beat *TGIF*'s release date by six months. Grossing nearly three hundred million dollars worldwide, the film was clearly superior to *TGIF*. Both would be considered "disco films," but clearly, *Saturday Night Fever* was *the* disco film. It captured the moment, the music, the culture, New York City at the time, everything. It also entrenched RSO firmly in the disco game, creating something of a rivalry with Casablanca Records. Casablanca was used to getting its way with things. They owned the charts, had hits galore, and never failed to impress. "There was only room for one picture centered on dancing . . ." Larry Harris says. "*Saturday Night Fever* left us in *the dust*."[12]

Even with a strong soundtrack, *TGIF* couldn't topple the disco monster *Saturday Night Fever*. The movies cost virtually the same amount of money to make (*Fever*'s budget is estimated at 2.5 million dollars, five hundred thousand more than *TGIF*'s). But *Saturday Night Fever*, anchored by its hot young star, John Travolta, out-grossed *TGIF* fifteen times over. To make matters worse, Casablanca, which rarely got outshined by anyone, also had an inferior soundtrack to *Fever*'s enormous-selling double LP. The Bee Gees struck gold, platinum, and diamond (ten million copies sold) in sales in various countries. The numbers brought in by *Saturday Night Fever*'s soundtrack were simply staggering, unlike anything seen in the film and music business up to that point. In Canada one million sales, certified diamond. In France over 2.1 million in sales, certified gold. In Germany 1.5 million in sales, certified gold six times over. Platinum in Hong Kong, with over 15,000 in sales. In the U.K. it went platinum, with over three hundred thousand in sales. And in the United States, the sales were extraordinary, fifteen million, establishing the album as platinum fifteen times over. Led by the Bee Gees' tunes "Stayin' Alive" and "How Deep Is Your Love," the album would spend twenty-four straight weeks, from January 1978 to July 1978, on top of the US charts. Casablanca released *TGIF*'s soundtrack months later, but it still ran into the tidal wave that was *Saturday Night Fever* and had the impossible task of getting out of its wake.

Donna Summer's track from *TGIF*, "Last Dance," may have been a mega-hit, but Casablanca didn't just want a number-one single. They wanted a number-one *album*. And despite RSO and *Fever*'s insane run on the charts, they thought they had them beat. Bill Wardlow, the man who controlled the charts—whom Casablanca knew all too well—was Casablanca's ultimate trump card. They intended to offer him a "deal," the likes of which only Casablanca would. As was their way, Casablanca owned the charts. In this case, *Fever*'s soundtrack was a huge problem. Larry Harris explains:

> *Bill promised me our soundtrack would be No. 1 for the week ending July 1 (in a favor exchange with Neil Bogart hooking Wardlow up with Merv Griffin). But as it turned out, even pulling Wardlow's strings couldn't elevate us to the top spot. I screamed at Wardlow over the phone for reneging on his promise. It was a good demonstration of how much ego and a sense of entitlement had grown [there].*[13]

Indeed, even the long reach of Casablanca, the ability to wheel and deal, to grease the wheels of whatever needed to get done, could not overcome the avalanche of RSO's mega album. Casablanca would take a backseat to *Saturday Night Fever* and have to accept it. *Saturday Night Fever*'s soundtrack would make history. It would win the Grammy that year for Best Album, unprecedented for a soundtrack. To date it is one of the top-ten selling albums of all time and the second-highest selling soundtrack of all time (behind Whitney Houston's *The Bodyguard*).[14] Casablanca didn't have a chance.

—◦—

Released in 1978, *Thank God It's Friday* received a tepid response, to be kind. Film critic Leonard Maltin didn't mix words and rated the film a "bomb . . . perhaps the worst film to have won some kind of Academy Award."[15]

The film indeed did garner an Academy Award. Donna Summer's "Last Dance" won the Oscar that year for Best Original Song. "Last Dance" featured a combination of a disco groove and elements of a slow ballad. The explosive combination drove the song to #1 on the US *Billboard* Hot Dance Club Play and #3 on the US *Billboard* Hot 100. The song and the movie further validated Neil's faith in his "diva" and Donna Summer's status as the "First Lady of Love." Over thirty-five years later, the song is still a celebration party staple.

"Last Dance" continued Summer's worldwide success and mass appeal; she was featured on movie screens around the world. Summer was becoming the larger-than-life figure Neil had concocted in his mind the moment he had listened to her moan the lyrics to "Love to Love You Baby" just a few years earlier. Summer was Neil's prized possession, a labor of love to whom he had hitched himself, personally as well as professionally. Neil was proud of Donna. He genuinely loved her—and loved that her success had come so quickly.

—◦—

Summer's continued addiction to prescription drugs and her work on the film and soundtrack to *Thank God It's Friday* unfortunately set her solo career back. After the film she found herself on an unplanned hiatus. She hadn't produced a new album in over two years. In 1979 some members of the press labeled Donna Summer a product of the disco era, which by the end of the decade was seemingly on its last legs. That was all about to change.

She finally went back to work. Donna Summer's next album, *Bad Girls*, took her from the Queen of Disco to something even bigger—something immortal. With the singles "Bad Girls" and "Hot Stuff," Summer became a music legend. The album, based on a concept surrounding the struggles of a prostitute, would go double-platinum. The album soared, and so did many of its singles. "Hot Stuff" landed #1 on both *Billboard* Hot 100 and Club Play Singles. The song "Bad Girls" landed #1 spots on *Billboard* Hot 100, Club Play Singles, and on Hot Soul Singles.

The compilation double album, *On the Radio: Greatest Hits Volumes 1 & 2*, was Summer's swan song with Neil Bogart and Casablanca Records. Shortly after the album's release, the relationship soured. Summer sued Casablanca and Neil Bogart to get out of her contract. In part she cited a conflict of interest with Neil's wife, Joyce, in her role as Summer's comanager, just as KISS had complained. Summer also was growing tired of being a "puppet." She wanted her freedom and no longer wanted to be the world's sex symbol.

Summer's family and her religious upbringing would be cited as part of the reason she needed to break free from the Bogarts. But there were other things at work. Summer later admitted:

> *I was one of the people that were selling mega-records at the time, but I wasn't being compensated for them. Let's put it like this, my original contract was not up to par and so there was a deficiency in what I should have been making. I was making the money for them, millions of dollars, which I wasn't seeing. At some point, I got a lawyer and started to investigate what was going on, and it wasn't pretty.*[16]

Summer also just wanted to move on; she had grown exhausted with disco. She wanted to remain relevant beyond it—perhaps sensing it was going to fade—and she said she'd "like to have as much validity as Streisand and Aretha Franklin."[17] Summer wanted to go back to her true musical love, rock music. Bogart was adamantly against Summer's desire to sing rock. "[Neil Bogart] saw dollar bills flying out of my pockets when I said I wanted to sing rock 'n' roll," Summer said. "[I was] feeling stuck doing something that had been choking me to death for three years."[18]

The tensions brewed at the worst time. Summer didn't know it, but Neil Bogart was suffering from cancer at the time. She left Casablanca in

1980, settling her lawsuit and moving on. Neil was heartbroken, as was Summer, who struggled with her decision even after Neil's death.

"Neil's passing was *very* painful," Summer said.

I sang at his funeral, but it was an extremely difficult moment for me. He was my Clive Davis. I couldn't see myself without him as part of my life because he was so in the making of it. It was a very tough time for me. Very tough, very lost . . . you didn't want to leave him. He was just magnetic. You love him. He was, for me, a mentor, he was a big brother, he was a protector, he was an educator, he was my parent when I needed him.[19]

Donna Summer would go on, but she would never recapture the massive success she achieved with Casablanca Records alongside Neil Bogart. She had one more successful album in the early MTV era with *She Works Hard for the Money* in 1983, but after that, her music failed to find the audience it once found. Summer's legacy at this point was well intact, with many hits and the label of "Queen," which stuck with her from her disco days. Summer would rack up five Grammy Awards and six American Music Awards during her career.

On May 17, 2012, Donna Summer passed away after a battle with lung cancer. The world mourned the loss of an incredible talent. Her influence on the world was so profound that her death prompted an official statement released from the President of the United States, Barack Obama, who said: "Her voice was unforgettable and the music industry has lost a legend far too soon." The president also referred to her by the moniker that Bogart pushed to bestow on her: "the Queen of Disco."

Neil Bogart and Donna Summer were an unlikely duo, but they shared a strong determination and belief in each other. Bogart welcomed the singer into not only his company but also into his family and his heart. Perhaps their loving relationship will go undefined, something only the two of them ever truly understood. Bogart believed so strongly in her talent, and he drove her to become one of the most successful female singing artists of all time. Together they cemented her place in the annals of music history. They were two electric personalities who, for a time, made music magic.

CHAPTER 14

Hollywood Bites Back

Peter never wanted to use company money. Neil was willing to gamble it all.

—BETH GUBER

As Neil helped hammer out his first hands-on feature film venture, his partner, Peter Guber, was developing another project. *Midnight Express* would do what both *The Deep* and *Thank God It's Friday* could not: bring acclaim and respect to the film department at Casablanca Filmworks. The film was the perfect combination of a stellar script (by a young writer named Oliver Stone), the right mix of creative types and businesspeople, and the stars in proper alignment. Peter Guber helped assemble a stellar crew behind the camera.

It all started with the autobiography written by Billy Hayes. The true story is a thriller set in a Turkish prison, where an American college student is incarcerated after being arrested for attempting to smuggle hashish out of the country. The Turkish police arrest him at the airport, and the young American's life is turned upside down by a harsh and inscrutable justice system and a far harsher prison. The film version of Hayes's book would be gritty, dark, and disturbing—and would scare straight a generation of would-be drug smugglers.

Guber assembled a young all-star team behind the scenes. In addition to young phenom Oliver Stone, British director Alan Parker (who would go on to more success with the film version of Pink Floyd's *The Wall*, *Evita*, and *Angela's Ashes*) was brought in to helm the dark film. Brits David Puttnam and Alan Marshall came in to produce. With a budget of

2.3 million dollars, the film was small in size. Turkey refused to allow the movie to be filmed on location in Istanbul, so nearly the entire movie was filmed at Fort St. Elmo in Valletta, Malta.

Peter Guber was a facilitator. One of his talents was for bringing the right people together and allowing them to do their thing. In many ways, his business prowess was a sharp contrast, almost the inverse, to his partner, Neil Bogart. A businessman first and foremost, Guber was a hands-off kind of guy. Alan Parker told Nancy Griffin and Kim Masters:

> *Guber left us alone to make the film. We re-created Istabul's Sagmalcilar Prison in an old fort in Malta, where the film was made in fifty-three days. Guber visited once briefly with a press junket of journalists. . . . Alan Marshall and I took the finished film to show to everyone in LA.*[1]

Guber knew where to go for the score to *Midnight Express*. The music behind the movie would come from Casablanca's "sure-thing," Giorgio Moroder. Moroder applied a soft electronic disco beat behind the film, which worked perfectly with the tone and setting.

Midnight Express premiered at the Cannes Film Festival and garnered serious buzz and positive reviews. The film wasn't an easy sell. It was violent and dark and, to an American audience, quite terrifying. Its initial theater run didn't provide an impressive haul, but with an Academy Award run featuring five nominations—for Best Picture, Best Director, Best Film Editing, Best Screenplay, and Best Score, the last two garnering wins—the film turned out to be a big winner. The award season helped re-spark film sales, with the final tally more than thirty million dollars for a film that cost just 2.5 million to make.

Despite the success involved in *Midnight Express*, and despite the accolades reigning down upon Casablanca, professionals in the film industry had an issue with what they perceived was going on at the company. After the success of *Midnight Express*, the whole operation seemed to turn into a facade of a movie company, something like an illusion. First off, the management at Casablanca didn't seem to have a plan. Scripts were coming in, but nobody was reading them, and there didn't seem to be any mechanism for pushing things forward. In 1978 the only movie Casablanca actually started producing was a film called *Foxes*, with Adrian Lyne attached as director. In 1979, again, only one film was given the green light, *The Hollywood Knights*, staring a young Tony Danza and a twenty-one-year-old Michelle Pfeiffer. The only thing Casablanca seemed to be really good at was using the industry trade papers to tout actors and directors attached to scripts and productions with big budgets on films they never intended to release. The reality was starting to become clear: Casablanca seemed to be great at one thing to the exclusion of all else—promotion.

The story of "repainting the building" and making things seem better than they were had always appealed to Neil Bogart. If things aren't going well, paint the building and make it *look* like everything was new and shiny, giving the appearance of success. Neil Bogart lived by the maxim that "perception is reality." He wanted people to think more was going on than perhaps was actually happening. He floated the idea that Casablanca was working to bring Cher and Gene Simmons together for a film,[2] as well as some other less-than-solid ideas. The reason the operation seemed to be an illusion is that, in many ways, it was.

Neil did make announcements. Casablanca Filmworks did have plans, but a litany of issues got in their way. There were issues with Columbia Pictures and the contract Guber had initially signed on the film *The Deep*. He had signed what was called a "Net Profit" deal, which generally only pays if there are properly accounted profits listed on the bottom line. However, the use of creative accounting limits the chances of those net profits coming to fruition, and this kind of creative accounting seemed to be the industry standard.

Both Neil Bogart and Peter Guber were frustrated and dismayed as the numbers rolled in from Columbia. First, they saw almost no money for *The Deep*, a film that cost a bloated 9 million dollars to make, but pulled in more than fifty million. Also, *Midnight Express*, a film with a reasonable budget of only 2.5 million dollars, raked in over thirty million. Frustrated by their lack of returns and Columbia's claims that its high expenses offset all the profit that rolled in, Casablanca turned to its attorneys to resolve the situation. Their contract with Columbia had a clause that said they could be released if there was an eighteen-month period in which no new production had been green-lit, which was the case.

The idea of making movies with Columbia lost its luster; the drive to complete more follow-up projects faded. Guber needed to get out of his deal with Columbia in order for Casablanca to salvage any chance of having an impact in the film industry. In June 1979, Casablanca Record and Filmworks broke free of Columbia.

Guber's displeasure with Columbia's accounting practices could be heard far and wide. He made no secret that he was pissed off about the situation. All of Casablanca was set ablaze with frustration. Their soundtracks were hits, but they weren't seeing any money from films that should have grossed millions in profits.

Bogart wanted a bigger piece of the pie as well. If expanding his record company to include a production wing wasn't big enough, then why not buy out an entire studio and do it all yourself? If you can't beat them, buy them out and kick 'em out the door.

Columbia Pictures was ripe for a buyout, and Bogart wanted to buy them out using PolyGram's large pile of cash. The potential of having a vast library of old hits was too good to resist, and Neil wanted badly to take a much greater leap into the film industry. He didn't have the money himself to buy a studio and produce movies, but he thought he might be able to get PolyGram to buy out Columbia. Then he would be able to install Guber as head of the studio. Not interested in investing that much in Columbia, PolyGram turned him down. They were more focused on making music and didn't see the value in buying a film studio. On top of that, PolyGram wasn't completely aware of what was going on at Casablanca, and handing Neil the keys to not only a music kingdom but a movie one as well was too much liability for the European company. Neil and Peter Guber had been but a heartbeat away from achieving their goal of owning a studio. Instead they were left with nothing but a mountain of frustration.

It would be a difficult blow for Bogart and Casablanca. They were forced to use the exit clause to escape the Columbia deal. They were creeping along making movies at a snail's pace—one or two a year, if that. And something else seemed to be brewing. During their short relationship, the Casablanca Records and Filmworks teams lived opposite lives. The Filmworks building was a corporate, businesslike atmosphere.

Their employees arrived in the morning and worked throughout the day. Next door was like the Delta Tau Chi House from *Animal House*; Casablanca Records might as well had John Belushi running through its halls. Much of the promotions staff didn't arrive until noon or later. They were all hung over or exhausted from late-night partying or "mingling" with the musicians they scouted until the early morning hours. The music at Casablanca Records was played loud; the drugs were there for the taking. The difference between the two worlds was astronomical. Sadly, so were the differences between their two leaders, old friends Neil Bogart and Peter Guber.

Neil's first wife, Beth, eventually married Peter Guber's brother, Charlie. She remembers a conversation she had with Peter explaining the difficulties he and Neil were having. "Peter told me their relationship was never working. They were very different in their viewpoints. Peter is very conservative, which has served him amazingly well. Neil was very creative but a poor businessman. Neil spent huge amounts of money. Neil was really not closely involved in the films. His realm was music."

Guber took care of the film department, but it was stalled due to the difficulties with Columbia. Neil's idea of owning the studio, the production wing, and the soundtracks was a great idea, but only in theory. It just never materialized. Neil's willingness to push the financial envelope was admirable and aggressive, but to a man like Peter Guber, it was frightening from a business standpoint. "Peter never wanted to use company money. Neil was willing to gamble it all," Beth Guber says.

And that was the problem. Neil was the ultimate gambler, comfortable—maybe even eager—to risk it all. He pushed the envelope to any extreme necessary. Peter Guber did not. He was not an "all-in" guy. Risking everything meant possibly losing everything. Guber had far too savvy a business mind to ever do something so risky. This would be the root of the issues between Neil Bogart and Peter Guber going forward. There could be no future for the two friends as business partners.

Neil Bogart's run at being a movie producer would begin and end with *Thank God It's Friday*. Casablanca would produce five feature films, but lacking the promise of their first three films, their film division faded out with a whimper.

~

Everything changed with the arrival of 1979. Neil Bogart and Peter Guber grew apart. Casablanca Filmworks was barely operational. "The Casbah" proved to be too much for Peter Guber to handle. If Neil had dreams of making more movies, they ended here. Peter Guber moved on to a new prospective business partner—producer Jon Peters, boyfriend to Barbara Streisand.

The Guber-Peters production team was born officially in 1983 and had a strong critical and commercial run in the mid to late 1980s with *An American Werewolf in London*, *Rain Man*, *Batman*, *Tango and Cash*, and *The Witches of Eastwick*, garnering them five Oscar wins, including Best Picture for *Rain Man*. Although they were complete opposites in personality—Guber, a driven, focused businessman, and Peters, a self-professed ladies' man—the two found enormous success together in Hollywood. They parted ways shortly after joining forces with Sony Pictures in 1989, when Guber fired Peters in an attempt to go it alone at Sony, until he eventually fell out of favor at the large film company. The one thing Neil Bogart, Peter Guber, and Jon Peters all had in common was their propensity to think big, and if that didn't work, think bigger.

~

Neil Bogart was a successful creative man, but at his core he was just a dreamer. He loved the *idea* of making movies. Movies were larger than life, and Bogart's personality fit perfectly on the grand screens. Film embodied the notion of fantasy that drove so much of his music choices. He had conquered music, and he so badly wanted to conquer the challenges of movies. Sadly, he would never get his chance.

CHAPTER 15

Hang Out with All the Boys:
The Village People

*Hey, if I can, through Casablanca, create a fantasy for people, give
them a couple hours of music with which to dance their asses off, to
make them forget that they have a payment to make tomorrow, then I
think I'm doing a public service.*[1]

—NEIL BOGART, 1979

By the mid-1970s Neil Bogart was beginning to amass an empire. Around
this time, French music composer Jacques Morali and his business partner, Henry Belolo, were tinkering around with a band called the Village
People. They were ready to cast a wide net for the right label, only they
didn't need to go that wide. They instinctively knew where they had to go:
Neil Bogart and Casablanca Records.

In hindsight, it's easy to see this as a watershed moment of the disco
era. In fact, a cultural critic might break the period into two specific eras:
Before the Village People and After the Village People. The group, its
look, and its sound would become an iconic part of late 1970s disco music
and culture. Morali's vision was to bring the caricature of the "American
Man" that he saw on the streets of Greenwich Village in the 1970s to the
mainstream. And so the Village People were born.

Broadway singer and actor Victor Willis was the center of the group,
and around him were cast men who fit the American male archetypes
Morali had envisioned. Morali had the idea and wrote the music, and
then he essentially cast people to play the band. He and Belolo knew

Bogart from his previous successes with KISS and Donna Summer, but there was another reason they went to Bogart, something more sentimental. Belolo remembers: "I am born in Casablanca. So I was always attracted about the idea of having someone in America establishing a company called Casablanca." Not only was the timing right for the music, but when Bogart was finally introduced to Victor Willis, the group's de facto leader, the two hit it off right away.

The Village People found success with their first album via their lead single, "San Francisco (You Got Me)." Morali's goal was to collect a following first in discotheques and clubs—aware that the scene itself could lift the song up the charts. (Bogart's decision to extend Donna Summer's "Love to Love You Baby" was made for similar reasons.) Belolo recalled bringing "San Francisco" to the people first, to see if it would play:

[Jacques and I] went to a club and we convinced the DJ to play ["San Francisco"]. It was a big studio, 4,000 to 5,000 people, and I was scared to death. . . . The first 30 seconds the floor got empty! I said to myself, "My God, it's a failure!" And when the chorus came . . . 5,000 people were screaming back on the dance floor and everyone kissing us, congratulating us. I said "Jacques, we got an idea there, there is something!"[2]

Bogart also began to consider an emerging demographic he now viewed as buyers. Gay audiences were flocking in droves to discotheques, and the unique all-male group was the perfect group to invest in. After conquering the clubs, the Village People were set to explode onto mainstream America.

By 1978 Bogart had a new wife, another son on the way, mounds of money coming in from hit acts, and, to top it all off, less stress than he'd had in a while: He had shifted much of the financial burden of running his business onto European giant PolyGram. Neil Bogart was once again king, and he was about to climb atop the flashy world of disco.

Upon arriving in New York in 1973, Jacques Morali was taken with the diversity and various cultural influences he found on the streets and in the clubs. A vision began brewing deep inside of him. He didn't quite know what it was yet, but he was on the verge of putting together the key components to create a supergroup that would be the voice of a community, a lifestyle, and a genre. In 1975, attempting to find a voice in the disco genre, Morali found himself working—with limited success—with a group calling themselves the Ritchie Family. He continued to tinker with the band, unhappy with its various iterations. The flamboyant, openly gay Frenchman was a dreamer. He wanted more, and he was about to find it.

Horace Ott, a talented studio man and musical conductor, was meanwhile working with burgeoning Broadway performer Victor Willis. In 1976 Willis played the lead in an Australian version of *The Wiz* (an urban take on *The Wizard of Oz*) and was the understudy in the United States version as the Tin Man and the Cowardly Lion.

Willis was hungry for the fame and attention he felt had eluded him up to that point. He brought his powerful voice into the studio and recorded a demo with Horace Ott. The two enjoyed working together. As chance would have it, Ott was working with Morali in the studio and saw the connection immediately. He had to get Willis and Morali together. However, laying down some background vocals for the Ritchie Family album, *Arabian Nights*, wasn't something the Broadway professional had any interest in. Willis always saw himself as a star. Singing backup wasn't part of his MO.

Because of their compatible working relationship, Ott insisted and eventually got Willis into the studio. Victor Willis was the kind of man who commanded attention upon entering a room. He arrived wearing a flashy hat, a large chalice hanging from his neck, and an accompanying outfit that just lured all eyes onto him. And he had the voice to match. A group of people gathered in the studio to watch. Willis enjoyed an audience, but someone in particular was looking him over. As Willis belted out the vocals, Jacques Morali watched closely; the French producer had something percolating in his brain. He began to pace, keeping his eyes on Willis, an idea forming in his mind.

As Willis sang, he noticed Morali's unconventional stare. When Willis finished, Morali beckoned him over, waving for him to step out of the recording room and join him. Somewhat confused, Willis obliged.

"Victor," Morali said, "I had a dream. You were a singer doing lead vocals for an album. We became a big success. I can't pay you a lot of money right now, but if you can record for me, I know I can make you a big star."[3]

It was a pitch made many times by all types and levels of producer to countless gullible showbiz wannabes, but Willis was curious nevertheless. Impressed by Morali's enthusiasm, Willis accepted the offer and recorded the first studio album of what would become the Village People.

As Willis and Ott began studio work, Morali and his business partner, fellow Frenchman Henri Belolo, began to throw ideas back and forth about the group they envisioned. They weren't looking for the standard fair; they wanted something different, cutting edge—of the time. They wanted a band representative of the people and the culture of New York City as they experienced it. Both men lived in Greenwich Village, an artistic area of New York City known for its creativity and personalities. There was far less judgment of sexual preference in Greenwich Village than there were in some other parts of New York. The Village had historically welcomed all types.

In a 2000 interview, Henri Belolo recalled:

One day Morali and I were walking in the streets of New York. I remember clearly it was down in the Village, and we saw an Indian walking down the street and heard the bells on his feet. We followed him into a bar. He was a bartender—he was serving and dancing on the bar. And while we were sipping our beer and watching him dancing, we saw a cowboy watching him dance. And Jacques and I suddenly had the same idea. We said, "My God, look at those characters." So we started to fantasize about what were the characters of America. The mix, you know, of the American man . . . and we named it the Village People.[4]

The French duo knew they had something unique in this concept. With the strong vocals of Victor Willis guiding the sound, Morali's development of the music, and a first cut of the album ready to be distributed, the group was ready to launch. The only thing left to consider was which music label to approach first about signing the group.

A name had been popping up over and over again in the music business in the mid-1970s. On the basis of the strength and success of popular acts like KISS, Parliament, and Donna Summer, Neil Bogart and Casablanca Records seemed to be the center of things. Morali and Belolo knew where to bring the Village People. "[Neil] understood immediately where we wanted to go," Belolo remembers. "Neil Bogart already had a reputation of being a talent scout and a music man—someone that will fast understand an idea."

Cofounder of Casablanca Records, Larry Harris, recalls in *And Party Every Day*:

> *They figured the act would have a built-in audience in gay nightclubs. The two had picked up on Casablanca's maverick approach to the music biz, and they were impressed that we'd developed KISS and Parliament-Funkadelic, two fairly out-there acts that many of the major labels wouldn't have looked at twice. Morali and Belolo knew their vision for the Village People was likely to be met with ambivalence or derision if they pitched it to the likes of Capitol or Columbia. But with Neil they felt they'd found the perfect match.*

Bogart loved the album immediately and, specifically, Victor Willis's voice. The Village People would be packaged as disco. Since Neil had had so much success with Donna Summer, Casablanca Records was morphing into what would be known as the disco label. It wasn't all disco of course, but when the label struck success with Donna Summer and the Village People, it was all but done—Neil was to be christened the "Disco King." Disco would become Neil Bogart's new "bubblegum." Willis and Morali finalized the album. The Casablanca machine needed to package it and promote it. Bogart considered it a low-maintenance risk for Casablanca; he'd already had success with the "gay" audience through Donna Summer and was looking to strike gold—or platinum—again.

Neil Bogart had a history of making decisions quickly—sometimes to his benefit, sometimes less so. His decision to sign the Village People to a contract was no different. Just as he had with KISS, he signed them without meeting Willis first. "Casablanca Records and Neil Bogart immediately recognized a potential winner, and we signed a deal in an hour,"[5] said Henri Belolo. Neil clearly saw things in black and white and knew an opportunity when it came along. He loved the concept and the sound. What else did he need to know?

There was only one thing left to do. With their lead singer intact, it was time to recruit the band's other members. At this time, the demo was essentially a one-man show. Relying on powerful vocals from a single talent, the production team could fashion the vision of a group around the lead vocal—similar to how the bubblegum craze of the 1960s was built. The other members of the group would essentially be hired to fill roster spots. The group would then be assigned a style, something high-energy to capture the audience's attention at live performances. With the producers and their lead vocalist establishing the studio sound, actors and performers could step in and out of the remaining roles when on tour.

They got to work casting the characters that would fill out the rest of the Village People roster. Open auditions were held. The influx of performers coming through the door was reminiscent of a male burlesque show. A tollbooth collector named Glenn Hughes was hired as the "Leatherman." Alex Briley, the son of a minister, was the "Soldier" (he would switch to the "Sailor" for the famous "In the Navy" video). A male stripper named Felipe Rose, actually born to a Lakota Sioux father, was the "Indian." Randy Jones, a singer raised on a farm in North Carolina, would become the "Cowboy." David Hodo, a struggling singer and actor, would be the "Construction Worker."

It was a strange situation as Victor Willis sat in with Jacques Morali during the rehearsal process. Willis was a classically trained vocalist, a professional who had toured and been on Broadway. Morali was asking him to share the stage with what amounted to a variety act. Like the bubblegum era Neil spearheaded at Buddah Records in the late 1960s, the Village People were a studio-driven creation, and their music was meant to be upbeat, joy-inspiring. The voice would be Victor Willis. The men singing behind him during recordings would be professional studio singers. However, on the road, the performers would be standing behind him in an assortment of gimmick-driven ensembles—what Morali saw as Americana. Willis did not love this arrangement. For Willis, singing on stage with an assortment of dancers, actors, and non-classically trained singers was tantamount to lying. Karen Willis, Victor's current wife, told us:

Victor was troubled by the fact that just dancers were on stage with him. He felt the performances were a sham. Sometimes their mics were dead. Background performers were not even singing. Jacques didn't care about singing—he wanted the "look" and the dancing. Jacques convinced Victor to do it. He convinced him it would be a big success.

The only song off the Village People's self-titled debut album that would find its way onto the charts was "San Francisco (You've Got Me.)" It hit #46 as a single on the U.K. pop charts and scored recognition for the group. It was a sensation in discotheques across the country. Morali wanted to go a different direction with the songwriting. He remembered how well he had liked the Victor Willis demo he had developed with Horace Ott. Morali wanted Willis's input on the writing. It was a smart and fortuitous move. Morali and Willis would go on to write and develop the songs that would become the biggest hits for the Village People.

After the album *Village People* hit #54 on the US Top 200 charts and #36 on the R&B charts, *Macho Man* arrived next, released in February 1978. The album soared and officially landed the Village People on the map. The album hit #24 on the US Top 200 and #31 on the US R&B charts. The title track, "Macho Man," would hit #25 on the US charts and become something of a phenomenon. The Village People were taking off and were touring all around the United States and Canada. Their performances were synchronized high-energy dance numbers behind Victor Willis's powerful voice. Audiences were enamored with the show, and the band's songs were getting huge in underground clubs. After *Macho Man* hit, the band began to gain momentum as a successful mainstream act—and they were about to strike gold.

This was all before their signature song, "Y.M.C.A.," had even been written. Morali was like Bogart, always at work, thinking about the next song, the next album, the next venue. He was constantly humming to himself, working on rhythm, chorus, melody. He kept going back to one tune he liked but had yet to work out completely. Deeply embedded into the gay culture as he was, he noticed that the community spent a lot of time at the local YMCA. He became curious and began to ask about the place. Victor Willis, who was straight, informed him that it was a place "urban" kids went to hang out. It was a place they could go to swim and play sports, somewhere they could just be themselves. This fascinated Morali, and he wanted to write a song about it.

Unlike the first album, for which Victor Willis never wrote a lyric or developed the music, Morali and Willis worked hand in hand this time around. Morali and Willis began to work the melody together and quickly developed the tune. With a melody in place, Willis began to write the lyrics while on tour. While in Vancouver, Willis completed the lyrics on one of the greatest dance anthems the world has ever known.

The "Young Men's Christian Association," founded by a British farmer for Bible study purposes in the 1840s, had become a staple in many US communities and a nonprofit haven for youth of all ages for decades. Willis knew it well. He used his own personal experiences to create a more universal depiction of the place. The lyrics were reminiscent of a young urban boy just looking for a place to belong, somewhere to be accepted where he could be himself and have a good time.

Village People member Randy Jones would tell *SPIN* in the article "'Y.M.C.A.' (An Oral History)": "The guy who really deserves the credit is Horace Ott, who arranged the horns and strings. Jacques had the ideas, but Horace transformed them into songs."[6]

With Ott's arrangements, Morali's concepts, and Willis's ability to create melodies and write lyrics, the Village People were finally hitting their stride. Horace Ott said of the song: "What I loved about 'Y.M.C.A.' was, to be honest, everything. Great beat, great voice with Victor, great timing in the midst of the disco boom. Now, was it a gay song? I don't know. It certainly appealed to a lot of people who embraced that lifestyle."[7]

People began to assume the group was gay, and the song began to be targeted as a "gay" song. The YMCA even threatened to sue the band over trademark infringement and its concerns of "dual meanings" embedded within the song's lyrics. However, when their membership significantly increased due to awareness of the organization through the song's popularity, they dropped their lawsuit. Today the organization is happy to be associated with the song.[8] Willis rejected the gay associations. His publicist said that Willis "was appalled by the homosexual subtext [the songs] took on, fearing that catering to a 'niche' market would doom the group to failure."[9]

Although nearly all the members actually were gay, Victor Willis was not. He was married to actress Phylicia Ayers-Allen (of *The Cosby Show* fame) at that time. Certainly the song was a hit in gay clubs, but patrons of black as well as Latin clubs enjoyed it too. The Village People's music was big in the underground music scene, where "Macho Man" and "Y.M.C.A." would both become ubiquitous.

Although "Y.M.C.A." became a gay anthem, Randy Jones claimed this was a misinterpretation. Jones would say: "It was not intended as a gay anthem. Do you have the lyrics in front of you? There's nothing gay about them. Victor wrote the words, but it's all a big fucking mystery."[10]

Released in 1978, "Y.M.C.A.," the final song added to the *Crusin'* album, would help propel the album to #3 on the US Top 200 and #5 on the R&B charts. Bogart's ears knew a smash hit when they heard it. After Neil Bogart heard "Y.M.C.A.," he wanted it placed front and center as the lead single on the album. The song itself would shoot to #2 on the US charts and all the way to #1 on the U.K. charts. The single itself would go platinum, sell over twelve million copies (one of only three disco songs to do this), and become one of the top twenty highest-selling singles of all time.[11]

In an interview, Village People member David Hodo was asked about Neil Bogart's part in the Village People's success:

> *Neil had a very big part. I loved Neil. Of all of the people I disrespected in the music business, I really respected Neil. Neil taught me what a hook was . . . that's the thing you can sing by the time the song is over upon hearing it for the first time. Jacques, our writer, was great at writing hooks, but Neil was great at picking the hooks that were going to be hits. For example, "Y.M.C.A." was meant to be filler on an album. Neil said "No, no. This is the hit. This is the one we're gonna push." Neil was very fresh, young, a genius in his field.[12]*

Bogart's ear for great hooks pushed "Y.M.C.A." to where it ended up—thirty-five years later it's still the song people most associate with the group. Joe Ermilio, director of MIS at Casablanca at the time, remembers:

The promotions department was caught by surprise with the success of "Y.M.C.A." The group and the song caught on so fast. Neil lit a fire under that department to push them hard. They went into hyperdrive promoting the group. Neil marketed the hell out of them because they were such a unique group in the disco era.

The origin of the famous "Y.M.C.A." dance—outstretched arms imitating the four letters—is hard to nail down. One story is that Neil's good friend Dick Clark had the Village People on *American Bandstand* on January 6, 1979. As the group performed, the audience members spontaneously began displaying the letters *Y.M.C.A.* with their hands during the song. Clark caught Willis's attention after they finished singing and replayed the song just for the audience. Willis watched and saw the hand movement and gestures the audience was doing.

Clark turned to Willis and said, "Victor, think you can work this dance into your routine?"

Willis responded, "I think we're gonna have to."

But Randy Jones remembers it slightly differently:

We were flying up from South America for the show, and we worked on the choreography on the airplane—handclaps-turning, marching in place . . . stuff like that. Well, the audience at this particular taping was a bunch of kids bused in from a cheerleader camp. The first time we got to the chorus, we were clapping our hands above our heads. And the kids thought it looked like we were making a Y. So they automatically did the letters.[13]

David Hodo said, "When I saw the movements, I thought, wow, that is so stupid. Then everyone in America started doing it, and I thought, Wow, that is so brilliant. It took on a life of its own."[14]

"Y.M.C.A." spent twenty-six weeks on the *Billboard* Top 100. As success for the band grew, trouble began to brew as well. The group started to fracture as bandmates became jealous of Victor Willis and his first-class treatment—literally. Many times when the band traveled across country, Willis would be the only one up front while the rest flew coach. He was the star, not only because he was the lead singer but because he recorded most of the vocals—lead and background—in the studio. Some professional background singers were brought in to lay tracks, but the majority of the members of the Village People performed only on stage.

Not only was Willis making money off his singing and the performances, but he also made a ton of money off the residuals from writing the music. His bandmates saw this and, as is typical for the industry, animosity began to set in. From Willis's point of view, he never saw the Village People as a group. He saw himself as the main event. As Willis hauled in millions of dollars for his work, other members were bringing in thousands—mainly for their performances.

Another issue started to arise when Morali and Belolo banned Willis from visiting Neil Bogart. They were terrified Neil was going to steal Willis right out from under them. In fact, in renegotiating contractual agreements with the Village People, Bogart made sure to add one clause: If Willis left the Village People for any reason, Casablanca would own the rights to produce Willis's solo album. Morali and Belolo eventually caved and gave Neil what he wanted. "What Neil wanted, Neil got. Neil wanted Victor and he was going to get him," Karen Willis told us.

Willis and Bogart were close. In fact, despite Morali and Belolo's efforts to keep Willis away from Neil, the two were often together in LA. That's when the fun usually began. Karen Willis told us:

Every time Victor came to Neil's office he had a different woman or groupie there. They hung all over him. It was like he was the rock star. Victor was always amazed by that. Neil would lock his office door, and Victor and Neil would snort coke—a lot of coke. In fact, Victor was introduced to powder cocaine by Neil Bogart. They regularly did all kinds of drugs in his office. I don't know who snorted more, Neil or Victor!

It was no secret that Bogart and Willis did lots of cocaine. And every time Willis walked through the doors of Casablanca, he'd see beautiful women—different ones every time—exiting the offices. Models were there for music artists. Actresses would be moving about for Filmworks. Casablanca was like one big circus, and Neil Bogart was its ring leader. Women, drugs, celebrities, and music seemed to always be on tap. Even though Casablanca had many beautiful women wandering about, Willis, even as the star, didn't partake. He was a dedicated husband. Drugs were the vice he shared with Neil Bogart.

The Village People were blowing up, becoming a huge hit across the country. Their shows were enormous. As with KISS, Donna Summer, and George Clinton's Parliament, Neil believed in doing things big or not doing them at all. Karen Willis remembers: "They used to have to haul our set around in four to six Mack trucks. We had a huge amount of equipment. We had a million-dollar set thanks to Casablanca."

Morali and Willis often spoke about how to make the shows big and then bigger. Bogart supported the huge stage shows and provided the group with whatever they needed. In typical Bogart fashion, he kept wanting more. In fact, to promote the song "In the Navy," Neil had his entire staff at Casablanca Records dress in sailor outfits for the launch of the album. Executive Producer Henri Belolo was even contacted by the US Navy, which was considering using the song in an upcoming recruiting campaign. Belolo agreed to give them the rights for free on the condition that the Village People be allowed to shoot a music video aboard the USS *Reasoner*. The Navy provided them with the warship, several aircraft, and the ship's crew.

The video footage was another brilliant promotional score for the band, despite the US Navy canceling the campaign after protests erupted over using taxpayer money for a music video of a controversial group. The promotions combined with huge set displays had "In the Navy" climbing all the way to #3 in the United States and #2 in the U.K. The album *Go West* would hit #8 in the US Top 200 and #14 on the US R&B charts. "In the Navy" would be the last Top 10 hit for the Village People. *Go West* also marked the last album Victor Willis would write and record for the group.

Victor Willis saw himself as *the* Village People. This view combined with his consistent drug use, namely cocaine, created a volatile situation between Willis and other bandmates. David Hodo told a reporter in 2006: "Villages are notoriously fractious places, and the early days of the Village People involved a lot of knife pulling, spitting, insanity, and lessons I didn't really want to learn."[15]

With infighting getting near its height and the backlash against the disco era coming to a crescendo, Willis and the other band members couldn't sustain their amazing run. The tipping point was a "disco movie" titled *Can't Stop the Music*. Willis knew disco's days were numbered and had little interest in being involved in the film. In late 1979 Willis parted ways with the Village People. Drugs, egos, and success had worn down the tread on the Village People's tires, but disco was coming to an end whether they liked it or not. Victor Willis saw himself as a star and wanted a big solo career that just never came to be.

Ray Simpson, who recorded backup vocals in the studio for the Village People, would step forward and take Willis's place as the group's lead singer. Alice Wolf, Victor Willis's more recent publicist, released a scalding statement about Simpson's replacing him: "[Simpson] has pranced around on stage for years attempting to imitate Victor Willis. Ray's thin vocals absolutely murder those songs Victor's voice made famous. What a rip-off to fans."[16]

Despite the scathing press release, Ray Simpson remains the lead singer of the Village People to this day. The group would never record another hit. Despite the lack of success with its new music, the group, with many of its names and faces changing over time, continues on. They remain an energetic novelty act and still perform all over the world.

The Village People will be remembered for a lot of things. Their producer, Jacques Morali (who died from AIDS in 1991), told *Newsweek* in 1979:

"Everyone finds what he wants in the group. I am sincerely trying to produce songs to make the gay people more acceptable. But a song can't remake the world. And you can't scare the mass audience too quickly. I don't want to kill my success."[17]

The Village People's success will live on in its anthem, "Y.M.C.A.," still played in venues around the world. In summer 2008, at the Major League Baseball All-Star Game at Yankee Stadium, the current cast of Village People performed "Y.M.C.A." with the Yankees grounds crew during the seventh inning stretch.

In a 2011 ESPN.com article covering the victory of the Stanford football team versus rival Notre Dame, the author described the atmosphere inside the locker room as the team showered the victorious quarterback with praise: "'Macho, macho man!' teammates bellowed, singing the lyrics to the Village People's famous song. 'I want to be a macho man!'"

That was the group's reach. With a steady diet of promotion from Casablanca spearheaded by Neil Bogart's vision for their success, the Village People's run was somewhat unparalleled. From 1977 to 1980, the Village People enjoyed a lifetime of success in just a heartbeat of time. "Neil tried to have them cut as many records as possible in as short a period as possible," Joe Ermilio, whom Neil would hire around this time as director of MIS, told us. "He knew the success may not last long and wanted to capitalize on their theatrical appeal the best he could as quickly as he could."

The team at Casablanca understood a simple fact about disco culture and its audience that made Casablanca and their artists such influential figures during that time. It was about the community, about the performers merging with the audience. As Neil Bogart himself put it, "The people in the clubs wanted to be the stars."[18]

CHAPTER 16

Highs and Lows

In 1978, around the time of the *Macho Man* EP, all was right creatively at Casablanca Records. Financially, however, the company was still spending more money than they were making; and as the company grew, the flow of information (or lack of it) was becoming a major issue.

On a basic level, Neil Bogart's trouble was with infrastructure. Information wasn't rising as quickly from the bottom up or from department to department as it needed to. He had a few rogue employees who were not keeping tabs on numbers—*any* numbers: financial, album sales, employee pay scales, etc. On top of all of that, a few underhanded employees were initiating purchase orders for themselves. Instead of buying a new Harley-Davidson for the local big-city radio jock, they grabbed one for themselves and wrote it off as another "promotional expense."

Purchase orders for thousands of dollars in furniture appeared when no furniture ended up inside Casablanca Records. Instead these items ended up at the home of a high-level employee who took advantage of an archaic system of checks and balances. Things were slipping through the cracks. Although money was rolling in, it was also rolling out. Something had to change as far as Bogart was concerned, and he knew he needed help to do it.

What should have been a phenomenal fiscal year for Casablanca was turning out to be a little weaker bottom line than expected. Bogart decided that he needed someone he trusted to help, so he reached out to family—namely, his sister Bonnie's husband, Joseph Ermilio.

As an added bonus for Neil, Joseph Ermilio already had a previous relationship with PolyGram, Casablanca's overlord. Joseph was working as a computer expert on the East Coast with a company called Phonodisc, an information management subsidiary under PolyGram. Neil asked him to come to Los Angeles to establish a new computer system at Casablanca that could save the company thousands of dollars and resolve its current and growing problems. Joseph Ermilio remembers:

> *Neil was outsourcing computer services to two outside companies. The companies took two to three weeks to get figures and sales numbers back to Neil and, subsequently, to PolyGram. PolyGram and the artists were furious it took so long, and Neil was wasting thousands of dollars a month on the antiquated "batch" system. He offered to bring me out and set up an "in-house" computer system. . . . Keeping everything in-house saved Neil thousands every single month.*

With Neil interested in bringing his sister, Bonnie, and Joseph out west, Al and Ruth Bogart also wanted to come to Los Angeles. With everything going well, Neil was willing to allow his parents to join the party. But he wanted to maintain his distance and keep a safe barrier: the Santa Monica Mountains. In February 1978 Neil brought Ruth and Bonnie to Los Angeles to look at homes in the San Fernando Valley, a large suburb about thirty minutes from where Neil lived. Bogart arranged for a real estate agent to take Ruth and Bonnie around. Neil had little interest in joining the search; he had work to take care of. More than anything, Neil wanted his sister to keep his mother occupied.

After a day of house hunting, Neil invited his mother and sister to a launch party for *Macho Man*, which was set to be released in a couple of weeks. Neil was going to give his mother and sister a taste of the life he lived, even though he usually tried hard never to reveal his alter LA ego (the one that devoured cocaine and pills like a vacuum) to his family. The *Macho Man* party was to be his night at center stage.

Ruth and Bonnie arrived at Neil's house in Beverly Hills after their house hunting. Bogart had a hair stylist and makeup artist there to doctor him up for the evening. He introduced Bonnie as his sister and then, unprovoked, introduced his mother to his assistants: "This is my mother,

Ruth. She's the one that used to lock me out of our apartment naked as a child when she got upset at me."

Neil delivered the information with chilling candor. Bogart had a vengeful side, and this would not be the last time he sought to embarrass his mother in this exact way. He seemed to get a kick out of introducing Ruth in this humiliating manner, a story recounted by many family members in different settings.

Mortified, Ruth ran up the stairs and locked herself in the bathroom, wailing and sobbing. Certainly no one could blame Neil for being bitter toward his mother, but the timing was something else. This comment came clear out of left field, eerily reminiscent of how his mother used to behave toward him and Bonnie when they were little.

Bonnie wasn't sure what to do. She was shocked by what Neil had said, but she had lived through the same atrocities her brother did. Their mother wailed from the upstairs bathroom: "I'm going to kill myself! Is that what you want?! I'm going to kill myself!"

Ruth's hysterical sobbing echoed throughout the entire house. Although Neil had started the scene, he had little empathy for his mother and wanted a quick end to the embarrassing display in front of his guests. Bonnie remembers Neil roaring: "You go up there and tell that fuckin' mother of mine to get the fuck out of the bathroom or I'm going to break that fuckin' door down and I'm going to send her on the fuckin' plane home!"

Bonnie's role was clear. She was to be their mother's keeper. Her job was to keep their mother away from Neil. Bonnie was supposed to be the buffer, but now she had to be enforcer too. Bonnie went upstairs and attempted to reason with Ruth. This pattern would repeat itself—the price for the homes Neil would purchase for both his sister and his parents. Bonnie would continuously need to deliver Neil's brutal messages to their mother.

Upon hearing Neil's response to the breakdown, Ruth gathered herself. She had to. Although she was angry and embarrassed, she knew Neil wasn't lying, and she wanted to be in Los Angeles more than anything. She wanted a place at her son's table. Ruth exited the bathroom quietly, the episode over. She straightened herself up and headed downstairs with Bonnie.

There was no exchange of words, no apologies for past or current crimes. Neil and Ruth shared some striking similarities. They were both unapologetic to an extreme. And they both had boiling tempers that could erupt at a moment's notice.

Joe and Bonnie moved out to LA, as did Ruth and Al. Their homes were purchased just a few blocks away from one another in Encino, California. Bonnie told us:

My brother gave me strict instructions when we moved out to Los Angeles. I was to keep an eye on my mother. She was not allowed to bother him or pester him to go to parties or for autographs. I was given the responsibility of being her babysitter. And if she called him and upset him, I'd get a phone call from my brother demanding I speak to her. Neil didn't want to deal with our mother anymore. In California he changed toward us. Neil would invite [Joe and me] to events and he would kiss us hello and then tell us, "I won't see you anymore." That is who he had become to us. We were more a nuisance at times than family.

Shortly after moving to California, Al and Ruth also changed their last name from Bogatz to Bogart. Children have long taken on the stage names of their parents, but the reverse is unconventional, almost unprecedented. They were proud of what their son had accomplished, even if he didn't have a great interest in sharing his life with them. There was some confusion for the Bogatzes. With their son Neil "Bogart" having so much success, they were already associated with his last name. Al and Ruth wanted to be known as the parents of Neil Bogart. They felt incredible pride in his achievements, even if they rarely shared in them.

This kind of "success by association" was good enough for the Bogatzes, and thus it was an easy decision to forgo their name for their son's professional one. Changing one's name to be more successful was part of the business, they thought. "Everybody was calling my father Mister Bogart because of my brother. So they changed their name to Bogart," Bonnie says.

The hills separating the San Fernando Valley from Beverly Hills proved to be the ideal "Great Wall" Neil had hoped it would be to keep his family at a distance. He invited his parents and sister to special events every once in a while and shared a small part of his success with them. But bringing them out to Los Angeles, getting them into their homes, and inviting them to a few choice holiday gatherings was pretty much as far as he was willing to go. Neil did not have a desire to rekindle any kind of relationship.

Neil had grown accustomed to his lifestyle. He was the ultimate party host, a man who glided through rooms like he owned every inch of them. His family acted like confused tourists in this atmosphere. By bringing them to the party, Neil not only felt as though he did his part but also highlighted how far he had come. His parents and sister were not part of Neil's new persona. They were only passengers on the journey, permitted to view the action from time to time—and then from a distance. Inviting his family to an exclusive gala was the only service he was interested in providing. Once there, they were on their own to mingle.

This was indicative of how the family interacted. There was no closeness shared, no everlasting bond rekindled at every holiday dinner or birthday. Neil was on a different level, in a different world really. He was brushing shoulders with politicians and movie stars, and he had a vast rolodex of relationships within the music industry. He had grown up and didn't want to be reminded of his childhood, the good or the bad. Ruth longed to be closer to that world, but he only let her get occasional sniffs. This was his world, his sanctuary. His family reminded him of a past he had left behind.

***

Neil's cancer would arrive less than three years after his parents and sister arrived in Los Angeles. It is difficult to say where their relationships might have gone had he not gotten sick. In the short term, however, Neil was entrenched in a massive wave of disco success; there were simply too many moving parts for him to break away from his busy world. Too much was happening too quickly. Neil continued to be the life of the party and the living embodiment of Casablanca Records, its success, and its round-the-clock party ethos.

On the surface, everything at Casablanca seemed right. The Village People's *Cruisin'* went platinum, and the label's songs seemed to be everywhere. However, all this success only fed into the mirage. Neil projected this success everywhere. He hobnobbed with the likes of former President Gerald Ford and California Governor Jerry Brown at political fund-raisers hosted by Bogart himself. Neil commanded the attention of his colleagues and of music artists around the world. He partied with superstars of all walks: music, sports, fashion, and film. He spent weekends at Studio 54, becoming good friends with legendary owner Steve Rubell. Bogart was a regular in the deep dark bowels of the party palace, a location he relished. At one time Neil was even close to *buying* Studio 54 from Rubell. The deal never materialized, but Neil remained a loyal patron. Everything seemed to point to Neil Bogart remaining an unstoppable force. Just as things were rolling along, a crack appeared in the armor.

It was in 1978, in this King Midas environment, that Bogart inexplicably made the decision to release the four solo albums by the members of KISS (and pumped out two million records). The error proved costly, and Casablanca took a financial hit. Neil's greatest miscalculation was not being more in tune with what was going on in the KISS camp. Casablanca allowed KISS to operate on autopilot. The band had gotten big fast and ridden a wave of tremendous success, but they had become overplayed and, some claimed, uninspired. The solo albums didn't live up to the hype—and didn't pique the interest of their fans.

Casablanca also started signing any and all disco artists on the market. Their music roster expanded at an alarming rate. So did their employee payroll, which swelled to nearly two hundred people, not including a massive number of musicians, writers, and producers under contract. Just a few years earlier, Casablanca was operating with closer to fifteen employees. Things had ballooned, almost to an inoperable size. In *Hit Men*, PolyGram's Rick Bleiweiss remembered:

Everything was at such a fevered pitch. You walked into Bruce Bird's office, music was blaring, twelve phones ringing. You never could talk

*in that building. You had to shout. I think the average person walking
in there would have been floored by the electricity and volume. Everything in that company was an exaggeration, a caricature.*[1]

Jerry Sharell, Casablanca's tenured promotions man, had a similar
take on the extraordinary atmosphere. He told us that "Neil started his
own echelon at Casablanca. It was known as the 'house of other things.'
A lot more smoking and blow going on at Casablanca. The company
was the hottest place in town—thank God he had music to back up his
wishes."

❧

PolyGram had a banner year in 1978, reaping the spoils from Casablanca and its films *Thank God It's Friday* and *Midnight Express*. Donna
Summer's song "Last Dance" was a huge success, as was the rest of the
soundtrack from *TGIF*. KISS's *Double Platinum*, released in April that
year, went platinum. *Macho Man* and *Cruisin'* were turning the Village
People into a household name. RSO, another PolyGram subsidiary, had
the monster films *Saturday Night Fever* and *Grease*, as well as their game-
changing soundtracks.

When the dust settled, PolyGram had racked up over one billion
dollars in sales in 1978, making them the undisputed music industry
leaders. PolyGram was blinded by some of the overall results, failing
to look at the bottom line. They were basking in the glory of being out
front, while behind the curtain, they were about to find out the cruel
little secret. They failed to keep track of what was happening at Casablanca. Their supposed "mole," David Shein, was the controller, but he
did little to control what was going on with the money. In *Hit Men*,
Shein said: "Neil had a unique way of co-opting people. It was real hard
not to believe what Neil said."

Neil Bogart used a variety of tools to manipulate and control people.
He was a virtual "Don." Bogart was that breed of show business impre-
sario who seemed to bend things to his will. When he spoke, people listened. If people didn't listen, he garnered their attention and *made* them
listen. Joseph Ermilio remembers a music industry event:

There were numerous music executives in the audience, and Neil was
speaking. There was some chatter in the audience, and Neil paused. He
stared out into the crowd and waited. He waited silently, and every-
one slowly turned to cock their heads back onto the stage. He stared
viciously out into the audience until he had silence. Once he had the
"floor" again, he spoke. That was his control. You were going to hear
what he had to say on his own terms.

Other executives despised Bogart. He had no problem letting loose
his feelings on them if he was upset, and this rubbed a lot of them the
wrong way. But meanwhile, he was simply beloved by many of his artists.
He spent so much on promoting his artists, it was sometimes impossible
for him to make a profit. Artists saw what Bogart did for other bands, and
they wanted to be a part of it. Other music executives felt pressure from
Neil's "gunslinging" promotional practices. His recklessness put massive
industry pressure on everyone else. The apex of this was the four solo
KISS albums. Larry Harris wrote:

It wasn't just PolyGram that was pissed at us, it was the entire indus-
try. Neil's aggressiveness had always been the subject of water-cooler
gossip in the various record companies. At first we'd seemed like ambi-
tious underdogs. But then raised eyebrows became contempt because
we started to promote to ridiculous extremes—and worse, we even
promoted ourselves, as record execs. This unquestionably made life dif-
ficult for our counterparts at other record companies. Now Warner
execs, for instance, had to field calls from artists asking, "Why can't you
promote us like Casablanca promotes their acts?" Our rampant spend-
ing was forcing other labels to keep up with the Joneses, whether they
wanted to or not.[2]

If 1978 was the apex, then 1979 was the crash. By the end of that year,
the bubble would burst. Peter Guber, a smart businessman, had inklings
that things weren't all perfect, despite the parties and celebrations. Asked
by a reporter whether Casablanca needed better controls, Guber said he
thought it did: "We're not flying in the dark, but it's dark, and we're flying."[3]

Clearly Guber sensed there were issues on the horizon. His spidey-sense proved correct—1979 was a bad year and the beginning of the end for Neil Bogart and Casablanca. Things quickly went from business as usual to business grossly unusual as the Germans atop PolyGram finally caught on to the shenanigans inside Casablanca. Aside from one major success, Donna Summer's *Bad Girls*, Neil Bogart's stock started to seem vastly overinflated. One PolyGram alumnus told Fredric Dannen: "Neil always spent everybody's money, and everyone always acted so surprised. Finally, the Germans woke up. Wait a minute! If he goes on like this, he'll bankrupt us! Well, of course!"[4]

PolyGram began to notice that things were unaccounted for. They started to pester Bogart for his business practices and tried to crack down on him. Everyone they sent out to Los Angeles, however, Neil turned to his side. One of Bogart's great talents was his ability to seduce; with the parties he was throwing and the money he was spending, it was easy for anybody to get swept up in the illusion. Even though David Shein, PolyGram's mole, had been sent out to report back on the activities at Casablanca, he was unable to resist Neil Bogart's allure. That was Neil's way. He was infectious, and everybody wanted to be along for the ride.

But PolyGram knew something was wrong, and the millions of dollars being spent and lost weren't going to get past them. As 1979 wore on, they started to tighten the reins on Bogart. Finally PolyGram's eyes were starting to open. "No amount of cooking the books was going to hide truckloads of unwanted records," Larry Harris writes, "especially since those trucks were backing up to their doorstep, not ours."

＊＊＊

As the stresses from PolyGram started to wear on Bogart, another issue arose. Neil was suffering a great deal of back pain, excruciating at times. He saw doctors, acupuncturists, everyone and anyone to solve his issues. Neil even brought massage therapists into the office to work on him. The debilitating back pain caused him serious problems, even prevented him from working. He took Quaaludes and pain killers and smoked a lot of pot to help. Doctors finally discovered what the issue was. Bogart got the news that he had cancer hiding behind his kidney. It was lymphoma; the silver lining was that, even in 1979, this type of cancer had a very high cure rate.

In *And Party Every Day*, Larry Harris wrote of how he got the news:

News of his illness did not spread quickly. Neil had always been very guarded about his health. Once, in 1979, he didn't show up at the office for several days. There were no phone calls, no messages, nothing—he was completely MIA. Fearing that something was terribly wrong, I went to his house and knocked on the door. When Joyce answered, I said to her, "I haven't been able to reach Neil on the phone, and he hasn't been in the office, and no one seems to know what's going on." She assured me that everything was fine.[5]

But things weren't fine. Neil's guarded approach to his health had worked. Nobody knew except a very small circle of trusted people. Bogart had to go through cancer treatments and, in doing so, lost his hair. Ever the promotions man, he wore a wig to conceal his hair loss. It was important to Bogart that he keep his profile in tact; he didn't want to show any weakness. In fact, despite his seeing doctors and undergoing treatments, nobody knew about Neil's illness. But with him missing so much work, rumors began to circulate.

"People started to talk around the office," Joe Ermilio remembers. "The rumors about Neil's health started to spread. The rumors were everywhere. The *Hollywood Reporter* kept speculating what was wrong with Neil."

The chemotherapy and cancer medication were causing Bogart to look bloated, "puffy." The wig he wore also vastly altered his appearance. The changes were more than noticeable. As word began to spread about Neil's health, he called his family together and revealed to them the big secret. Joseph remembers Neil's chilling words: "I have cancer. I've been taking treatments and the prognosis is good. I'm going to beat this thing."

Neil's sister, Bonnie, remembers:

Neil never told us anything. When he told us he had cancer, he acted like it wasn't that big a deal. He was very confident he would be okay.

The doctors had assured him he would be all right. During this time, Neil was detached from us. For the most part, the only time I heard from him was at family gatherings during the holidays or to complain about our mother. We had a few moments when we would confide to one another about life and the past. They were very few moments that happened during the holidays, but they were nice.

❦

By the end of 1979, things at Casablanca Records were a mess. The numbers were bad, there were far too many unsuccessful acts, and staples like KISS and the Village People had faded. Disco was becoming overhyped, a dirty word in fact. The worldwide phenomenon would receive a death blow from a bizarre event in Chicago.

In the middle of a particularly lackluster season for the Chicago White Sox, an anti-disco demonstration was organized by local radio DJ Steve Dahl and supported by the Sox. Dahl encouraged fans to bring their disco albums to Comiskey Park on July 12, 1979. During a break in the doubleheader against the Detroit Tigers, the records were set on fire in center field. The fans got overzealous, and soon a riot broke out. Fans tore out seats and then stormed the field and began taking out chunks of the green. Police were called in, and the second game of the doubleheader was canceled. Fans were arrested. It was a seminal moment in American music history: the death of disco. The American pastime would be the setting for the death of an American phenomenon.

Disco's demise meant trouble at Casablanca Records, a company heavily invested in the craze. Neil Bogart had helped drive disco into the mainstream, bringing it from underground clubs into suburban homes. The wheels were coming off disco's wagon, and Casablanca, hitched to that wagon, was about to get run off the road.

Promotion man Danny Davis had recently left Motown after being lured in by Bogart and the glow of Casablanca's success. It was not a good match; Davis hated the experience. Davis's son, who also worked at Casablanca, told him, "Dad, this is a very 'loose' joint. Every Friday I go to Monarch to pick up records. When I move the truck again on Sunday, there are no records there." Things indeed were "loose." Danny Davis told us:

I came there and it was not the Casablanca I was assured it was. What was apparent to the industry was not apparent to me: the drug abuse. And Neil didn't spend a lot of time at the office. He wasn't as flamboyant or outgoing as he was earlier in his career. I always thought Casablanca was top of the line and Neil was a great inspiration to many. I thought Casablanca was the "golden triangle." He built what "appeared" to be a giant joint. It was not as I perceived it. I made a lot of money with Neil and I was grateful. But it was not as I perceived it. Not at all.

As Casablanca dealt with millions of its records being returned—far too many had been pressed to meet demand—disco's end became abundantly clear. With Bogart's battle with cancer sapping his energy, he was simply too distracted to save Casablanca. Another miracle was not in the cards.

In 1980 Neil took another hit. Donna Summer sued to be let out of her contract. The lawsuit stemmed from a personal disagreement between Summer and Neil over the direction of her music. Neil wanted to keep her in the box she was so successful in—disco—and Donna desperately wanted to transition to more challenging material such as rock music. With disco dying quickly, a change probably would have done Summer well. But Neil stood his ground. Summer had had enough.

The focus of the ten-million-dollar lawsuit was the "conflict of interest" created by her comanager, Joyce Bogart. "It's like having an artist and you don't even know what in the hell they're about,"[6] Summer would tell *Rolling Stone*. In another interview about her wanting to forge her own path away from disco, Summer said: "I felt like Marie Antoinette or Joan of Arc—great women of their time who had to deal with ridicule and misunderstanding."[7]

The move was a slap in the face to the Bogarts. Certainly Summer had a point—there was indeed a conflict of interest. It was, however, that particular conflict of interest that had created the disco queen and developed Donna Summer into the superstar she became.

It was clear that Neil Bogart loved Donna Summer, and her lawsuit cut him deep. Equally, Donna loved Neil; she ended up regretting her decision to sue the Bogarts until the day she died. She justified her decision through her religion, claiming the Bogarts had pushed her too hard to become the world's sex symbol, a stark contrast to her Christian upbringing. Summer spoke few words on the subject, but it was clear the Queen of Disco embraced the spotlight. Though she claimed the Bogarts had trapped her, she would never have achieved her dreams without Neil Bogart's support.

Summer had no idea Neil was sick at the time, but his mother, Ruth, would later comment: "Donna Summer's lawsuit and PolyGram killed my son." Though not literal, this was on point. The suit did account for the avalanche of stress Neil incurred while battling his life-threatening illness.

The lawsuit was terrible PR for PolyGram. The only thing worse was Casablanca's bottom line. The dollars and cents were horrifying. The company was completely mismanaged. Joseph Ermilio knew it was just a matter of time before PolyGram got into the computers and saw what was going on. Wanting to protect his brother-in-law from certain secrets, Ermilio asked Neil if he wanted him to wipe the hard drive clean of a lot of the "under the table" payments. In particular, he wanted to hide the payments made to Beth, Neil's ex-wife using PolyGram and Casablanca's personal piggybank. Ermilio remembers: "I asked Neil if he wanted me to remove the information out of the computer. He was paying Beth child support with company funds. Neil told me, 'No, Joey, I don't want you to get in trouble. I did it. It's my responsibility. Don't erase anything.'"

The Donna Summer lawsuit pushed PolyGram over the edge. The lawsuit, combined with extraordinary accounting issues, forced Poly-Gram's hand. In February 1980 PolyGram forced Neil Bogart out. Neil, whose cancer had started to go into remission, was given a golden parachute, and PolyGram bought the other 50 percent of the company. This time, though, they were purchasing a company plummeting into the abyss. Donna Summer was leaving, KISS was struggling and the band imploding, the Village People had lost their lead singer, Victor Willis, and were in steep decline, Parliament-Funkadelic's sales had stalled, and nearly all of disco was dead. Casablanca's music catalog contained a tremendous amount of overproduced disco albums. The flood of albums into a dead market combined with a poor global economy in 1979 left PolyGram with virtually nothing but a deep black hole when they assumed 100 percent control of the company. The kingdom Neil Bogart had built with his blood and sweat had forced him out.

Neil's departure was swift and sudden. Everyone at Casablanca was stunned, and all they had was a note left by their fearless leader to console themselves with.

> *February 8, 1980*
> *To all my dear friends:*
> *The attached sheet from my biography gives the facts. Legally, I can say no more. I shall miss you. I love you all. We really did it. We became a solid #3 behind WEA and Columbia. Under Bruce Bird's direction, I hope you will go even further. Although I have resigned my position as President and sold the majority interest of my stock, I'll still be around (I'm your landlord).*
> *Please understand, I did what I felt I had to do. I wish you all love and happiness. Here's looking at you!*
> *Neil*

In typical fashion, Bogart left the company mostly on his terms and with a modicum of dignity. He would "move on" rather than risk being viewed as the victim of a firing. The truth was, Neil was paid more than ten million dollars to walk away from his own company. PolyGram needed to start over, and Neil Bogart was the ring leader of what they perceived to be a long line of terrible business decisions. They knew that although Bogart may have had incredible business sense, he was actually a terrible businessman. Bruce Bird would assume Neil's position as president, at least for a short time. PolyGram cleaned house.

Casablanca's in-house newsletter, *INSIDE*, contained Neil's personal biography, his parting gift and comments to the employees. It read:

> *On February 8, 1980, Neil Bogart announced that he has resigned his Presidency of Casablanca Record and Filmworks, the post he has held since he created Casablanca records in 1974. Through this action, and the sale of his stock, Bogart has signaled the termination of his*

*partnership with the PolyGram Group, the European conglomerate
that has distributed Casablanca's product for the past two years. Bogart's decision to end his leadership of Casablanca and to sell his inter-
ests in the company mark the beginning of Casablanca as a wholly
owned PolyGram company.*

*Commenting on his decision, Bogart observed that "this really is
the beginning of a new chapter for Casablanca as well as for me. When
you've struggled to create something successful, as I struggled for Casablanca, you want to see it grow and prosper. Like any proud parent, I
hope Casablanca's success will continue. But for me, the philosophical
gap between myself and a multi-national corporation like PolyGram
was simply too wide. I knew that an important chapter in my life
needed to end, and a new one to begin.*

*"It is very gratifying that I leave Casablanca at a time when it
is flourishing, fulfilling the dreams I have had for it all along. When
I see* Billboard *chart positions showing Casablanca placing third in
the singles' market, fourth in album sales, right up there with the
giants WEA and CBS, I realize what an incredible success story it has
become. I am proud to have been a part of it.*

*"My good wishes for Casablanca are matched only by my excite-
ment over the challenges that lie ahead. I'm remembering how good
it feels to begin something brand new, when you dare to attempt the
'impossible' dreams. If my new chapter were to have a heading, it
would simply say 'Bogarts . . . An Entertainment Company,' and I
guarantee you it will make interesting reading."*

TO BE CONTINUED . . .

Neil Bogart remained a promotions man until the end. It was obvious the company was on its way down, but he continued to sell a version of it that looked good to others. As poorly as Neil may have run a
company from a business standpoint, he was brilliant when it came to
parachuting out. Bogart always had impeccable timing: with his artists,
with his music, with his decisions to jump ship. He escaped Buddah at
just the right time—as bubblegum music faded and the company started
to waffle. Now, with Casablanca, his own creation, he saw disco quickly

falling out of favor. The combination of PolyGram's fury and Neil's sense that his time had passed led to a necessary parting of the ways.

PolyGram had more decisions to make besides ousting Bogart. The company loved Peter Guber, in whom they saw the same magic that Neil possessed—but with the vital additive of corporate responsibility. Guber's Filmworks division was always far more sedate and professional than Casablanca's music division. Guber too saw the writing on the wall regarding Neil Bogart and PolyGram, even if Bogart had been such an important part of his rise. As Nancy Griffin and Kim Masters noted in their book *Hit and Run*: "[Guber] loved his partner, his dark twin. . . . Bogart had been Guber's soul mate and springboard, but now he was a liability."[8] Guber's only choice was to leave Bogart behind and move forward without him. Bogart was enraged, charging that his partner had deserted him.

Guber would make a sweetheart deal with PolyGram and establish a 50/50 partnership with them. Wolfgang Hix served as a consultant to PolyGram and explained to Griffin and Masters the difference between the two men—and why PolyGram felt Guber was so valuable:

> *With Guber you felt, well, you can talk to this guy; what he is saying makes sense and he is not humming a tune all the time and snapping his fingers and doing crazy things. If you went into Neil Bogart's office, with the camels [Bogart had put stuffed camels in the lobby at Casablanca Records]—it was very, very strange. It was a very weird situation.*[9]

Casablanca Records went on in name without Bogart, but it would never be the same. From 1981 to 1986 Casablanca limped along and failed to have any sort of impact in the music world. Bruce Bird, vice president of promotion, assumed control and attempted to keep the ship afloat, but the company had too many issues. For one, it was still hemorrhaging money. By this time disco was dead, KISS was struggling with internal strife as well as other issues, the Village People were essentially finished, and Donna Summer was free of her contract. The company was a mere shell of its former self. Aside from releasing Robin Williams's debut comedy album, *What a Concept*, and the 1983 soundtrack from the hit movie *Flashdance*, Casablanca failed to live up to its incredible run of the 1970s.

Casablanca's final album, released in 1986, was Animotion's *Strange Behavior*. PolyGram would eat losses for years to come as massive amounts of returned records and bad business practices, combined with the death of disco, crippled the company. PolyGram closed up shop in 1986 and either released all of its artists on Casablanca's label or shifted them over to Mercury, another label under its control.

━ ❧

Neil Bogart built a palace of excess in the 1970s—which, considering the behavior of his peers, is really saying something. Success came fast; the end came even faster. Feeling abandoned by his friend Peter Guber, hung out to dry by a cracking-down PolyGram, and feeling the effects of his cancer, Bogart kept his head up for the next chapter. He continued spinning his own brand of truth as he again marched into the great unknown. This time, however, Bogart would march with millions of dollars in his pockets along with the many ideas swirling in his head. He had not been out of work in years, and he wouldn't be for long. It was time for Bogart to figure out a new game plan. He was determined not to walk away from the music business with his tail between his legs. When asked if Neil could succeed again in the business, Joyce Bogart said: "He's a schemer and a dreamer. He can pull it off."[10] Bogart's ego and bravado would win out, and he set to begin a new adventure to prove, yet again, that he was still king.

CHAPTER 17

Boardwalk and Beyond

I'm in competition against myself, really.

—Neil Bogart,
People magazine,
May 1980

In 1980, fresh off resigning from the company he built, Neil Bogart convinced himself and everyone around him that he could prove himself yet again. Despite going through rigorous cancer treatments at the time, this is exactly what he did. His cancer was in remission, and he had a huge stockpile of cash from PolyGram to fund his next venture. He was hell bent on re-creating an empire. Fortunately, Neil Bogart was just the kind of guy who could embrace such a daunting task. He saw it as a challenge, an opportunity. Boardwalk Entertainment Company was born and named for the most prized stop in the game Monopoly.

This time Neil would do things differently, or at least try to. He was still recovering from his illness and exhausted from his battles with Poly-Gram and his lawsuit with Donna Summer. He was no longer young and full of piss and vinegar; he was now an industry veteran who had been through life's mental and physical wringer. Bogart was wise enough this time around to know he couldn't do it alone. He sought to bring some big guns from Casablanca and elsewhere to help.

In May 1980 he brought on Jon Peters, who would run Boardwalk's film division, and Peter Guber, who would lend his name to Boardwalk but run his projects through PolyGram. Peters had befriended Peter Guber and had quickly become an ally as they started developing films together. Guber and Peters were made from a similar mold and shared a passion for success in the movie business.

The move to add Jon Peters's name to the roster was orchestrated by Guber to make amends for the way things had gone down with Poly-Gram. Bogart had felt betrayed when Guber stayed on at PolyGram as he was being pushed out. Guber was hoping this would help smooth things over.

Bogart had lofty goals for his new company. He wanted Boardwalk to succeed not as just another fledgling record company but as a large entertainment group with the capacity to compete against the biggest players in show business. However, Boardwalk turned out to be a "triangle," with no clear leader. Roles were not identified, and Neil seemed to be left on an island all by himself.

The dynamic among Neil, Peters, and Guber was odd to say the least. From the start, Peter Guber was there in name only, leaving Jon Peters to carry the torch for the film division, but essentially all Guber was doing was sending business PolyGram's way. Peters and Guber were close and shared a similar goal—to make a lot of money in the film industry—but this left Bogart spread thin to build up the music division on his own. He would have to create another successful empire virtually by himself. Dealing with cancer treatments and attempting to build a company of Casablanca's size in half the time would be too much; Neil's lofty goals would leave him stranded. Both Bogart and Jon Peters vied for Guber's attention, and Peters was winning out.

Peters and Guber were working on building their own relationship and film empire, but through PolyGram, not Boardwalk. Boardwalk just wasn't factoring into their plans. Meanwhile, Boardwalk Entertainment Company was more a stagnant music company than the "entertainment group" Neil had hoped for. Bogart attempted to build Boardwalk using the same formula and blueprint he had done with Buddah and Casablanca, mixing veteran acts with new talent and promoting the hell out their live tours while pushing music sales. Bogart knew that the "old" acts would provide legitimacy for his start-up, which would allow him to take chances on new talent. He brought together Curtis Mayfield and the Ohio Players from his previously relationship with them at Buddah

Records and then signed such up-and-comers as Joan Jett and the Blackhearts and Night Ranger.

Though this formula had printed money for Bogart in the past, he ran out of time with Boardwalk. Although the announcement of the formation of Boardwalk and its top brass made it seem as though it was a "super-team," the reality ended up being a one-man show. Neil Bogart was ironically now the front man for a mirage, not unlike the way some of his bubblegum acts or the Village People were designed. Guber decided to split up his 50 percent share in PolyGram and combine it with Peters's profits from the 1980 hit *Caddyshack*, thus creating their own film production company. Bogart was then officially on his own, with nothing to show for his work with Peters and Guber.

Neil spent nearly two years attempting to put Boardwalk Entertainment Company on the map and once again catch lightning in a bottle. He tried, but he became exasperated by the effort to find the right collection of talent.

He found one legitimate success story in Joan Jett. Joan Jett and the Blackhearts' first studio album together, *I Love Rock 'n' Roll*, was released on November 18, 1981. It proved to be Boardwalk's most successful album, selling over ten million copies. The album, heavily driven by the title track, charted in six other countries besides the United States, hitting #1 in four of them. In the United States, "I Love Rock 'n' Roll" struck #1 on the US *Billboard* Hot 100, US *Billboard* Top Tracks, and on US *Billboard* Hot Dance Club Songs. The success of "I Love Rock 'n' Roll" was epic. The single achieved platinum sales status as well and has remained a jukebox and radio favorite for more than thirty years. The album's second big song, "Crimson and Clover," an energized cover of Tommy James and the Shondells's 1968 hit, reached #7 on the US *Billboard* Hot 100.

In September 1981, at Bogart's suggestion, Jett recorded the huge 1960's hit "Louie Louie," though she did it under protest. She explained, "This was a song I did not want to do. But Neil Bogart (who had given me a shot when nobody else would) asked me to, so we did. All that stuff at the beginning of the song is me trying to ensure that the song would suck. Didn't work. I thought it came out well."[1]

Jett also had success with a cover of Eddie Cochran's anthem "Summertime Blues," which the band also recorded at Bogart's request. Kenny Laguna, Jett's longtime producer and co-collaborator, remembers recording the song: "Neil thought this song sounded like a follow-up to 'Bad Reputation.' We recorded it for him, but he never put it out. We got frustrated and sent the tapes to all the AOR stations, without the label's knowledge. The record went to Top 10 at AOR. Bogart flipped out when he saw in the trades that there was a song out on his label that he didn't know about."[2]

Unfortunately, much of Jett's success occurred after Neil passed away. *I Love Rock 'n' Roll* was a bright spot for Neil, but it proved to be his swan song. Boardwalk cost Neil financially; the company had lost millions by the time Joan Jett broke out. It was too little too late for Neil to really cash in on his final successful act. In theory, Boardwalk may have had a chance to be big on the heels of *I Love Rock 'n' Roll*. Ultimately, however, it failed to live up to Neil's lofty expectations.

─ ⌒ ─

The pressures and stresses over the course of a wild decade had taken its toll. Neil was growing tired of it all. "My father and Joyce were looking for homes and schools in New York," Jylle Bogart Barker told us. "He had grown tired of Los Angles."

Neil finally wanted to take a break. He'd always loved his kids and now wanted to make them the center of his universe which meant work would have to take a back seat. Those were the plans, anyway. Somehow, some way, Neil's plans always seemed to work. But this time, sadly, they would not.

Despite Bogart finally getting a successful act with Boardwalk after nearly two years of failure, things were far worse than anyone realized. In 1981 Neil had gotten terrible news: His cancer had returned. The lymphoma had spread all over his body, ravaging his insides and attacking all his organs. With Bogart now entrenched in a second battle for his life, Boardwalk was quickly placed on the back burner. Boardwalk Entertainment Company would become an expensive failure. Perhaps facing his own mortality, Bogart was quite aware of the reality of what Boardwalk just couldn't be.

Just before Christmas 1981, Joseph Ermilio had a very candid conversation with his brother-in-law. The family often got together just prior to Christmas for a few moments of normalcy, exchanging presents and sharing good food and rare moments of bonding. Ermilio remembers that Neil looking calm and tired as he spoke about his career and where he thought the record industry was heading. He expressed his vision to use music videos to promote record artists; he said he regretted staying in the music business and not transitioning to the movie business while he could.

"He was a different person," Ermilio recalls. "He was willing to open up to us and share his thoughts and was very warm and caring."

"Joe, Boardwalk was the biggest mistake of my life," Neil admitted. In addition to the candid reflection about his career and the music business, Neil mentioned that he had provided for his sister and his family. Ermilio didn't understand what Neil meant or why he was even saying it at this moment. It was incredibly rare for Neil to open up like this; it just wasn't like him. He played a lot of things close to the vest, especially his feelings. Neil must have sensed something. Indeed, it would be Neil's last holiday season.

Neil began to reflect on his life with those he allowed close to him. Perhaps he knew the end was near. Or maybe he simply fretted over his legacy now that his time at Casablanca was done and Boardwalk continued to flounder. Either way, Neil let it be known that he had never gone after what he truly believed—and was 100 percent correct about—was going to be the future for music artists: music television. Neil had conceptualized a music television station back in the mid-1970s, but he only flirted with the idea, never fully jumping in. He had worked hard to get promotional videos and spots made for his artists as a way of garnering interest in them. His KISS promotional video gave people a crucial firsthand view of the new group before they launched, he placed the Village People on top of a US battleship to promote "In the Navy," and he employed Bill Aucoin and Joyce Biawitz, who produced *Flipside*, to produce promotional videos for his artists.

He also saw great opportunities in the visual medium for music artists by way of full-length music videos, which could be an asset in promotion and save record companies millions of dollars that would normally have been spent mounting expensive tours around the country. "Neil always talked about wanting to make music videos and create a television station to showcase his artists," Joseph Ermilio remembers. "This would save him huge costs on touring and bring the artists right into the living room of the consumers. Near the end, it was just too late."

As someone who grew up loving old Hollywood, it was a natural leap that Bogart would try to merge together music and movies—he just wasn't around long enough to see it become the norm. Fate had another path for Neil Bogart. He was fighting like hell to stay alive.

Once it was confirmed that the cancer was back and was exponentially worse, Neil pooled his resources and began to travel the world, searching for cures. Any experimental treatments were on the table. Neil was desperate to find an answer and had the means to do so. He flew to Asia, to Europe—anywhere—to meet with anyone who thought he or she could provide a cure. He was willing to try any kind of alternative medicine, herbal remedies, or acupuncture to counterbalance all the toxins he was pumping into himself with the chemotherapy and radiation. It was all for not, and he had to face a sobering fact: Neither his money nor his influence nor his reputation could save him.

Irv Biegel, president at Boardwalk during the time of Neil's demise, told the *Los Angeles Times*:

> *"He just didn't understand the word 'no.' He was always determined to do things that everybody else thought were out of the range of possibility." Ten weeks before his death, Neil told Irv Biegel about his illness. "He said, 'I'm gonna whip it, I promise you,'" said Biegel. "I think that was the only promise Neil ever made to me that he didn't keep."[3]*

Throughout his battle with cancer, Neil kept a guarded approach when it came to the public. In fact, not too many people even knew about his fight. He wore a wig to hide the effects of the chemotherapy and continued to make appearances at industry events despite all that he was going through, maintaining relationships as the cancer ravaged his body.

By 1982 it was clear Neil's treatments weren't working and he was getting worse. He was restricted to his bed, and his mobility was down to almost nothing. Neil's old pal from Buddah Records, Ron Weisner, visited Neil in April 1982, weeks prior to his death. Weisner told us:

It was depressing. I remembered someone very alive. It was heartbreaking to see him. It was very upsetting. It was upsetting personally. It was sad to see him wind up like that. He had lived his life. He was the epitome of the person who didn't take "no" for an answer. He could always find a way.

It was apparent that Neil Bogart's final days were coming. On May 8, 1982, Mother's Day, Neil Bogart lay dying at Cedars Hospital in Los Angeles, California. He was only thirty-nine years old.

While other family members were on a break from keeping Neil company, Bonnie stood by his side, holding her brother's hand. She whispered in his ear, assuring him he would be all right. "You are loved," she said. "Everything will be all right. Everything will be okay," she whispered over and over again.

Joseph Ermilio was on the far side of the room. One final breath and the nurse told Bonnie and Joseph what they could already see: Neil Bogart—lying in his hospital bed with a wig covering his balding, sickly head, his body emaciated by the disease—was gone.

The Bubblegum King, the Disco King, the young father of four children and husband to Joyce Bogart, had died. He passed quietly in his hospital bed, the larger-than-life figure departing this world in near silence, with only the loving words of his sister to console him.

Even in death, Neil Bogart put on a grand show. His funeral was a spectacular gathering of singers, politicians, and mega-entertainers, including Bob Dylan, Joan Jett, Danny Thomas, and California Governor Jerry Brown to name a few. The funeral played like an enormous music production put together at a moment's notice. In the *Los Angeles Times* article on Bogart's death, Steve Pond wrote:

The record industry lost one of its most flamboyant and audacious gamblers in the late morning hours of May 8th, when Neil Bogart died of cancer at the age of thirty-nine. A man whose idol was P. T. Barnum, Bogart had apparently known about his illness for a year but kept it private as he continued to run the Boardwalk Entertainment Company in the go-for-broke style that had helped him establish such stars as Donna Summer, the Village People, KISS, and Joan Jett, and that made him an industry leader in both commercial victories and near-debilitating defeats.

Billboard magazine's Paul Grien wrote, "What makes Bogart's career so extraordinary is that he scored No. 1 hits at all four labels he headed." He added that "Bogart went out the way he'd probably have wanted to— with the biggest record of the year." All that week *Billboard* printed in its pages testimonials to the man that Neil was from friends and admirers both inside and out of the music industry.

The unlikely choir of Neil Diamond, Donna Summer, Burt Bacharach, Marvin Hamlisch, Gladys Knight, Curtis Mayfield, the Isley Brothers, and members of KISS sang a spiritual ballad, "Gonna Keep His Eye on Us," at the memorial.

Bette Midler gushed: "Neil Bogart. He was sunny and full of life. He was the first person in the music business who said he believed in me. I will never forget him."

Even PolyGram management, who'd battled with Bogart, found it fitting to recognize his contribution to the industry: "It is with profound regret that we mourn the passing of a true music man."[4]

Neil's lifelong relationships with family members and friends could be described as distant in the end. While he was a gregarious and fun-loving guy, not many people truly knew him. Neil rarely opened up, preferring to make secret visits to a psychologist to express what he maybe couldn't share with others. Even as a teenager, Bogart surrounded himself with his work and didn't play with other kids. As an adult, he was a driven man who had few close friends, clinging to a cloak of secrecy that prevented him from opening up to almost anyone. In sickness and close to death, Neil had limited contact with much of his family. When the second round of cancer struck him, it was a shock to everyone. Only Neil's inner circle and very close relatives knew of his failing health, and most of them found out just prior to the end. When Bogart finally told Bonnie about the cancer, there was little time remaining. There was only enough time to say good-bye.

Neil Bogart was laid to rest in spectacular fashion, a going-out party he himself would have been proud of. The final tribute to the music giant was indicative of his larger-than-life persona—he passed away just prior to "I Love Rock 'n' Roll" hitting #1. In life, Neil was responsible for some of the world's most memorable musical anthems of all time—from "Y.M.C.A." to "I Love Rock 'n' Roll" to "Love to Love You Baby," to "Rock and Roll All Nite." His musical legacy still can be heard around the world in bars and clubs every single day, in the artists who were influenced by his roster of clients, and in the stories and legacy that he left in his wake. The fans may know the artists and the songs, but Neil Bogart was the man behind the curtain, putting together the spectacular show.

CHAPTER 18

The Afterlife

Boardwalk Entertainment drifted along like a sailboat without its mainsail, mast, and jib, floundering around until it finally came to its inevitable demise. Neil Bogart's death was a difficult time for his family and his employees. The mogul and heart of the company left behind giant footprints. He was loved and hated by many in his business, but ultimately he was respected.

Neil Bogart's passing also left a void in the Bogart/Bogatz family. The star, the success, in many ways its center, was dead at thirty-nine. The family struggled to bridge the gap between the Neil they knew and the one he created, some could say was reborn as, in Los Angeles. Those left on the East Coast simply didn't know the man anymore, nor did they know exactly how to react to the news of his death. Once Neil moved to California and found Joyce, that part of his family became a secondary part of his life. His relationships with the people he grew up with back East, his many cousins he had hosted at his home with ex-wife Beth in the early 1970s, as well as his friends, were part of his past—and Neil was a man consumed by his present successes. He had inconsistent contact with his children Jylle, Timothy, and Bradley after the divorce from Beth. His son Evan lived with him but was young when Neil passed away. The roller-coaster ride of his life, successes, and subsequent illness and death consumed Neil's time from the early 1970s to 1982.

The gap between Neil's immediate family—his children, sister, and parents—would be pronounced for a long time after his death. Neil loved his family, but he was not a traditional family man by any means. Once Neil passed on, the family would only remain in distant contact with one another, lacking the closeness that Neil once enjoyed himself as a kid in Brooklyn.

It was a particularly difficult time for Al and Ruth. They had worked so hard to foster Neil's talent and support his ambition. They had even moved out to Los Angeles to bask in some of his success and be close to their children and grandchildren. But Neil was first diagnosed with cancer just a year after they arrived. Then, just two years later, Neil received the terrible news that his cancer was terminal. Al and Ruth would always feel as though they were robbed of time with their son. His passing was sudden and difficult for them, despite the lack of any reconciliation.

Al and Ruth moved past their son's death using their close-knit group of friends and family for support. Bonnie and Joseph lived nearby with their two children, giving Al and Ruth a needed family connection. Joyce lived "over the hill" in Neil's Beverly Hills home, while Al, Ruth, Bonnie, and her family lived in Encino in the San Fernando Valley. Just as they did when Neil was alive, the hills would mark a distinct divide between the family members.

Ruth never talked about the past or her impact on Neil and Bonnie during their youthful years. Ruth, like Neil, was unforgiving and lacked the ability to conjure up any regret over past indiscretions. For Ruth, being in the wrong was a subjective thing. "It may have been shorter than expected," she said to a reporter about her son's life, "but he did everything he ever wanted or dreamed of and there are people who live to be a hundred who can't say that."[1]

Three years later after Neil's death, Joyce would move on, marrying Neil's doctor, Josh Trabulus. With Neil's estate and insurance money, Joyce became a philanthropist, raising money using her best attribute: her ability to mingle with entertainment elite. In 1984, just two years after Neil passed away, the Bogart Pediatric Cancer Research Program was founded in Neil's memory. Established by Joyce Bogart along with songwriter Carole Bayer Sager, the foundation sought to celebrate Neil Scott Bogart's life and raise money for those in need. The Bogart Pediatric Cancer Research Program linked up with Children's Hospital Los Angeles to help kids coping with cancer. The program has grown immensely over time and today successfully supports several research programs affecting patients and doctors alike around the world. According to its website[2] the foundation has raised more than twenty-five million dollars to its various causes. In addition to running a charitable foundation, Joyce also helped raise Neil's first three children—even though they were not her own. They had rooms at her Beverly Hills home and she always supported them, according to those who are close with the family.

Neil's four children, Jylle, Timothy, Bradley, and Evan, all now live in California. Both Timothy and Evan have followed their father into the entertainment industry. Timothy has made a run at writing/directing/producing feature films and television shows. Evan has enjoyed success in music as a writer and producer. The two brothers have teamed up to reignite Boardwalk Entertainment in honor of their father. The company's first big project is a feature film entitled *Spinning Gold*, a film based on the life of their father, Neil Scott Bogart, written by Timothy Scott Bogart. The company will also produce the soundtrack.

Neil Scott Bogart ultimately lived life his way. Donna Summer, in the liner notes to her 1982 self-titled album, dedicated the record to Bogart's memory and memorably wrote: "He made the world believe . . . they could see right through his eyes."[3]

Despite his five-foot, six-inch frame, Bogart was always the largest man in the room. He not only knew how to find a band or singer with promise, he knew how to deliver. His acts are responsible for innumerable hits that have since spanned decades and continue to be played around the world for fans of all ages. Very few producers have burned up the charts with music that has withstood the test of time like Neil Scott Bogart. He rose from the streets of New York as a boy with a dream to step atop the music world as one of the most recognizable and influential music producers of all time. He was a powerhouse, a steam engine that quit for nothing and for no one.

Neil saw the world differently than most—he was always ahead of the game, seeing the next move before anyone else could. He didn't follow trends but instead went with his gut, which led him to succeed with an array of eclectic acts, from punk rock to disco to metal to funk and pop music. He never limited himself to one kind of music. He had an ear for good music and didn't care about the genre. It takes a special (and brave) man to sign a band within an hour of hearing a single song over the phone.

⚬

No matter how much running Neil did, he couldn't run far enough away from who he was: Neil Bogatz, the poor abused Jewish kid from Brooklyn. "No matter what my father did, he could never please his mother," Jylle says. "He could never be successful enough." That identity had to die, and it seemed no amount of coke and no amount of success could completely put Neil's past to rest and set his present self at ease. Initially Neil didn't get into the entertainment business because he wanted to be rich or famous; he always loved what he was doing.

> *The goal was to enjoy myself. To take all the fantasies that I thought I'd enjoy seeing and doing and hearing and present them for people to enjoy. I never thought I'd be a successful businessman and make a lot of money."*[4]

Neil was a complicated man, and so was his relationship with the public. On the one hand, the population outside of music's inner circles barely knew who he was. He was the puppet master, the man behind the curtain. Despite this, there were moments when Neil hungered for the limelight. When he needed the public's adulation, he had no problem appearing from behind the veil to revel in his successes. Neil was also the most recognizable music mogul of his time. He made it his business to personally introduce his bands at big venues. He was a brilliant promoter, of both his artists and himself. It ran deep in his blood.

"We run the promotion of a record the same way you would an army going to war," he said. "You have to have a war plan. You have to know exactly how you want to promote it, where you want to advertise, when you want the record to break, when you are going after certain stations, when you're going to advertise to help get those stations. You really run a whole war game."[5]

No promotion was big enough. The implementation of any idea, no matter how ridiculous, was pursued in the name of promotion.

Neil lived a lifetime in just thirty-nine years on this earth. He could never get enough—never enough power, never enough money, never enough drugs, never enough. With the world at his fingertips, Neil fell deeper into hard drug use. Walk down Sunset Boulevard at any point during Casablanca's heyday and you'd hear about the insane, never-ending party going on over there at all hours of the night. The sad thing about all the partying was that Neil started to become a caricature of an industry mogul. He fell so far away from his childhood dream, from that idealistic dreamer, from the hardworking, stop-at-nothing streetwise kid, that he ended up becoming something else entirely. Neil knew the party would end, but he had no idea it would be so soon and when he was so young— though maybe he did. Bogart once told a reporter: "I think I'm lucky to still be living in my childhood, but when I get to my forties, I think that'll be enough."[6]

Neil Bogart's life ended with his closest childhood ally, his sister, by his side. It was a peaceful end for a man of great fury. For all his faults, and for all his gifts, he admirably made his own path. His life can best be summed up by words engraved at his final resting place:

Two roads diverged in a wood, and I,
I took the one less traveled by,
And that has made all the difference.[7]

—ROBERT FROST

Acknowledgments

Brett's Acknowledgments

I was asked to begin this endeavor on behalf of my family by my mother, Bonnie, and my Grandma Ruth. It was a truly amazing journey retrieving the steps of my uncle, Neil Bogart. Although I began this challenge by myself, I had a tremendous amount of support and help along the way. I'd like to begin by thanking my coauthor, Josh Levine. Josh is a good friend and a talented writer. It has been a true pleasure to take on this extremely personal project with him by my side. To our amazing editor, Jon Sternfeld: You have brought my uncle's story to life and added magic to this book.

To my mother, Bonnie, who partook in this difficult journey looking deep into the past. In addition, my mother and my sister, Shere, have been my personal editors and guinea pigs for what feels like three lifetimes of my writings. To my father, Joseph, who has supported me in many ways during and before this long journey. To Jylle Bogart Barker, my cousin and my uncle's oldest child, I thank you with all my heart. Her memories and support have added compassion and truth to this journey. To Laura Duane and Josh Lynn, friends who offered me tremendous guidance and support when I stood alone during the infancy phase of this biography. I'd like to thank Chuck Zahler for his invaluable memories and his lifelong support. To Beth Guber for revisiting a past from many moons ago to provide invaluable detail into my uncle's life that only she could do. To Seymour Bogart, Ira Bogart, Eileen Friedman, Lynn Campolo, Sheryl Feinberg, David Bogatz, Jerry Sharell, Ron Weisner, Danny Davis, Jeff Goldblum, Buck Reingold and Karen and Victor Willis for standing by my side during this journey and helping me make important connections to a history I was searching for. To my agent, Jennifer Hebert, I thank you for your daily support and tireless work on my behalf. I'd also like to thank our literary representation on this project, Andrew Paulson and Zachary Shuster Harmsworth Literary Agency.

I'd like to extend a special thanks to my wife, Ashley, without whom I could not have taken on this important task. Her undying love and support mean everything to me, and I thank her for putting up with all the late nights I spend writing in the dark in my own personal bubble. And for my children, Phoenix, Bailey, Tyler, and Ella; I love you all dearly.

To my Uncle Neil, I'd known you all my life, but this journey allowed me to truly understand who you were and your incredible, but much too short, life. I am proud to be called your nephew. Finally, to my beloved grandparents, Ruth and Al Bogart, I love you both dearly. My Grandpa Al was an amazing man, a light in the lives of many. His influence and creativity are the cornerstones of all our family's success. Thank you, Grandpa, for guiding and supporting me in my life and making this family what it is today. You truly were a gift to us all. I hope we are all making you proud and you have found peace and happiness on the other side together.

Josh's Acknowledgments

First and foremost I wish to thank my coauthor, Brett Ermilio, for the opportunity to latch onto this magic carpet ride, as well as Neil Bogart's family, friends, and business partners for opening up to us. I would also like to thank our editor, Jon Sternfeld. The appreciation I feel for Jon can best be encapsulated by the absolute thrill I get whenever an e-mail from Connecticut appears in my inbox. To our first agent, Andy Paulson, who sat down in my office one day and asked to hear what I was working on. I would also like to acknowledge the following: Mitch Shernoff, Siew Lin Cheah, Jim Dawson, Joel Selvin, Gerhard Wimmer, Kevin Anderson, David Gregornik, Howard Wilf; my brother-in-law, friend, and legal counsel, David Gabor; my mentors at the writing program at USC, Dr. James Ragan and the late great Hubert Selby Jr.; and my aunts, Laura Levine and Eileen Sacherman, who, whether knowingly or not, helped spark the fire.

To my parents, Michael and Barbara, who neither pushed too much nor pulled too hard but supported just right. I love you both so much.

My Dear Alexandra,

One day I told you I was writer. You asked me what that meant. I told you I put the words inside books. Whether at the time you understood that or not, the look of wonder on your face will always be embedded in my heart.

My Dear Jack,

When I'm older and grayer than I am today, remember, your diapers didn't change themselves.

To my lovely, talented, and beautiful wife, Amanda,

May the wondrous and glorious chapters continue for eternity. . . . I love you.

Sources

INTERVIEWS CONDUCTED BY THE AUTHORS:

Al Bogart, 1993–96
Ruth Bogart, 2000–03
Joe Ermilio, 2000-12
Bonnie Ermilio, 2000-12
Chuck Zahler, January 2012
Ira Bogart, November 2011
Seymour Bogart, October 2011
Eileen Freidman, October 2011, December 2012
Lynn Campolo, October 2011, December 2012
Beth Gruber, November 2011, January 2012, December 2012
Sheryl Feinberg, October 2011
Russ Bach, November 2011
David Bogatz, October 2011
Jerry Sharell, December 2011
Ron Weisner, December 2011
Danny Davis, December 2011
Karen Willis, November 2011
Peter Guber, November 2011
Jim Dawson, July 2013
Jylle Bogart Barker, March 2014
Buck Reingold, March 2014
Jeff Goldblum, March 2014

Endnotes

Prologue

1 - Anthony Cook, "Play It Again, Neil," *New West* magazine (October 10, 1977).

Chapter 1: The Creative Seed

1 - Geffen Records, Donna Summer, liner notes (1982).
2 - Jim Gaffney, "Bogey's Beat," *Topside Watch* (1945).
3 - *Patrol* (November 15, 1944).

Chapter 4: The Dreamer Casts Off

1 - *The New Yorker* (July 1958).
2 - Anthony Cook, "Play It Again, Neil," *New West* magazine (October 10, 1977).
3 - Ibid.

Chapter 5: Trading Up

1 - Interview with Russell H. Tice, mark-stein.com/interview/mintview.htm.
2 - Ibid.
3 - "Bogart Joins Cameo/Parkway," *Billboard* magazine (October 23, 1965).
4 - Author interview (January 2013).

Chapter 6: The Bubblegum King

1 - W. K. Knoedeleseder Jr., "Bogart's Biz: Play It Again, Neil," *Los Angeles Times* (February 4, 1979).
2 - Carl Cafarelli, "An Informal History of Bubblegum Music," *Goldmine* (April 25, 1997).
3 - W. K. Knoedeleseder Jr., "Bogart's Biz: Play It Again, Neil," *Los Angeles Times* (February 4, 1979).
4 - Carl Cafarelli, "An Informal History of Bubblegum Music," *Goldmine* (April 25, 1997).
5 - Anthony DeCurtis, ed., *The Rolling Stone Illustrated History of Rock and Roll: The Definitive History of the Most Important Artists and Their Music* (New York: Random House, 1992): 452.
6 - W. K. Knoedeleseder Jr., "Bogart's Biz: Play It Again, Neil," *Los Angeles Times* (February 4, 1979).

7 - Anthony DeCurtis, ed., *The Rolling Stone Illustrated History of Rock and Roll: The Definitive History of the Most Important Artists and Their Music* (New York: Random House, 1992): 452–53.

8 - Kim Cooper and David Stray, *Bubblegum Music Is the Naked Truth: The Dark History of Prepubescent Pop, from the Banana Splits to Britney Spears* (Port Townsend, WA: Feral House, 2001): 84.

9 - "Pop: Tunes for Teeny-Weenies," *Time* magazine (July 19, 1968).

10 - "Jerry Kasenetz and Jeff Katz," home.comcast.net/~bubblegumusic/kk.htm.

11 - Artie Wayne, *I Did It for a Song*.

12 - "Donna Summer: Is There Life After Disco?" *Rolling Stone* (March 23, 1978).

13 - "Record Company Success Laid to Dazzling Performers," *Hollywood Reporter* (November 1, 1976).

CHAPTER 7: BUDDAH RECORDS

1 - Larry Harris, *And Party Every Day: The Inside Story of Casablanca Records* (London: Backbeat Books, 2009).

2 - Ibid.

3 - Ibid.

4 - Ibid: 23.

5 - "Pluggers War on Old Curse," *Billboard* magazine (October 29, 1949).

6 - Larry Harris, *And Party Every Day: The Inside Story of Casablanca Records* (London: Backbeat Books, 2009).

7 - Fredric Dannen, *Hit Men: Power Brokers and Fast Money Inside the Music Business* (New York: Crown, 1990).

8 - *The Hollywood Reporter* (November 1, 1976).

CHAPTER 8: THE BEGINNING OF CASABLANCA

1 - www.classicbands.com/BillAucoinInterview.html.

2 - "Post-Kiss, the Village People and Donna Summer, Neil & Joyce Bogart Redo Their Own Lives," *People* magazine (May 26, 1980).

3 - Gene Simmons, *Kiss and Make-Up* (New York: Crown, 2001).

4 - *Village Voice* (December 14, 1972).

5 - Matthew Wilkening, "41 Years Ago: KISS Perform Their First Concert," ultimate classicrock.com/kiss-first-concert/.

6 - Larry Harris, *And Party Every Day: The Inside Story of Casablanca Records* (London: Backbeat Books, 2009).

7 - Ibid.

8 - Ibid.

9 - Peter Criss and Larry Sloman, *Makeup to Breakup: My Life In and Out of KISS* (New York: Charles Scribner's Sons, 2012).

10 - Gene Simmons, *Kiss and Make-Up* (New York: Crown, 2001).

11 - Peter Criss and Larry Sloman, *Makeup to Breakup: My Life In and Out of KISS* (New York: Charles Scribner's Sons, 2012).

12 - Ace Frehley, Joe Layden, and John Ostrosky, *No Regrets* (New York: VH1 Books, 2011): 92.

13 - "Post-Kiss, the Village People and Donna Summer, Neil & Joyce Bogart Redo Their Own Lives," *People* magazine (May 26, 1980).

14 - Peter Criss and Larry Sloman, *Makeup to Breakup: My Life In and Out of KISS* (New York: Charles Scribner's Sons, 2012).

15 - Larry Harris, *And Party Every Day: The Inside Story of Casablanca Records* (London: Backbeat Books, 2009).

16 - Peter Criss and Larry Sloman, *Makeup to Breakup: My Life In and Out of KISS* (New York: Charles Scribner's Sons, 2012).

17 - Ace Frehley, Joe Layden, and John Ostrosky, *No Regrets* (New York: VH1 Books, 2011): 118.

18 - Fredric Dannen, *Hit Men: Power Brokers and Fast Money Inside the Music Business* (New York: Crown, 1990).

19 - "Post-Kiss, the Village People and Donna Summer, Neil & Joyce Bogart Redo Their Own Lives," *People* magazine, May 26, 1980

20 - Fredric Dannen, *Hit Men: Power Brokers and Fast Money Inside the Music Business* (New York: Crown, 1990).

21 - Anthony Cook, "Play It Again, Neil," *New West* magazine (October 10, 1977).

22 - "Post-Kiss, the Village People and Donna Summer, Neil & Joyce Bogart Redo Their Own Lives," *People* magazine (May 26, 1980).

23 - Ibid.

24 - W. K. Knoedeleseder Jr., "Bogart's Biz: Play It Again, Neil," *Los Angeles Times* (February 4, 1979).

25 - Ibid.

26 - Anthony Cook, "Play It Again, Neil," *New West* magazine (October 10, 1977).

27 - "Larry Harris of Casablanca Records Talks KISS, Angel and the Golden Age of Vinyl with LRI," legendaryrockinterviews.com/2011/06/15/legendary-rock-interview-with-larry-harris-of-casablanca-records/.

CHAPTER 9: THE GLORY DAYS

1 - *Los Angeles Times* (February 4, 1979).

2 - Larry Harris, *And Party Every Day: The Inside Story of Casablanca Records* (London: Backbeat Books, 2009): 96–97.

3 - Joan Anderman, "A Radiant Summer's Night," the *Boston Globe* (July 14, 2008).

4 - Larry Harris, *And Party Every Day: The Inside Story of Casablanca Records* (London: Backbeat Books, 2009): 206.

CHAPTER 10: KISS TAKES OFF

1 - Peter Criss and Larry Sloman, *Makeup to Breakup: My Life In and Out of KISS,* (New York: Charles Scribner's Sons, 2012): e-book, 3,138.

2 - Gordon Fletcher, *Hotter Than Hell* album review, *Rolling Stone* #153 (January 1974).

3 - Ed Naha, "Kiss," *Rolling Stone* #179 (January 30, 1975).

4 - Gene Simmons, *Kiss and Make-Up* (New York: Crown, 2001): 83.

5 - David Leaf and Ken Sharp, *KISS: Behind the Mask: The Official Authorized Biography* (New York: Grand Central Publishing, 2005): 219.

6 - Ibid.

7 - Peter Criss and Larry Sloman, *Makeup to Breakup: My Life In and Out of KISS*, (New York: Charles Scribner's Sons, 2012): e-book, 1,744.

CHAPTER 11: THE KISS EXPLOSION

1 - Ibid: pg. 90.

2 - Ibid: pg. 111.

3 - Peter Criss and Larry Sloman, *Makeup to Breakup: My Life In and Out of KISS*, (New York: Charles Scribner's Sons, 2012): 90.

4 - Gene Simmons, *Kiss and Make-Up* (New York: Crown, 2001): 99.

5 - Peter Criss and Larry Sloman, *Makeup to Breakup: My Life In and Out of KISS*, (New York: Charles Scribner's Sons, 2012): 134.

6 - Simmons, *Kiss and Make-Up* (New York: Crown, 2001): 139.

7 - Fredric Dannen, *Hit Men: Power Brokers and Fast Money Inside the Music Business* (New York: Crown, 1990): 175.

8 - Gene Simmons, *Kiss and Make-Up* (New York: Crown, 2001): 139.

9 - Peter Criss and Larry Sloman, *Makeup to Breakup: My Life In and Out of KISS*, (New York: Charles Scribner's Sons, 2012): 168.

10 - Gene Simmons, *Kiss and Make-Up* (New York: Crown, 2001): 159.

11 - Peter Criss and Larry Sloman, *Makeup to Breakup: My Life In and Out of KISS*, (New York: Charles Scribner's Sons, 2012): 179.

12 - Ibid: 187.

13 - Scott Zamost and Poppy Harlow, "The Most Recognizable Band on Earth? Inside the World of KISS Inc.," CNN Money (October 24, 2011).

14 - Gerhard Wimmer, kissnews.de/NewsUSA.htm.

CHAPTER 12: SUMMER DAYS

1 - "The Long Hot Summer," *Newsweek* (April 2, 1979).

2 - Larry Harris, *And Party Every Day: The Inside Story of Casablanca Records* (London: Backbeat Books, 2009): 96.

3 - Ibid: 117.

4 - "The Long Hot Summer," *Newsweek* (April 2, 1979).

5 - "Donna Summer: Is There Life After Disco?," *Rolling Stone* (March 23, 1978).

6 - Michael Freedburg, *Rovi*.

7 - John Rockwell, "Records: The Disco Fever Is Spreading" *New York Times* (February 26, 1978).

CHAPTER 13: THE FILMWORKS MARRIAGE

1 - Nancy Griffin and Kim Masters, *Hit & Run: How Jon Peters and Peter Guber Took Sony for a Ride in Hollywood* (New York: Simon & Schuster, 1997): 90.

2 - Fredric Dannen, *Hit Men: Power Brokers and Fast Money Inside the Music Business* (New York: Crown, 1990).

3 - Larry Harris, *And Party Every Day: The Inside Story of Casablanca Records* (London: Backbeat Books, 2009): 134.

4 - Ibid.

5 - "Sink or Swim: The Making of *The Deep*," Bernews (January 12, 2011).

6 - Nancy Griffin and Kim Masters, *Hit & Run: How Jon Peters and Peter Guber Took Sony for a Ride in Hollywood* (New York: Simon & Schuster, 1997): 85.

7 - Nancy Griffin and Kim Masters, *Hit & Run: How Jon Peters and Peter Guber Took Sony for a Ride in Hollywood* (New York: Simon & Schuster, 1997): 90.

8 - Ibid: 89.

9 - Larry Harris, *And Party Every Day: The Inside Story of Casablanca Records* (London: Backbeat Books, 2009): 212.

10 - Ibid: 213.

11 - Nancy Griffin and Kim Masters, *Hit & Run: How Jon Peters and Peter Guber Took Sony for a Ride in Hollywood* (New York: Simon & Schuster, 1997): 93.

12 - Larry Harris, *And Party Every Day: The Inside Story of Casablanca Records* (London: Backbeat Books, 2009): 213.

13 - Ibid: 214.

14 - RIAA (2012).

15 - Leonard Maltin, ed., *Leonard Maltin's 2008 Movie Guide* (New York: Signet, 2007): 1373.

16 - Christian John Wikane, "Casablanca Records: Play It Again," popmatters.com.

17 - "The Long Hot Summer," *Newsweek* (April 2, 1979).

18 - Ibid.

19 - Christian John Wikane, "Casablanca Records: Play It Again," popmatters.com.

CHAPTER 14: HOLLYWOOD BITES BACK

1 - Nancy Griffin and Kim Masters, *Hit & Run: How Jon Peters and Peter Guber Took Sony for a Ride in Hollywood* (New York: Simon & Schuster, 1997): 94.

2 - Marilyn Beck, *Valley News* (October 21, 1978).

CHAPTER 15: HANG OUT WITH ALL THE BOYS: THE VILLAGE PEOPLE

1 - Terry Atkinson, "Neil Bogart: Paving Casablanca with Gold," *Rolling Stone* (1979).

2 - "A Tribute to Henri Belolo and Jacques Morali," disco-disco.com.

3 - "Village People," *Rolling Stone*, Vol. 289 (April 19, 1979).

4 - "A Tribute to Henri Belolo and Jacques Morali," disco-disco.com.

5 - Ibid.

6 - Jeff Pearlman, "Y.M.C.A." (An Oral History)," *Spin* (June 2008).

7 - Ibid.

8 - Ibid.

9 - "'Macho Man,' 'Y.M.C.A.' about Straight Fun: Publicist," ctvnews.ca/macho-man-y-m-c-a-about-straight-fun-publicist-1.251160.

10 - Jeff Pearlman, "Y.M.C.A." (An Oral History)," *Spin* (June 2008).

11 - "Glenn Hughes," *The Telegraph* (London: Telegraph Media Group, 2001).

12 - Interview with Gary James, classicbands.com.

13 - Jeff Pearlman, "Y.M.C.A." (An Oral History)," *Spin* (June 2008).

14 - Ibid.

15 - Ed Vulliamy, "Every Day People," the *Observer* (November 11, 2006).

16 - Ibid.

17 - "Disco Takes Over," *Newsweek* (April 2, 1979).

18 - Sherrie A. Inness, ed., *Disco Divas: Women, Gender, and Popular Culture in the 1970s.* Sherrie A. Inness (University of Pennsylvania Press, 2003): 187.

CHAPTER 16: HIGHS AND LOWS

1 - Fredric Dannen, *Hit Men: Power Brokers and Fast Money Inside the Music Business* (New York: Crown, 1990): 169.

2 - Larry Harris, *And Party Every Day: The Inside Story of Casablanca Records* (London: Backbeat Books, 2009): 219.

3 - Anthony Cook, "Play it Again, Neil," *New West* magazine (October 10, 1977).

4 - Fredric Dannen, *Hit Men: Power Brokers and Fast Money Inside the Music Business* (New York: Crown, 1990): 177.

5 - Larry Harris, *And Party Every Day: The Inside Story of Casablanca Records* (London: Backbeat Books, 2009): 257.

6 - "Is There Life After Disco?,"*Rolling Stone* (March 23, 1978).

7 - "The Long Hot Summer," *Newsweek* (April 2, 1979).

8 - Nancy Griffin and Kim Masters, *Hit & Run: How Jon Peters and Peter Guber Took Sony for a Ride in Hollywood* (New York: Simon & Schuster, 1997): 100.

9 - Ibid: 107.

10 - "Post-Kiss, the Village People and Donna Summer, Neil & Joyce Bogart Redo Their Own Lives," *People* (May 26, 1980).

CHAPTER 17: BOARDWALK AND BEYOND

1 - Joan Jett and the Blackhearts website, joanjettbadrep.com.

2 - Ibid.

3 - Steve Pond, "Neil Bogart: 1943–1982," *Los Angeles Times.*

4 - *Billboard* (May 22, 1982).

CHAPTER 18: THE AFTERLIFE

1 - Lynda Collins, "LV Stars to Raise Funds in Honor of Old Friend," *Las Vegas Times* (November 29, 1995).

2 - The Bogart Pediatric Cancer Research Program, bogartfoundation.org.

3 - Geffen Records, Donna Summer, liner notes (1982).

4 - Anthony Cook, "Play it Again, Neil," *New West* magazine (October 10, 1977).

5 - Ibid.

6 - Ibid.

7 - Robert Frost, "The Road Not Taken" (1916).

Index

About the Authors

Brett Scott Ermilio

Brett Ermilio attended the University of California, Santa Barbara, and California State University, Northridge, to complete his bachelor's in History and a minor in Film Studies. A screenwriter since the age of sixteen, Brett won the Sherill C. Corwin Writing Award for Best Screenplay for his work *Jacob* at age twenty-three. *Jacob* would go on to be optioned but never produced.

Brett has worked as a freelance screenwriting consultant on numerous projects and joined "The Peanut Gallery," a writing group headed by screenwriter/producer Mark Brown in 1999. Brett was commissioned soon after to turn director Paul Hunter's short story *Bundy* into a full-length screenplay. In 2006 Brett wrote, directed, and produced his first feature film, *2 Hitmen,* distributed worldwide by York Entertainment in November of 2007. Currently Brett is working on numerous film and television projects.

Josh Levine

Josh Levine attended the Master of Professional Writing Program at the University of Southern California and graduated with a master's degree in creative writing. His writing credits include the documentary *On Moral Grounds,* based on the Holocaust restitution case *Stern v. Generali.* The documentary appeared at the Wisconsin and Telluride Film Festivals and was subsequently sold to Screen Gems, a subsidiary of Sony Studios. He is currently working on the third draft of his first work of fiction, as yet untitled. He lives in Los Angeles with his lovely wife, four-year-old daughter, and two-year-old son.